BABY NAMES

DRIAN

STEPHAN

KELC

CLARE   MARILYN

HARRY

FABIENNE   RUTH   ADR

HAVILAH

PARIS

TAWNIE   JOCASTA

ACOB   GARNER CORNELIU

LYA MARGARET   LINDSAY

PHIE CHARLOTT

PERDITA RICHARD

JOSEPH

NALD VICTORIA

FINLAY

ACK SAPPHIRE   ADRIEL

NABEL

ROYSTON   GEORG

BABY NAMES

This edition published in Great Britain
in 2003 exclusively for WHSmith,
Greenbridge Road, Swindon SN3 3LD
by Hamlyn, part of the
Octopus Publishing Group Limited,
2–4 Heron Quays, London E14 4JP

Copyright © 2003
Octopus Publishing Group Limited

ISBN 0 600 60921 9

Printed in Finland

CONTENTS

FEATURES

NAMING
YOUR BABY

Ascribing personal names to people differentiates them from one another and also gives them an identity and a place in the community. Naming is a very old and widespread custom and one that varies greatly in practice within different societies.

In some African and Asian cultures, for example, children are named according to their position in the family – such as 'first-born son' or 'eldest daughter', while people with a Hispanic background like to honour deceased relatives. Chinese tradition dictates that males are given different names at various milestones in their life. In Great Britain, we generally have one or more first names followed by a surname, a family name that may or may not convey information about our roots.

When to start thinking about baby names

Choosing a name for your baby is one of the most important things that you will ever do for him/her. Deciding on the name can be as lengthy a process as the gestation period so it is a good idea to start thinking about the names you like early on. There are bound to be disagreements between you and your partner, and between yourselves and your families and friends. But remember, at the end of the day it is your choice as parents as to how to name your child that must take precedence.

However much we may dislike the name given to us by our parents, comparatively few of us actually go to the trouble of changing it legally. This means that most of us really are named for life, so it is important to get it right. Start collating a list of favourites – go through this book and highlight the names that appeal the most. Over time you should, between you, be able to whittle them down to a shortlist of just one or two.

Unisex names

Some names, known as unisex or gender-neutral names, can be used for both boys and girls, although confusingly this can vary between different English-speaking countries. For example, Jordan is both a girl's and a boy's name in the UK and in America but is only used for boys in Australia. Girls – and perhaps more importantly their parents – seem happy to use a boy's name but it is perhaps understandable that boys are not so agreeable to having girls' names.

Alternatively a girl's name may simply be a version of a boy's name but with a new spelling, for example Kelsey (for boys) and Kelcie (for girls).

KELSEY

RICHARD

GILLIAN

NINA

KELCIE

FINLAY

LANGUAGE AND THE
ORIGIN OF NAMES

As you will see from the directories later in this book, many of the first names used in European countries today have an ancient pedigree, coming from Hebrew, Ancient Greek or Latin or from one of the early Germanic or Celtic languages (Breton, Cornish, Gaelic and Welsh). With the expansion of Germanic rule in the first millennium Germanic (Frankish and Saxon) names like Charles, Henry and Matilda spread across Europe to France, Spain and Italy and eventually featured in many European royal families.

Names of Germanic origin tend to consist of two vocabulary elements, many of which include the words for 'war', 'wolf', 'bear', 'counsel' and 'protection'. Edmund, for example, derives from 'ed' (happy, fortunate) + 'mund' (protection/protector).

Edward and Edith are Anglo-Saxon names that have survived to modern times, but most Old English names were replaced by the French/German names brought over by the Normans in 1066 – names such as William, Ferdinand, Hugo and Ella.

Although the Celts were at one time spread right across Europe, it is only in the UK and English-speaking countries (particularly North America and Australia) that their names and Anglicized equivalents have greatly increased the pool of first names that are used (see page 112).

The blurring of cultural identities

Some first names have religious or cultural connotations that still provide a clue as to their heritage. Names like Reuben and Isaac, for example, are obviously Jewish, while names like Xavier are associated with the Roman Catholic Church. However, today's melting pot of cultures and heritage means this labelling is becoming less and less apparent. Joseph and Rachel, for example, are no longer considered as primarily Jewish.

Today's stock of names

There is now a larger stock of names than ever before to choose from, making the decision very hard! The choice of names includes all those (first names and surnames) inherited throughout history from different cultures and religions, as well as those borrowed more recently (such as Michelle from France and Natasha from Russia – both became popular in the second half of the 20th century). There are also nicknames (like Rusty and Tex) and short names (such as Harry and Pam) that have become names in their own right, place names (Chelsea and Iona) and vocabulary words (such as Summer, Emerald and Blossom). Authors and showbiz personalities have also often invented new names.

The trait of naming boys after their fathers, coupled with the acceptability of giving girls vocabulary words, made-up names, unusual spellings of existing names and even boys' names, accounts for the fact that there are more names used for girls than for boys. In England and Wales in 2002, for example, 3,089 different girls' names were registered, compared with just 2,430 boys' names.

MAKING
WISE CHOICES

There are no hard and fast rules when it comes to choosing a name , other than that you both like the name you decide upon. However, the following points are worth consideration. Firstly, never name your child on a whim. A name is usually permanent. It has to last your offspring throughout his/her life and demands rigorous testing. Try and think of all the connotations – the sound of the name(s) with the surname, any likely short or pet names or undesirable words the initials might spell – to try and forestall any playground teasing and the use of cruel nicknames. You might also want to avoid names that have unpleasant associations for you personally – be it the name of an 'ex' or a particularly nasty boss.

It is best to steer clear of cute names that suit a baby but do not wear well in later life. In addition, bear in mind that the name for the new baby must go with the names of any older children already in the family. For example, a Bart and Lisa in the same family might prompt jokes about the Simpsons while a William and a Harry together will obviously have royal connotations.

WILLIAM
HARRY
BART LISA

Sound and rhythm

Try saying any potential name, together with the surname, out loud a few times to determine how well the names go together. Some combinations trip off the tongue more easily than others. For example a first name that ends with the first letter or sound of your baby's surname, like Paul Letterby or Jasmine Nash, requires you to pause to get your tongue around the awkward combination of letters. A real test is to try shouting the name out the back door a few times as though calling your child in for supper. If this makes you cringe it is time to think of another name!

Consider the number of syllables in the name. If you have a particularly long surname a short first name is probably best and vice versa, for example Anne Wardle-Cardew and Isabella Burns are better options than Victoria Wardle-Cardew and Jane Burns, respectively.

You might be proud of yourself for coming up with first names that rhyme with your surname (Fay May or Scott Watt) and appealing puns (Stan Dupp or Honey Moon) but your poor child certainly won't find it so amusing. Zowie Bowie for one, son of pop star David Bowie, was quick to change his name as a teenager...

JASMINE
DAVID
ZOWIE
FAY MAY

Unusual names

Although classic names are popular, there is an increasing tendency these days for parents to seek individuality for their child by giving them an unusual appellation. Unusual names are certainly remembered, even if always misspelt. Again, think of your child's feelings – he or she is likely to be the only one in the class with the spelling 'moniker' and may enjoy feeling special. However, he/she may well not like the attention that it warrants, especially if you give your son a girl's name.

Even as adults some people find it humiliating to have an unusual name and to be constantly explaining and/or spelling it – even if others find it a good conversation starter! There are many instances of the children of celebrities being saddled with an off-the-wall name and changing it as soon as possible. For example Free, son of actress Barbara Hershey, changed his name to Tom.

If you have an unusual surname it is even more important to opt for a familiar first name. If your surname is Smith or Jones, however, you can afford to be a little more adventurous...

Take care with initials

Do think carefully about the initials of the intended name, particularly where more than one first name is chosen. It may be that you simply need to swap the order of names or choose alternatives to avoid some unfortunate combinations, such as Clare Diana Player (CD Player), William Charles Seet (WC Seet), Bernie Ursula Matthews (BUM) or Tom Witt (which could be read as Twit).

Keeping the family happy

Appeasing relatives, especially the grandparents, for one reason or another may have an influence over the choice of name for your baby. Some families, for example, have a tradition of naming the first son after their father, or prefer certain names for religious reasons. Using a family name will certainly give your child a sense of history and belonging, but, whatever the persuasive arguments, the final decision is up to you and your partner and you should never give in to a name that you dislike. Choosing a relative's name as a middle name is one compromise, however, that may help to keep the peace.

The best approach is to be open to ideas but keep your chosen name under wraps until the baby is born. Then name your baby as you please, as it will be too late to give in to family pressure.

WILLIAM

CLARE

CHARLES DIANA

TOM

URSULA

REGISTERING YOUR
BABY'S BIRTH

By law, all births in the UK must be registered within six weeks (three weeks in Scotland) of your baby's date of birth – and usually in the district in which the child was born.

The General Register Office (GRO) is the body responsible for recording all births within England and Wales (see www.statistics.gov.uk/registration). You can also visit the websites www.gro-scotland.gov.uk and www.groni.gov.uk for information on registering your baby's birth in Scotland or Northern Ireland, respectively.

You should be able to locate the whereabouts of your local registrar simply by looking in the telephone directory or by contacting your local council. Often, the registration of a birth can be carried out at the hospital where the baby was born, before mother and child leave for home.

Who can register the birth?

If the baby's parents are married to each other, either parent can register the birth. If they are not married, and the father's details are to be entered in the register, both parents are required to visit the registrar and sign the register together. Alternatively, one parent can register the birth provided that he or she can produce a signed declaration of paternity (this document is readily available from any local registrar's office).

What details are recorded?

The registrar requires details of the baby's sex, full name, date and place of birth – plus the time of birth if it is a multiple birth – as well as details of the parents. The latter includes the parents' full names, their dates and places of birth and occupations. The mother will also need to provide her usual address, her maiden name if appropriate, her date of marriage if married to the child's father and details of any previous children.

The information given to the registrar is usually recorded both on computer and in the birth register, which the person registering the birth signs. Do check the information, particularly the spelling of names, before you sign as it is difficult to change it afterwards.

Once you have registered your baby's birth you will receive, free of charge, a basic birth certificate, which contains your baby's details. Further copies and a fuller version, which contains the parents' details, may be purchased.

AUGUSTINE
DAVINIA
AURILIA COLVIN
GISELLE
NOAH

OFFICIALLY NAMING
YOUR CHILD

Just as there are now a range of civil ceremony options available to couples getting married, instead of just the traditional church wedding, there is also more choice when it comes to an official ceremony for naming your child.

Traditionally the formal Christian baptism provided by the church was the only option. Nowadays parents can opt for either a baby blessing in church or a civil naming ceremony, neither of which has to involve godparents, the sprinkling of water at the font or the lighting of candles.

Baby blessing ceremony

An alternative to a baptism/christening, the baby blessing offered by the Church of England is a Service of Thanksgiving and Blessing, which thanks God for the gift of a child and its safe arrival, asks God's blessing on the baby and asks God to help you be a good parent. A less formal acknowledgement of a new baby than a baptism, the celebration is aimed at non-church-going parents who want to welcome their child into the world without appearing hypocritical. Instead of asking such parents – and godparents – to profess their Christian faith, prayers are said that ask for the child to 'come through faith and baptism to the fullness of God's grace'.

This ceremony allows you to celebrate your new arrival without committing your child to a particular faith. A child who has been through such a service could be baptised later in life if they wish to be.

Civil naming ceremony

Another alternative to the traditional christening, the civil naming ceremony is a formal celebration conducted by a Celebrant and held at a register office or some other approved building. The occasion allows parents without religious beliefs, from any cultural background and regardless of their marital status to make a public declaration to be a good parent to their child, while at the same time bringing together family and friends to celebrate and welcome the new arrival into the family.

A civil naming ceremony is a very personal and flexible event, created especially to suit parents' wishes. For example, the ceremony can include poems and readings and the presentation of a special gift to the child. 'Supporting adults' take the place of godparents and they promise to support the baby through childhood. Grandparents, too, can have a role in the ceremony and make their own appropriate promises.

A naming ceremony has no legal status – it is simply a celebration – and the Record of Ceremony cannot be used as proof of identification. This is the function of the birth certificate (see page 15). A civil naming ceremony gives the child the choice to follow a religion they have picked themselves later in life.

Civil naming ceremonies are offered by a number of councils around the country – contact your local council or register office for details.

HOW TO USE
THIS BOOK

The book contains two main directories, one for boys and one for girls, and both list the names alphabetically. Each entry provides the language of origin, if known, its meaning and any commonly used short or pet forms. Names in brackets at the end of an entry offer alternative spellings (these are pronounced the same way). However, a name that sounds different will have been given its own entry.

The use of 'Greek' throughout refers to the language of Ancient Greece rather than the modern language.

ADRIEL CRISTIAN
DIONE MEGAN
CHARLOTTE
OSCAR DARCY
HADRIAN

Special features

An alternative option to simply browsing through the directories searching for a name that appeals to both parents is to look at the 18 themed special features that are scattered throughout the book, which group names together according to topic. The aim of these features is to provide you with inspiration for finding a suitable name for a particular reason rather than through random choice.

The topics covered in these features range from literary, mythological and biblical characters through to ideas for naming your baby according to the time of year he/she is born, after the colour of his/her hair or after a particular plant. There are also lists of the favourite names in the country, both currently and in previous decades.

By consulting the feature sections together with the main directories you should find plenty of names to appeal to you and your partner from which you can compile your shortlist of favourite choices. Don't forget that you need to choose an option for both genders, unless you are 100 per cent sure of the sex of your unborn baby or you particularly wish to use a unisex name (see page 7).

AURILIA BENICE
ETHAN
NICHOLAS IMOGEN

ARON
SEYMOUR DOUGLA
BARNABY MADDOCK
PATRICK
FLYNN
ELDWIN
VAUGHA
GARSON VAUGHA
AIMIE XAVIER IAN
RLANDO ZIRCON ANTONI
QUENTINSTEFFAN
DAVID URIAH
HAMILTO
ENNON NIGEL
WALDEN DARIEN
LKENER
TRISTAN YORK
HANDLER PRESTON
ALPH

A-Z DIRECTORY OF
BOYS' NAMES

It appears that tradition and conservatism play a much more important role when it comes to naming boys than girls. This does result in a slightly smaller stock of names from which to choose a boy's name. There is a tendency to give boys a family name – perhaps one that is carried by the boy's father and/or grandfather. Some parents might be thinking ahead to their son's future career when they choose a 'respectable' name over a more unusual one when both are on their shortlist. However, there is something to be said for an unconventional name as it is far more likely to be remembered!

ADRIAN

AARON

ADELBERT

A

Aahmes	Egyptian – child of the moon
Aaron	Biblical name believed to be of
	Egyptian origin, meaning 'descended
	from the gods', 'high mountain' *(Aron)*
Abba	Variant of Abbot
Abbas	Arabic – austere, lion-like
Abbot	Hebrew – head of the abbey, father
Abdel	Arabic – servant
Abdiel	Hebrew – servant of God
Abdul	Swahili – servant of the Lord
Abel	Hebrew – breath, vapour
Abelard	Old German/Anglo-Saxon – of
	noble firmness
Abner	Hebrew – father of light
Abraham	Hebrew – eternal father of the
	multitudes. Name of the first
	patriarch and father of the Hebrews.
	Short/pet forms: Abe, Abie
Abram	Favoured British form of Abraham
	until after the Reformation
Abran	Spanish form of Abram
Ace	Latin – unity, first-rate
Achilles	Greek – strength
Ackerley	Anglo-Saxon – from the
	oak-tree meadow

Adair	Gaelic – oak-tree ford
Adalbert	Old German/Anglo-Saxon – noble,
	bright, illustrious. Short/pet forms:
	Bert, Bertie
Adam	Hebrew – red earth. Name of
	the first man
Addis	Variant of Adam
Addison	Anglo-Saxon – son of Adam
Adelar	Old German or Anglo-Saxon –
	noble eagle *(Adlar, Adler)*
Adelbert	Variant of Albert
Adelfrid	Old German/Anglo-Saxon – noble,
	peaceful
Aden	Arabic – fiery one. Also a place name
Adil	Arabic – just, fair
Adlai	Hebrew – refuge of God
Adlar	Alternative spelling of Adelar
Adler	Alternative spelling of Adelar
Adley	Hebrew – just
Admetus	Greek – untamed
Adolfo	Spanish form of Adolph
Adolph	Old German – noble hero.
	Short/pet forms: Dolf, Dolph
Adon	Hebrew – lord
Adoni	Aborigine – sunset
Adonis	Greek – of manly beauty
Adrian	Latin – dark one, dark riches. From
	the Roman name Adrianus, which
	describes a man from Adria

AHMED

ALADDIN

ALARIC

A

Adriel	Hebrew – of God's flock. Also derived from a Native American word, meaning 'beaver'
Aeneas	Greek – worthy of praise
Afton	Celtic – from the Afton River
Agustin	Alternative spelling of Augustin
Ahearn	Celtic – lord of the horses (Ahern)
Ahern	Alternative spelling of Ahearn
Ahmed	Arabic – praiseworthy
Ahmik	Hebrew – strength of God's flock
Ahren	German – eagle
Ahrens	Old German – power of the eagle
Aidan	Phonetic spelling of the Celtic name Áedán, meaning 'little fiery one'
Aiken	Made of oak. An Anglo-Saxon name that has a second meaning in the North of England – 'little Adam', implying that the baby is the image of his father
Aimery	Old German – industrious ruler
Ainsley	Anglo-Saxon – my meadow (Ainslie)
Ainslie	Alternative spelling of Ainsley
Ajax	Greek – mourner. Name of one of the Greek heroes in the Trojan War in Greek mythology
Aki	Japanese – autumn
Akins	Egyptian – brave
Akiva	Hebrew – protect
Akram	Arabic – noble, generous

Aladdin	Arabic – nobility of faith
Alair	Latin – cheerful, merry
Alan	Celtic – harmony. Also possibly Gaelic – handsome, rock solid. Short/pet form: Al (Allan, Allen, Allin, Alun, Alyn)
Alano	Spanish form of Alan
Alanus	Variant of Alan
Alaric	Old German – ruler of all. The Visigoth King, Alaric I, was responsible for the sacking of Rome in AD410
Alasdair	Scottish form of Alexander, meaning 'defender of men' (Alastair, Alisdair, Alistair, Alister)
Alastair	Alternative spelling of Alistair

AIDAN

A · ALDWIN · ALFRED · ALCANDER

Alban	Latin – white, blond, fair. St Alban was the first British martyr. A Romano-Briton, he lived in Verulamium, now the city of St Albans *(Alben)*
Albany	Derived from Alban. Also US place name
Alben	Alternative spelling of Alban
Alber	Old German – agile mind
Albert	Derived from Adalbert. Short/pet forms: Al, Bert
Alcander	Greek – strong
Aldan	Alternative spelling of Alden
Alden	Anglo-Saxon – old friend, wise protector *(Aldan, Aldon)*
Alder	Species of tree
Aldo	Old German – old, rich
Aldon	Alternative spelling of Alden
Aldous	Derived from the Latinized form of the Old German word, which means 'old'
Aldridge	Anglo-Saxon – from the alder tree ridge
Aldwin	Anglo-Saxon – old friend
Alec	Short/pet form of Alexander, now also an independent name *(Alek, Alick)*
Alejandro	Spanish form of Alexander
Alek	Russian form of Alec
Aleksei	Russian form of Alexander

Aleksy	Polish form of Alexander
Aleron	Latin – on the wing
Alex	Short/pet form of Alexander, it is now also an independent name *(Alix)*
Alexander	Greek – helper and defender of men. A name bestowed upon many saints, martyrs and kings, it has been popular for over 3,000 years. Short/pet forms: Alec, Alek, Alex, Alick, Alix, Sandy
Alfie	Short/pet form of Alfred, now also an independent name
Alfons	Alternative spelling of Alphonse
Alfonso	German form of Alphonse
Alfred	Anglo-Saxon – elf-counsel. In early English history elves were regarded as powerful spirits of nature. The name also means 'wise advice'. Short/pet forms: Al, Alf, Alfie, Fred, Freddie, Freddy

Alger	German – clever warrior
Algernon	French name, meaning 'with a moustache'. Supposedly a nickname given to an 11th-century Count of Boulogne, named Eustace, to avoid confusion with his father who had the same name
Ali	Arabic – noble, kind
Alick	Alternative spelling of Alec
Alisdair	Alternative spelling of Alasdair
Alistair	Phonetic spelling of Alasdair, the Gaelic form of Alexander
Alister	Alternative spelling of Alistair
Alix	Alternative spelling of Alex
Allan	Alternative spelling of Alan
Allard	Old German – nobly resolute
Allen	Alternative spelling of Alan
Allin	Alternative spelling of Alan
Alpheus	Name of a river god in Greek mythology
Alphonse	Anglo-Saxon – eager, noble, ready for battle. Short/pet forms: Alf, Alfie (Alfons)
Alroy	Gaelic – red-haired
Alston	Anglo-Saxon – from the old manor
Altair	Arabic. Name of bright star in the constellation of the eagle, Aquila
Alton	Anglo-Saxon – old town
Alula	Latin – winged one
Alun	Alternative spelling of Alan
Alvin	German/Anglo-Saxon – noble friend, friend of all. Possibly a more modern form of the Anglo-Saxon name Alwyn
Alworth	Possibly Old German – respected by all
Alwyn	Anglo-Saxon – friend of the elf
Alyn	Alternative spelling of Alan
Amadeus	Latin – lovable
Amado	Latin – loving deity
Amador	Latin – lover
Amaro	Portuguese – dark, like a Moor
Ambar	Sanskrit – sky
Ambrose	Greek – pertaining to the Immortals. Ambrosia was the food of the gods, as nectar was their drink
Amiel	Hebrew – God of my people
Ammon	Egyptian – the hidden
Amon	Hebrew – trustworthy
Amos	Hebrew – worried, troubled, or messenger (of God). Name of one of the Old Testament prophets
Anand	Sanskrit – happy
Anarawd	Welsh – eloquent, pronounced 'a-na-rod'
Anatole	Translates literally as 'rising sun'. The Greek name for the main part of Turkey, and a meeting place for traders in ancient times

ANOKI

ANDERSON

ANTONIO

A

Anders	Swedish form of Andrew
Anderson	Variant of Andrew
Andre	French form of Andrew
Andreas	Variant of Andrew (*Andreus*)
Andrei	Russian form of Andrew
Andres	Spanish form of Andrew
Andreus	Alternative spelling of Andreas
Andrew	Latin/Greek – manly, brave. Name of the first apostle. Short/pet forms: Andie, Andy, Drew
Andries	Variant of Andrew
Andros	Variant of Andrew
Aneurin	Welsh – gold. Name of the Welsh Labour politician, Aneurin Bevan (1897–1960). Short/pet form: Nye
Angelo	Greek – (saintly) messenger
Angus	Gaelic – unique choice, chosen one. Originally a Scottish name, Aonghus. Short/pet form: Gus
Angwyn	Welsh – handsome
Anieli	Variant of Andrew
Anker	Variant of Andrew
Anlon	Phonetic spelling of the Gaelic name Anluan, meaning 'great champion'
Anoki	Native American – an actor
Ansel	Anglo-Saxon – blessed
Anselm	Old German – protector, helmet of the gods
Anson	Anglo-Saxon – son of Agnes or Ann
Anthony	Latin. Derived from an Old Roman family name, meaning 'priceless' and 'flourishing'. Name given to many saints, including St Anthony of Padua (1195–1231), a famous preacher and patron of lost property. Short/pet forms: Ant, Tony (*Antony*)
Antol	Variant of Anthony
Anton	Russian form of Anthony
Antonio	Variant of Anthony
Antony	Alternative spelling of Anthony
Archer	Old German – bowman, archer
Archibald	Old German – very bold. Another of the names brought to England by the Norman Conquest. Short/pet form: Archie
Archie	Short/pet form of Archibald, now also an independent name
Arden	Latin – eager, fervent, ardent (*Ardin*)
Ardin	Alternative spelling of Arden
Ardley	Anglo-Saxon – from the domestic meadow
Ardon	Hebrew – bronze
Aren	Nigerian – eagle
Ares	God of war in Greek mythology, equivalent to the Roman god Mars, meaning 'war-like'
Argus	Greek – watchful. Short/pet form: Gus

ARMAND   ARUNDEL

ASHFORD

Ariel Hebrew – God's lion. Name of a Shakespearean spirit of the air

Arlen Celtic – pledge

Arley Latin – bowman

Arlin Gaelic – pledge

Arlo Anglo-Saxon – fortified hill

Arman Persian – desire

Armand German – of the army

Armande French form of Armand

Armando Italian form of Armand

Arne Old Norse – eagle

Arno Variant of Arne

Arnold Derived from the Old German *Arenvald*, meaning 'eagle power', this modern name is probably a later development from the Latin form, *Arnoldus*. Short/pet forms: Arnie, Arny

Arnon Hebrew – rushing stream

Arnvid Old German meaning 'eagle of the forest'

Aron Alternative spelling of Aaron

Arran Scottish place name

Arsen Greek – strong

Arsenio Greek – manly, virile

Arthur An old name of uncertain roots. It is probably of Latin origin, as there was an Old Roman family name Artorius, although it could be from the Celtic *artos*, meaning 'a bear', or Gaelic *art*, 'a stone'. The name may also derive from the Norse god of war, Thor. It is the name of the legendary sixth-century British monarch. Short/pet forms: Art, Artie, Arty

Artur Gaelic form of Arthur

Arturo Italian and Spanish form of Arthur

Arun Hindi – sun

Arundel Anglo-Saxon – eagle's dell. Also an English place name

Asa Hebrew – healer, physician

Ascot Anglo-Saxon – cottage. Also an English place name

Asher Hebrew – lucky, blessed, happy. Short/pet form: Ash

Ashford Anglo-Saxon – dweller by the ash tree ford. Short/pet form: Ash

ARTURO

Ashleigh	Alternative spelling of Ashley. Short/pet form: Ash
Ashley	Anglo-Saxon – ash field/wood. Used for both boys and girls, although the spelling Ashleigh is usually preferred for girls. Short/pet form: Ash *(Ashleigh)*
Ashlin	Variant of Ashley. Short/pet form: Ash
Ashton	Anglo-Saxon – town by the ash trees/dweller at the ash tree farm. Short/pet form: Ash
Astley	Anglo-Saxon – eastern wood. A place name and the family name of the barons of Hastings
Atherton	Anglo-Saxon – dweller in the forest
Atlas	Greek – not enduring. Name of the Titan in Greek mythology who was forced to bear the world on his shoulders
Atsu	Egyptian – twin
Auberon	Variant of Aubrey
Aubrey	Old German – elf ruler
Audley	Anglo-Saxon – prospering
Audric	French – old and wise ruler
August	Variant of Augustus
Augustin(e)	Variant of Augustus *(Agustin)*
Augustus	Latin – worthy of honour, venerable, revered, exalted. This esteemed title

	was awarded by the first Roman Emperor, Octavius Caesar, to himself. Short/pet form: Gus
Auriga	Unknown origin – charioteer
Austell	Name of a Cornish saint, and a place name
Austen	Alternative spelling of Austin
Austin	Derived from Augustine. Also a US place name *(Austen, Austyn, Awstin, Ostin)*
Austyn	Alternative spelling of Austin
Avery	Anglo-Saxon – ruler of the elves
Avi	Hebrew – father
Avon	English place name
Awstin	Alternative spelling of Austin
Axel	Hebrew – divine reward
Aylsworth	Unknown origin – cf great wealth
Aylwin	Old German – devoted friend
Aymon	Old French – ruler of the home
Azal	Unknown origin – mountain's foundation
Azi	Nigerian – a youth

BAILEY BARNIE

BANNING

B

Bailey	Old French – enclosure
Bainbridge	Anglo-Saxon – of the sea/water
Baird	Celtic – singer, poet *(Bard)*
Balbo	Latin – inarticulate
Balder	Old Norse – god of light
Baldric	Old German/Anglo-Saxon – warrior's sash or belt
Baldwin	Old German – bold/brave friend
Balfour	Gaelic – pasture
Balin	Anglo-Saxon – soldier of distinction
Balint	Latin – strong and healthy
Ballard	German – a dancing song
Bancroft	Anglo-Saxon – bean field
Banister	Unknown origin – wild pomegranate
Banning	Gaelic – blond child
Baptista	Latin – baptized
Barclay	Anglo-Saxon – birch-tree meadow
Bard	Alternative spelling of Baird
Barden	Anglo-Saxon – barley valley
Bardo	Old Norse – son of the earth. Also Aborigine – water
Barnabas	Aramaic – son of consolation. In the New Testament, Barnabas was a companion to St Paul and urged St Mark to write his gospel
Barnaby	Modern derivative of Barnabas. Short/pet forms: Barn, Barney, Barnie, Barny
Barnadin	Variant of Bernard
Barnard	Variant of Barry and Bernard
Barnes	Anglo-Saxon – bear
Barnett	Anglo-Saxon – nobleman
Barney	Short/pet form of Barnaby and Bernard, now also an independent name *(Barnie, Barny)*
Barnie	Alternative spelling of Barney
Barnum	Anglo-Saxon – barley store
Barny	Alternative spelling of Barney
Baron	Old German/Anglo-Saxon – warrior, free man. The ancient feudal title for a king's tenant is now the lowest rank of British nobility, and a first name
Barr	Derived from Barrett

TOP 10
UK BABY NAMES

Children's names tend to follow trends and cycles of popularity. Whether you are looking for a popular name for your baby or are trying to avoid using one, the following lists of current top 10 names may help you make up your mind!

Parents have a legal obligation to register their child's birth (see page 14). From these records lists are produced to show the most popular first names for all new babies born in the UK. Although some parents will always be influenced by showbiz personalities and other celebrities (see page 134) when it comes to naming their children, it appears from the Office for National Statistics' records that traditional names are still generally the most common.

Jack and Chloe are currently the most popular names across the UK and have been the top choices for the last few years. However much you like these names, do bear in mind that your child – although unique to you – may be one of several Jacks or Chloes in the classroom in the years to come...

Jack

Chloe

Emily

Josh

Top 10 baby names in England & Wales for 2002

Boys
1. Jack
2. Joshua
3. Thomas
4. James
5. Daniel
6. Benjamin
7. William
8. Samuel
9. Joseph
10. Oliver

Girls
1. Chloe
2. Emily
3. Jessica
4. Ellie
5. Sophie
6. Megan
7. Charlotte
8. Lucy
9. Hannah
10. Olivia

Source: Office for National Statistics, England and Wales

Top 10 baby names in Scotland for 2002

Boys
1. Jack
2. Lewis
3. Cameron
4. Ryan
5. James
6. Jamie
7. Liam
8. Matthew
9. Ross
10. Callum

Girls
1. Chloe
2. Sophie
3. Emma
4. Amy
5. Erin
6. Ellie
7. Rachel
8. Lauren
9. Megan
10. Hannah

Source: General Register Office for Scotland (GROS)

Top 10 baby names in Wales for 2002

Boys
1. Joshua
2. Jack
3. Thomas
4. Dylan
5. Rhys
6. Daniel
7. Ethan
8. Luke
9. James
10. Benjamin

Girls
1. Chloe
2. Megan
3. Ellie
4. Emily
5. Jessica
6. Sophie
7. Caitlin
8. Lauren
9. Ffion
10. Lucy

Source: Office for National Statistics, England and Wales

Top 10 baby names in Northern Ireland for 2002

Boys
1. Matthew
2. Jack
3. Ryan
4. James
5. Adam
6. Joshua
7. Conor
8. Ben
9. Dylan
10. Daniel

Girls
1. Chloe
2. Caitlin
3. Katie
4. Megan
5. Emma
6. Amy
7. Lauren
8. Sarah
9. Hannah
10. Rebecca

Source: Northern Ireland Statistics & Research Agency (NISRA)

BARRY
BELTANE
BARTHOLOMEW

B

Barrett	Old German – bear-like
Barrie	Alternative spelling of Barry
Barrington	Common English place name and aristocratic surname, now also used as a first name. Short/pet forms: Barrie, Barry
Barry	Phonetic spelling of the Gaelic name Bearach, meaning 'spear'. Also a short/pet form of Barrington. Short/pet forms: Baz, Bazza *(Barrie)*
Barrymore	Variant of Barry
Bart	Short/pet form of Bartholomew, now also an independent name
Bartholomew	Hebrew – son of the furrow, ploughman. Short/pet forms: Bart, Barth, Barty, Batty, Tolly
Bartle	Derived from Bartholomew
Bartley	Derived from Bartholomew
Barton	Anglo-Saxon – barley farm
Bartram	Variant of Bertram
Baruch	Hebrew – blessed
Basil	Greek – kingly, brave. Always a very popular name in Eastern Europe, the Crusaders brought it back with them to England. Also a species of herb. Short/pet forms: Bas, Basie
Batista	Variant of Baptista *(Battista)*
Battista	Alternative spelling of Batista
Baxter	Anglo-Saxon – baker

Bayard	Old German – reddish-brown hair
Baynard	Anglo-Saxon – reddish-brown
Beau	French – handsome, beautiful
Beaumont	French – beautiful mountain
Beauregard	French – beautiful view
Beavis	Alternative spelling of Bevis
Beavys	Alternative spelling of Bevis
Beck	Old Norse – brook
Bede	Anglo-Saxon – prayer. An English historian, the venerable Bede (*c.*673–735) was a monk in a monastery at Jarrow
Beldon	Anglo-Saxon – unspoiled glen
Bellamy	French – beautiful friend
Beltane	Unknown origin – May Day
Ben	Short/pet form of Benedict and Benjamin, Ben is now also an independent name

BERKELEY
BENJAMIN
BEVAN

Benedick	Alternative spelling of Benedict
Benedict	Derived from the Latin *benedictus*, meaning 'blessed'. Short/pet forms: Ben, Benny *(Benedick)*
Benet	Alternative spelling of Benett
Benett	Derived from Benedict *(Benet, Bennet, Bennett)*
Benjamin	Hebrew – son of the right hand. (The right hand was traditionally linked with strength). Short/pet forms: Ben, Benjie, Benjy, Benny
Bennet	Alternative spelling of Benett
Bennett	Alternative spelling of Benett
Benson	Hebrew – excellent son, son of Benjamin
Bentley	Anglo-Saxon – from the field of coarse grass
Benton	Variant of Bentley
Berenger	French – courage of a bear
Bergren	Old Norse – mountain stream
Berk	Turkish – solid and firm
Berke	Variant of Burke
Berkeley	Anglo-Saxon – birch wood/meadow
Berman	Old German/Anglo-Saxon – keeper of bears
Bernard	Old German – brave as a bear, bold, bear-like. Short/pet forms: Barn, Barney, Barnie, Barny, Bern, Berne, Bernie, Berny *(Bernhard)*

Bernhard	Alternative spelling of Bernard
Berrigan	Aborigine – wattle
Berthold	Old German – ruling in splendour
Berton	Variant of Berthold
Bertram	Old German – bright raven. Short/pet forms: Bert, Bertie
Bertrand	Variant of Bertram
Bertwin	Old German – illustrious friend
Bes	Egyptian – brings joy
Bevan	Celtic – youthful warrior, son the of Evan
Bevis	French – beautiful view *(Beavis, Beavys)*
Bhima	Sanskrit – the mighty one
Bialy	Polish – white-haired boy
Bijan	Persian – ancient hero
Bill	Short/pet form of William, now also an independent name

BLAIR

BOYCE

BRADLEY

Billy	Short/pet form of William, now also an independent name
Bingham	Anglo-Saxon – crib. Short/pet form: Bing
Birch	Species of tree
Bishop	Anglo-Saxon – bishop
Bjorn	Scandinavian form of Bernard
Blade	Anglo-Saxon – glory
Blaine	Gaelic – yellow/yellow-haired
Blair	Scottish place name – a Celtic word implying a suitable place for a battle, such as a field
Blaise	Latin – lisping
Blake	Anglo-Saxon – black, dark-skinned, and also, confusingly, pale, fair-complexioned
Blaze	Latin – flaming fire. Name implies dynamism and energy
Boaz	Hebrew – in him is strength. In the Old Testament Ruth married the wealthy Boaz
Boden	French form of Boyden
Bogart	French – strong as a bow
Bolton	Anglo-Saxon – of the manor farm
Bona	Variant of Bonar
Bonar	Latin – good
Boniface	Latin – doer of good, benefactor
Bono	Variant of Bonar
Boone	French – good

Borden	Anglo-Saxon – from the valley of the boar
Boris	Russian – fighter, one who battles
Bowen	Celtic – son of Owen
Bowie	Gaelic – yellow-haired
Bowman	Anglo-Saxon – archer
Boyce	French – from the woodland
Boyd	Celtic – yellow. Probably describing the colour of hair
Boydell	Celtic – wise fair one
Boyden	Anglo-Saxon – a herald
Brad	Anglo-Saxon – broad. Also short/pet form of Bradley
Braden	Anglo-Saxon – from the wide valley. Also a variant of Bradley
Bradford	Anglo-Saxon – broad crossing. Also an English place name
Bradley	Anglo-Saxon – dweller in the broad meadow. Short/pet form: Brad

BRETON

BRAMWELL
BRODERICK

B

Bradney	Variant of Bradley
Brady	Anglo-Saxon – broad island. Also a variant of Bradley
Bram	Derived from Abraham
Bramwell	Anglo-Saxon – bramble well
Bran	Celtic – raven
Brand	Old Norse – sword blade
Brandon	Variant of Brendan, or of Anglo-Saxon origin, meaning 'gorse hill'
Brant	Old German – firebrand
Braxton	Anglo-Saxon – Brock's town
Brendan	Derived from the Gaelic Brenaian, believed to mean 'dweller by the beacon', a more credible and certainly preferable interpretation than 'stinking hair', the meaning given by some authorities. Short/pet form: Brend (Brendon)
Brendon	Alternative spelling of Brendan
Brennan	Variant of Brendan
Brent	Anglo-Saxon/Celtic – high, steep hill
Brentan	Variant of Brent
Breton	Latin – a Breton, a native of Brittany. Breton was the Celtic word for the people of north-west France and their form of the Celtic language (Britton)
Brett	Variant of Breton
Brewis	Variant of Bruno

Brewster	Anglo-Saxon – brewer
Brian	Celtic – two possible derivations: hill, or strong. Popular name in Ireland thanks to the hero king, Brian Boru (Brien, Brion, Bryan)
Briant	Variant of Brian
Briar	Variant of Brian
Brice	Celtic – speckled/freckled one (Bryce)
Brien	Alternative spelling of Brian
Brindley	Celtic/Anglo-Saxon – burning wood. A place name associated with a woodland clearing and also with the reddish-brown colour of wood
Brion	Alternative spelling of Brian
Britton	Alternative spelling of Breton
Brock	Anglo-Saxon/Celtic – badger. The traditional name for a badger in folk and children's stories, as Bruno is for bear
Broderick	Norse – brother. The name was traditionally given to a second son. Also thought to have an Anglo-Saxon origin, meaning 'from the broad ridge'
Brody	Gaelic – ditch
Bromwell	Anglo-Saxon – dweller by wild broom spring
Bronson	Anglo-Saxon – son of the dark-skinned one

BRYAN

BROOKLYN

BYRON

Bronson	Variant of Bruno
Brook	Anglo-Saxon – reward, pleasure. Adopted as a surname before it became a first name for both sexes (the girl's spelling is usually Brooke)
Brooklyn	US place name, more commonly used for girls than for boys
Brooks	Anglo-Saxon – running water
Bruce	Derived originally from a French place name Braose, now Brieuse, probably meaning 'brushwood thicket'. It came to Britain as a surname with the Norman Conquest. Scottish parents began using it as a given name in the 19th century and its popularity spread
Bruno	Old German – brown, bear-like. The folk name for a bear, as Brock is for badger
Brutus	Latin – heavy, unreasonable. Name of the Roman soldier and statesman who helped assassinate Julius Caesar, and was immortalized in Shakespeare's *Julius Caesar*
Bryan	Alternative spelling of Brian
Bryant	Variant of Brian
Bryce	Alternative spelling of Brice
Bryn	Welsh – hill
Bryson	Anglo-Saxon – son of Bryce

Bryton	Anglo-Saxon – a Briton
Buchan	Scottish place name, meaning 'little hut'
Buck	Anglo-Saxon – male deer
Bud	German – off-shoot
Budi	Indonesian – the wise one
Buddy	From the US nickname for 'friend'
Burian	Slavonic – lives near the weeds
Burke	Old German – castle
Burnet	Alternative spelling of Burnett. Also a species of plant
Burnett	Anglo-Saxon – brown *(Burnet)*
Burr	Old Norse – youth
Burt	Derived from Burton
Burton	Anglo-Saxon – bright fame
Busby	Old Norse – dweller in a thicket. Short/pet form: Buzz
Buzz	Short/pet form of Busby, now also an independent name
Byrd	Anglo-Saxon – like a bird
Byrle	Unknown origin – cup bearer
Byron	Anglo-Saxon – at the cattlesheds, cowherd

CAINE

CALVIN

CALDWELL

C

Cadell	Welsh – battle spirit
Cadeo	Vietnamese – folk song
Cadeyrn	Welsh – battle king
Cadfael	Welsh – battle metal
Cadman	Welsh – strong in battle
Cadmus	Welsh – eastern
Cadoc	Celtic – war-like
Cadogan	Celtic – little battle
Cador	Cornish – shield
Caesar	Possibly Latin – head of hair. Name used by Roman imperial family
Cain	Hebrew – craftsman *(Caine)*
Caine	Alternative spelling of Cain
Cairbre	Gaelic – strong man, pronounced 'kar-bra'
Calder	Anglo-Saxon – stream
Caldwell	Anglo-Saxon – cold spring
Caleb	Hebrew – bold. In the Old Testament Caleb set out with Moses from Egypt and was, with Joshua, one of the two original migrants to enter the promised land. Short/pet form: Cal
Caley	Gaelic – slender
Calhoun	Celtic – warrior. Short/pet form: Cal

Callum	Gaelic form of Columba, meaning 'dove'. St Columba left Ireland with 12 companions to found a monastery on the island of Iona, off the West Coast of Scotland. Short/pet form: Cal *(Calum)*
Calum	Alternative spelling of Callum
Calvert	Anglo-Saxon – calf herder. Short/pet form: Cal
Calvin	Latin – bald. Short/pet form: Cal
Camden	Scottish – winding valley
Cameron	Gaelic – crooked nose
Campbell	Gaelic – crooked mouth
Canute	Old Norse – knot
Caradoc	Celtic – friendly, loving. This popular Welsh name, from Caradawg, honours their first-century hero who repelled the Romans and after whom the place Cardigan is named

C

CARRICK

CASPER

CAVANAUGH

Carbury	Unknown origin – charioteer
Carew	Gaelic – castle/fort
Carey	Alternative spelling of Cary
Carl	Old German – free man, farmer. Origin of the English name Charles (*Karl, Karle*)
Carleton	Anglo-Saxon – carl's (farmer's) town (*Carlton*)
Carlisle	Anglo-Saxon – carl's (farmer's) island
Carlo	Italian form of Carl/Charles
Carlos	Spanish form of Carl/Charles
Carlton	Alternative spelling of Carleton
Carr	Old Norse – from the marsh
Carrick	Phonetic spelling of the Gaelic name Carraig, meaning 'rock', 'dweller on the rocky headland'
Carroll	Phonetic spelling of the Gaelic name Cearbhall, meaning 'champion warrior'
Carson	Old Norse – son of Carr
Carter	Anglo-Saxon – cart driver
Carthach	Gaelic form of Caradoc
Carver	Anglo-Saxon – carver, sculptor
Cary	Uncertain origins. Possibly derived from an English place name Carew, meaning 'fort', or Welsh 'dweller in a castle', or, as one authority suggests, from the Latin 'dear' (*Carey*)

Casey	Gaelic – watchful, brave. Used for both boys and girls (*Kacy, Kasey*)
Caspar	Alternative spelling of Casper
Casper	German – imperial, precious, treasurer. The English equivalent is Jasper (*Caspar, Kaspar*)
Cassidy	Gaelic – clever
Cassius	Latin. Old Roman family name of uncertain meaning
Cathal	Gaelic – battle + rule, pronounced 'ko-hal'
Cato	Latin – knowledgeable, wise
Cavan	Derived from Cavanagh
Cavanagh	Gaelic – handsome (*Cavanaugh*)
Cavanaugh	Alternative spelling of Cavanagh
Cavell	French – active and bold
Cebert	Old German – bright. Short/pet form: Bert, Bertie

CASSIDY

CESAR

CHANDLER
CHESTER **C**

Cecil	Latin – blind. Derived from an old Roman family name, and the name of the son of Vulcan, the god of fire and craftsmanship in Roman mythology. Also an ancient surname of Welsh origin. Short/pet form: Ces *(Cecile)*
Cecile	Alternative spelling of Cecil
Cedric	Invented by Sir Walter Scott in his 1819 novel *Ivanhoe*
Cesar	Variant of Caesar
Chad	Anglo-Saxon – battle, warrior. Name of a seventh-century saint. Also a place name
Chadwick	Variant of Chad
Chae	Alternative spelling of Chay
Chaim	Hebrew – life
Chale	Spanish – strong and manly
Chalmers	Scottish – son of the lord
Chance	Derived from Chancellor
Chancellor	Anglo-Saxon – keeper of records, secretary
Chandler	French – candlemaker
Chapin	French – clergyman
Chapman	Anglo-Saxon – merchant
Charles	English form of the German name Carl. A favourite royal name since it was adopted by the House of Stuart in the 17th century. Short/pet forms: Chae, Charley, Charlie, Chars, Chas, Chay, Chaz, Chuck
Charleston	US place name
Charley	Alternative spelling of Charlie
Charlie	Short/pet form of Charles, now also an independent name *(Charley)*
Charlton	Anglo-Saxon – settlement of peasants
Chase	French – hunter
Chauncey	Latin – chancellor, academic
Chay	Short/pet form of Charles, now also an independent name *(Chae)*
Chen	Chinese – great, vast
Cheney	French – from the oak forest
Chenzira	Shona – born on a journey
Chester	Latin – fortified castle, town. Also a place name
Chet	Derived from Chester
Chevalier	French – knight

HERO
WORSHIP

Heroes are people we tend to idolize for possessing superior qualities – be it courage, fortitude, nobility, talent, beauty or even superhuman ability. They may figure in the world of entertainment (film stars, musicians, TV celebrities or fictional screen heroes), politics (respected politicians or world leaders) or science (inventors and pioneers in medicine). They could be military or sporting heroes, or simply the first or the best in their field. This is one of the widest sources of names for your child – just think of the endless possibilities that are out there...

Since you really could choose any sphere and influence from around the globe, the relatively small number of names that follow will simply serve to point you in the direction of inspiration.

PIERCE AGATHA
AMELIA MARILYN
BRIDGET DAVID

Boys

Bobby Charlton, legendary Manchester United and England footballer
Charlie Chaplin, 20th-century comedian
David Beckham, English footballer of iconic status
Edmund Hillary, first European to climb Mt Everest
Elvis Presley, American rock 'n' roll star
Frank Bruno, British heavyweight boxer
Hercules, mythological hero of great strength

James Bond, 007, fictional British secret agent
John Lennon, Beatles singer/songwriter
John Wayne, American screen hero
Louis Armstrong, American jazz musician
Luke Skywalker, fictional hero of the *Star Wars* saga
Martin Luther King Jr, American clergyman and civil rights leader
Michael Owen, footballer with prolific goal-scoring record

Muhammad Ali, world-famous American heavyweight boxer
Neil Armstrong, first man to walk on the moon
Nelson Mandela, South African political leader imprisoned for anti-apartheid activities
Pierce Brosnan, British actor who plays James Bond
Roger Bannister, first man to run the mile in under four minutes (in 1954)
Winston Churchill, British statesman, author and historian

Girls

Agatha Christie, prolific writer of detective novels
Amelia Earhart (Putnam), the first woman to fly over the Atlantic
Anne Frank, young Jewish-Dutch diarist
Bridget Jones, fictional bumbling heroine created by Helen Fielding
Catherine the Great, 18th-century Empress of Russia
Cleopatra VII, first-century BC Queen of Egypt
Delia Smith, British TV cook

Diana Princess of Wales, 'the People's Princess'
Emmeline Pankhurst, British suffragette
Eva 'Evita' Duarte Peron, Argentinian political leader
Florence Nightingale, 19th-century British hospital reformer
Germaine Greer, feminist
Golda Meir, Israeli stateswoman and prime minister 1969–74
Joan of Arc, 15th-century French patriot and martyr

Lara Croft, fictional computer game heroine
Madonna, singer/actress
Margaret Thatcher, first British female prime minister
Marie Curie, Polish-born physicist, discovered radium
Marilyn Monroe, American actress and sex symbol
Martina Navratilova, famous tennis player who holds nine Wimbledon singles tennis titles
Mother Teresa, 20th-century Albanian missionary

CLARK
CHRISTIAN
CLAYTON

Cheyenne Native American – unintelligible speakers

Chicago Native American – powerful. Also a US place name

Chick Variant of Charles

Chill Derived from Chilton

Chilton Anglo-Saxon – town by the river

Chimalsi Swahili – young and proud

Christian Derived from the Latin *christianus*, meaning 'a Christian'. A name used by the Danish royal family since the 15th century. Short/pet forms: Chris, Kit, Kris *(Christien, Cristian, Kristian)*

Christien Alternative spelling of Christian

Christmas Name used for both girls and boys born at Christmastime, the annual Christian festival that celebrates the birth of Christ

Christoph Variant of Christopher *(Krystof)*

Christopher Greek – one who carries Christ. The legendary St Christopher carried the infant Jesus across a ford. He is the patron saint of travellers. Short/pet forms: all Chip, Chris, Christy, Kit, Kris *(Kristoffer)*

Christos Greek – Christ

Chuck American (short/pet) form of Charles

Cian Gaelic – ancient

Cicero Latin – historian

Ciro Spanish – sun

Clancy Gaelic – ruddy/red warrior

Clarence Latin – of Clare. Edward III created the title Duke of Clarence for his son Lionel on his marriage to a young lady of the de Clare family in 1362

Clarendon Latin/Anglo-Saxon – famous gentleman

Clark Latin – clerk, cleric, learned man. The original name for the church scholars who were the only people who could read and write. Was a surname, now adopted as a first name *(Clarke)*

Clarke Alternative spelling of Clark

Claude Variant of Claudius

Claudian Variant of Claudius

Claudio Variant of Claudius

Claudius Latin – lame. Name of the lame Roman emperor and historian who popularized the name within Roman Britain

Claus Variant of Claudius. Also derived from Nicholas

Clayland Variant of Clayton

Clayton Anglo-Saxon – from the clay town. A place name, referring to local clay pits or clay beds

COLBRAN

CLIFFORD

COLIN C

Cleavant	Anglo-Saxon – a steep bank
Cleave	Variant of Cleavant
Cleavon	Variant of Cleavant
Cledwyn	Celtic – blessed sword
Clemence	Variant of Clement (Clemens)
Clemens	Alternative spelling of Clemence
Clement	Latin – gentle, merciful, mild. Short/pet form: Clem
Cleon	Greek – glorious, famous
Cleveland	Anglo-Saxon – from the cliffs
Cliff	Short/pet form of Clifford and Clifton, it is now also an independent name
Clifford	Anglo-Saxon – ford by a cliff. Short/pet form: Cliff
Clifton	Anglo-Saxon – town by a cliff. Short/pet form: Cliff
Clint	Short/pet form of Clinton, now also an independent name
Clinton	Anglo-Saxon – headland farm, settlement on the summit. Short/pet form: Clint
Clive	Anglo-Saxon – cliff, steep hill
Clyde	Name of a Scottish river
Clydias	Unknown origin – glorious
Codey	Alternative spelling of Cody
Codie	Alternative spelling of Cody
Cody	Gaelic – uncertain meaning (Codey, Codie)

Coemgen	Breton form of Kevin
Colan	Alternative spelling of Colin
Colbert	Old German/Old French – bright, famous. Short/pet forms: Bert, Bertie
Colbran	Anglo-Saxon – firebrand
Colby	Anglo-Saxon – from the coal town/dark country
Cole	Anglo-Saxon – coal, black. Possibly also derived from Nicholas, meaning 'victory of the people'
Coleman	Anglo-Saxon – dark, charcoal burner (Colman)
Coleridge	Anglo-Saxon – dweller by the black ridge
Colier	Variant of Cole
Colin	French diminutive of Col, a short form of Nicholas. Also Anglicized form of the Gaelic name Cailean meaning 'dove'

CONNOR COOPER CORVIN

Colley	Anglo-Saxon – swarthy, black-haired
Collin	Alternative spelling of Colin
Collis	Variant of Cole
Colm	Gaelic – dove, pronounced 'coll-um'
Colman	Alternative spelling of Coleman
Colton	Anglo-Saxon – from coal/dark town
Columba	Dove. *See* Callum
Columbia	Variant of Columba
Columbus	Variant of Columba
Colvin	Unknown origin – dark friend
Conan	Celtic – wolf, hound
Conlan	Gaelic – hero, mighty. Short/pet form: Con
Connell	Anglicized form of the Gaelic name Conall, meaning 'wise chief'. Short/pet form: Con
Connor	Phonetic spelling of the Gaelic name Concobhar, meaning 'lover of wolves/hounds'. Short/pet form: Con *(Conor)*
Conor	Alternative spelling of Connor
Conrad	Anglicized form of the German name Konrad. Short/pet form: Con
Conroy	Variant of Conrad
Constantine	Latin – constant, faithful, resolute. Constantine the Great was the first Christian Emperor of Rome. He built the city of Constantinople on the site of ancient Byzantium, now called Istanbul. Short/pet form: Con

Conway	Variant of Conroy
Cooper	Latin – barrel maker
Corban	Alternative spelling of Korben
Corbet	Alternative spelling of Corbett
Corbett	Latin – raven *(Corbet)*
Corbin	Variant of Corbett
Corcoran	Gaelic – of reddish complexion
Corey	Anglo-Saxon surname, which was derived from Old Norse *(Cory, Kory, Korey)*
Corin	Latin – spear bearer
Cornel	Alternative spelling of Cornell
Cornelian	Derived from carnelian, a red or reddish-yellow gemstone
Cornelius	Latin – horn-like (cornucopia)
Cornell	Variant of Cornelius *(Cornel)*
Cort	German – bold
Corvin	Possibly Latin – raven, black

CURTIS
CRAWFORD
CYRUS C

Corwin	Anglo-Saxon – heart's friend
Cory	Celtic – helmet. Also an alternative spelling of Corey
Cosimo	Alternative spelling of Cosmo
Cosmo	Greek – harmony, universe *(Cosimo)*
Courtney	Aristocratic surname derived from a French place name, and now used as a first name for both boys and girls
Cowall	Phonetic spelling of the Gaelic name Comhghall, meaning 'pledge', 'hostage'
Cowan	Gaelic – stone mason
Craig	Gaelic – crag, rock
Cramer	Unknown origin – merchant
Crawford	Scottish place name, meaning 'ford where the crows gather', and a surname, now used as a first name
Creighton	Gaelic – border settlement
Crispian	Alternative spelling of Crispin
Crispin	Derived from the Latin *crispus*, meaning 'curled', it was made famous by the third-century patron saint of shoemakers. The name is often associated with boys that have curly hair *(Crispian)*
Cristian	Alternative spelling of Christian
Cronus	Possibly Greek – crow. Father of Zeus in Greek mythology

Crosby	Anglo-Saxon – dweller by the crossing
Cullen	Celtic – young animal, handsome
Culver	Anglo-Saxon – dove
Curran	Gaelic – hero
Curry	Gaelic – marsh, or a herb
Curt	Variant of Curtis. *See also* Kurt
Curtis	Old French – courteous. The old spelling was Curteis
Cuthbert	Old German/Anglo-Saxon – brilliant wisdom, splendour. Short/pet forms: Bert, Bertie
Cynric	Anglo-Saxon – with royal might
Cyrano	Greek – from Cyrene
Cyriack	Variant of Cyril
Cyril	Greek – lordly. Short/pet form: Cy *(Cyrill)*
Cyrill	Alternative spelling of Cyril
Cyrus	Derived from the Persian *kuru*, meaning 'throne'. The Puritans adopted this name, which occurs in the Old Testament

DAMIAN

DAIRMID

DANIEL

D

Dacre	Cumberland place name, meaning 'trickling stream', and an aristocratic surname, now used as a first name
Dafydd	Welsh form of David
Dag	Old Norse – day
Dagan	Hebrew – grain
Dahoma	Swahili – long life
Dai	Welsh pet form of David
Dairmid	Celtic – free from envy, pronounced 'der-mott' (*Diarmait, Diarmid, Diarmud*)
Dakota	Native American – ally. Also a US place name. Used for boys and girls
Dale	Anglo-Saxon – valley. A common surname, it has now been adopted as a first name for both sexes, but more usually for boys (*Dayle*)
Daley	Gaelic – assembly (*Daly*)
Dallas	Celtic – skilled, or from the water field. Also a US place name used for both boys and girls
Dalton	Anglo-Saxon – dweller in the vale
Daly	Alternative spelling of Daley
Dalziel	Celtic – from the small field, pronounced 'dee-yell'

Damek	Slavonic – earth
Damen	Alternative spelling of Damon
Damian	Greek – one who tames. Name of the fifth-century patron saint of doctors (*Damien, Damion*)
Damien	Alternative spelling of Damian
Damion	Alternative spelling of Damian
Damon	Variant of Damian (*Damen*)
Dan	Short/pet form of Daniel, now also an independent name
Dane	Anglo-Saxon – from Denmark
Daniel	Hebrew – God is my judge. A well-known name thanks to the biblical prophet who was thrown into the lion's den and survived. Short/pet forms: Dan, Danny

DALZIEL

DARIEN

DARRELL

DASAN

Dante	Italian – lasting
Danton	Variant of Dante
Darby	Gaelic – freeman
Darcy	Derived from the surname, D'Arcy, which came from a French place name and was brought to England with the Norman Conquest. Used for both boys and girls
Darel	Alternative spelling of Darryl. Also Aborigine – blue sky
Darell	Alternative spelling of Darryl
Darien	Variant of Darren *(Darrion)*
Darin	Persian – precious present
Dario	Spanish form of Darius
Darius	Name of several ancient Persian kings, one of whom invaded Greece and was defeated at the battle of Marathon in 490BC
Darnell	Anglo-Saxon – hidden nook
Darol	Alternative spelling of Darryl
Darragh	Gaelic – oak
Darran	Alternative spelling of Darren
Darrel	Alternative spelling of Darryl
Darrell	Alternative spelling of Darryl
Darren	Anglo-Saxon – dearly beloved. The same language root as Darryl, another surname popularized as a first name *(Darran, Darrin, Darryn)*
Darrin	Alternative spelling of Darren
Darrion	Alternative spelling of Darien
Darrol	Alternative spelling of Darryl
Darryl	Anglo-Saxon – beloved. A surname turned first name, helped by the name of the film producer Darryl Zanuck who founded 20th-Century Fox. Used occasionally for girls. Short/pet form: Darry *(Darel, Darell, Darol, Darrel, Darrell, Darrol, Daryl)*
Darryn	Alternative spelling of Darren
Darwin	Anglo-Saxon – lover of the sea. Also an Australian place name
Daryl	Alternative spelling of Darryl
Dasan	Native American – leader

DARIUS

David	Darling, derived from the Hebrew word 'beloved'. In the Bible it was the name of the boy who killed the giant Goliath and later became king of Israel, and father of the great King Solomon. A popular name in Wales thanks to the sixth-century patron saint of Wales. Short/pet forms: Dave, Davey, Davy
Davis	Scottish – David's son
Dayle	Alternative spelling of Dale
Dayton	Anglo-Saxon – cheerful town. Also a place name
Deacon	Greek – servant, messenger
Dean	Anglo-Saxon – valley, dweller in the valley. Also Latin – presiding official
Decker	Anglo-Saxon – roofer
Declan	Phonetic spelling of the Gaelic name Deaglan, meaning 'full of goodness'
Deepak	Alternative spelling of Dipak
Delano	French – of the night. Short/pet form: Del
Delbert	Anglo-Saxon – bright like daytime. Short/pet forms: Bert, Bertie, Del
Delvin	Greek – dolphin. Short/pet form: Del
Deman	Dutch – man
Demetrius	Derived from Demeter, the goddess of the harvest in Greek mythology

Dempsey	Gaelic — proud
Dempster	Variant of Dempsey
Denali	Native American – the great one
Denbeigh	Alternative spelling of Denby
Denby	Old Norse – from the Danes' settlement (Denbeigh)
Denham	Anglo-Saxon – from the home in the valley
Denis	Derived from Dionysus, the god of wine and revelry in Greek mythology. Used in the Middle Ages when it led to surnames such as Dennis, Dennison, Denny and Tennyson. Short/pet form: Denny (Dennis, Denys)
Denman	Anglo-Saxon – man of the valley
Dennis	More modern spelling of Denis
Denver	Anglo-Saxon – from the edge of the valley. Also a US place name
Denys	Alternative spelling of Denis
Denzel	Alternative spelling of Denzil
Denziel	Alternative spelling of Denzil
Denzil	Originally a Cornish place name before becoming a first name (Denzel, Denziel, Denzyl)
Denzyl	Alternative spelling of Denzil
Derby	Anglo-Saxon – place of the deer
Derek	Old German – ruler of the people. Short/pet forms: Derry, Rick, Ricky (Derik, Derrick, Deryk)

DEXTOR
DESMOND
DIONYSUS

Derex	Variant of Derek
Derik	Alternative spelling of Derek
Dermot	Phonetic spelling of the Gaelic name Dairmid. Short/pet form: Derry (Dermott)
Dermott	Alternative spelling of Dermot
Derrick	Alternative spelling of Derek
Derry	Short/pet form of Derek and Dermot. Also an Irish place name
Derwin	Anglo-Saxon – valued friend of the people
Deryk	Alternative spelling of Derek
Desiderio	Spanish – desire
Desmond	Derived from a Gaelic name, which means 'man from south Muster'. Short/pet forms: Des, Desi, Dezi (Desmund)
Desmund	Alternative spelling of Desmond
Devereux	Popular US name originally derived from a Norman surname, D'Evreux
Devlin	Gaelic – brave
Devnet	Gaelic – poet
Devon	English place name
Dewey	Welsh form of David
Dewitt	Flemish – blond, fair-haired
Dexter	Latin – skilful, dexterous. Short/pet form: Dex
Dhugal	Alternative spelling of Dougal
Dian	Indonesian – a candle

Diarmait	Alternative spelling of Dairmid
Diarmid	Alternative spelling of Dairmid
Diarmud	Alternative spelling of Dairmid
Dieter	German – the people's ruler
Digby	Anglo-Saxon – a settlement by a ditch
Dillan	Alternative spelling of Dillon
Dillon	Gaelic – faithful (Dillan)
Dilwyn	Welsh – blessed/fair truth
Dimitri	Variant of Demetrius (Dmitri)
Dino	Variant of Dean
Dion	Derived from Dionysus, the god of wine and revelry in Greek mythology, which produced the name Denis
Dionysus	God of wine and revelry in Greek mythology, equivalent to the Roman god Bacchus
Dipak	Sanskrit – light, little lamp (Deepak)
Dirk	Dutch/German form of Derek
Dixon	Old German – Richard's son
Dmitri	Alternative spelling of Dimitri
Doane	Celtic – dune dweller
Dolan	Gaelic – dark-haired
Domenic	Alternative spelling of Dominic

GEOGRAPHICAL
NAMES

In Anglophile countries, many of today's first names derive from Anglo-Saxon or Celtic words for geographical features and place names, which were originally used to describe where a person lived. Examples include Ainsley ('my meadow'), Ashley ('ash field'), Clayton ('from the clay town'), Hayley ('hay meadow'), Shelley ('clearing on a slope'), Shirley ('bright meadow') and Willoughby ('farm beside the willow trees'). Over time these descriptive place names became proper surnames, eventually becoming the first names we know today.

In recent years the trend has been to name children after cities, countries and other geographical places. The trend seems to be one particularly promoted by celebrities, for example, Madonna named her daughter Lourdes and actress Kim Basinger's daughter is called Ireland. Many place names can be used for children of either sex – Paris, Dallas, Memphis and Phoenix are all examples.

Your reasons for choosing a place name may be dictated by fond memories of a holiday somewhere. Do take care choosing a geographical name for your child. In your quest for a unique name, don't just shut your eyes and stick a pin in a map because you think it might be fun. Spare a thought for your child having to explain his/her unusual name or correct its mis-pronunciation throughout his/her life.

Boys

Aden	Denzil	Oxford
Albany	Derry	Paris
Arran	Devon	Pembroke
Arundel	Dudley	Perth
Ascot	Durham	Phoenix
Austell	Eden	Preston
Austin	Fife	Richmond
Avon	Hamilton	Rio
Bradford	Hudson	Rocky
Brooklyn	Jordan	Royston
Chad	Kent	Rye
Charleston	Kingston	Stirling
Chester	Lansing	Stoke
Chicago	Lincoln	Sydney
Cleveland	Lorne	Trent
Clyde	Memphis	Tyne
Dallas	Milan	Tyrol
Darwin	Milford	Tyrone
Dayton	Missouri	Whitby
Denby	Montgomery	Windsor
Denver	Orlando	York

Girls

Adelaide	Dominica	Petra
Ailsa	Etna	Phoenix
Alabama	Florence	Rhoda
Alexandria	Geneva	Rhona/Rona
Andorra	Georgia	Rhonda
Arcadia	India	Rochelle
Asia	Ireland	Roma
Asmara	Italy	Roslyn
Augusta	Jakarta	Shannon
Brittany	Kerry	Shenandoah
Brooklyn	Lorraine	Siena
Capri	Lourdes	Skye
Carmel	Malaya	Sofia
Cathay	Martinique	Tallulah
Chelsea	Memphis	Tara
China	Missouri	Valencia
Clare	Odessa	Verona
Dakota	Orissa	Victoria
Dallas	Paris	Winona

ROYSTON
CHELSEA
PARIS
LINCOLN
TALLULAH
JAKARTA

DONOVAN

DOMINICK

DREW

Dominic Latin – belonging to the Lord. Used by Roman Catholic families since the 13th-century saint founded the Dominican order of friars. Short/pet form: Dom *(Domenic, Dominick)*

Dominick Alternative spelling of Dominic

Don Short/pet form of Donaghan, Donahue, Donald and Donovan, it is now also an independent name in its own right

Donaghan Celtic – of dark complexion. Short/pet forms: Don, Donny

Donahue Variant of Donald

Donal Variant of Donald

Donald Gaelic – world ruler. Six Scottish kings were called Donald. Short/pet forms: Don, Donny

Donat Celtic – given

Donato Latin – gift from God

Donelle Variant of Donald

Donelly Variant of Donald

Donkor Akan – the humble one

Donovan Gaelic – dark brown. Short/pet forms: Don, Donny

Doran Two possible meanings. Possibly from the Greek, meaning 'gift' or from an Irish surname, meaning 'descendant of the exile'

Dorian Greek – a man from Doris (a place in central Ancient Greece)

Dory French – golden-haired boy

Dougal Phonetic spelling of the Gaelic name Dughall, meaning 'dark stranger', which was used to describe the Vikings. It became a surname and was later taken up by Scottish parents as a first name. Short/pet forms: Doug, Dougie *(Dhugal, Doughal)*

Doughal Alternative spelling of Dougal

Douglas Derived from the Gaelic word *dubhghlas*, meaning 'dark water'. Short/pet forms: Doug, Dougie *(Douglass, Duglas)*

Douglass Alternative spelling of Douglas

Dovel Anglo-Saxon/Old Norse – young dove

Dow Gaelic – black-haired

Doyle Variant of Dougal

Doyt Variant of Dwight

Drake Anglo-Saxon – serpent, dragon

Drew Old French – sturdy. Also the short/pet form of Andrew

Driscoll Derived from a Gaelic surname meaning 'interpreter' or 'messenger'

Drystan Celtic – tumult, din

Duane Gaelic – black *(Dwane, Dwayne)*

Dudley English family name meaning 'Dudda's clearing'

DUSTY

DUNSTAN

DYLAN **D**

Duff	Phonetic spelling of the Gaelic name Dubh meaning 'black', 'dark-haired', 'of a dark complexion'
Dugan	Anglo-Saxon – to be worthy
Duglas	Alternative spelling of Douglas
Duke	Latin – leader, guide. Also the short/pet form of Marmaduke
Dunbar	Gaelic – dark branch
Duncan	Gaelic – dark/brown warrior. It has remained most popular in Scotland and is the name of the Scottish king murdered by his cousin and featured in Shakespeare's *Macbeth*
Dunn	Anglo-Saxon – brown. Also the short/pet form of Dunstan *(Dunne)*
Dunne	Alternative spelling of Dunn
Dunstan	Anglo-Saxon – stoney hill, dark stone. Name of the tenth-century English saint who was Archbishop of Canterbury. Short/pet forms: Dunn, Dunne, Dusty
Durand	Latin – enduring, lasting *(Durant)*
Durant	Alternative spelling of Durand
Durham	Anglo-Saxon – stockbreeding. Also a place name
Durwood	Anglo-Saxon – unflinching guard
Dusan	Slavonic – God is my judge
Dustin	German – valiant fighter. Short/pet form: Dusty

Dusty	Short/pet form of Dunstan and Dustin, it is now also an independent name
Dutch	German – the German
Dwane	Alternative spelling of Duane
Dwayne	Alternative spelling of Duane
Dwight	An English surname derived from the French name, Diot
Dyer	Anglo-Saxon – colourer of fabrics
Dylan	Welsh – son of the wave, man of the sea. Name of a legendary Welsh hero who was the son of a sea god. Popularized by the Welsh poet Dylan Thomas
Dymas	Name of the father of Hecate, goddess of the underworld in Greek mythology

EDGAR

EARLE

EDUARDO

E

Eamon	Gaelic form of Edmund. Name of the Irish President Eamon de Valera (1882–1973) *(Eamonn)*
Eamonn	Alternative spelling of Eamon
Earl	Anglo-Saxon – warrior, chief. Derived from the British title *(Erle, Earle)*
Earle	Alternative spelling of Earl
Earnest	Alternative spelling of Ernest
Earnst	Alternative spelling of Ernst
Eason	Gaelic – son of Adam
Eaton	Anglo-Saxon – from the riverside
Ebenezer	Hebrew – stone of help
Eberard	Old German – hardy, strong *(Eberhard)*
Eberhard	Alternative spelling of Eberard
Ebert	Old German/Anglo-Saxon – of active mind. Short/pet forms: Bert, Bertie
Edan	Variant of Aidan
Eden	Hebrew – delight. Name of biblical paradise. Used for boys and girls
Edgar	Anglo-Saxon – prosperous spear. Name of the first publicly acknowledged King of England. Short/pet forms: Ed, Eddie, Eddy
Edgard	Variant of Edgar and Edward
Edison	Anglo-Saxon – son of Edward
Edko	Czech form of Edgar
Edmond	More modern alternative spelling of Edmund
Edmund	Anglo-Saxon – happy + protection. Made famous by two saints and two early kings of England. Short/pet forms: Ed, Eddie, Eddy, Ned, Ted, Teddie, Teddy *(Edmond)*
Edom	Hebrew – red
Edouard	French form of Edward
Edric	Anglo-Saxon – happy ruler
Edsel	Anglo-Saxon – rich in self
Edson	Anglo-Saxon – son of Edward
Eduard	Dutch form of Edward
Eduardo	Spanish and Portuguese form of Edward *(Edwardo)*

EDWIN EGBERT

ELJAH E

Edward	Anglo-Saxon – happy + protection. Edward is also a recurrent name in the English/British royal line. Short/ pet forms: Ed, Eddie, Eddy, Ned, Ted, Teddie, Teddy	**Eldred**	Anglo-Saxon – mature counsellor
		Eldwin	Anglo-Saxon – old friend
		Elek	Hungarian – helper and defender of mankind
Edwardo	Alternative spelling of Eduardo	**Elewa**	Swahili – very intelligent
Edwin	Anglo-Saxon – rich friend. A common name in the days before the Norman Conquest, which became fashionable again in Victorian times. Short/pet forms: Ed, Eddie, Eddy (*Edwyn*)	**Elford**	Anglo-Saxon – dweller by the ford
		Elgin	Anglo-Saxon – noble
		Eli	Hebrew – height, elevation (*Ely*)
		Elia	Variant of Elijah
		Elias	Variant of Elijah
		Elijah	Hebrew – Jehovah is God, God's own given one
Edwyn	Alternative spelling of Edwin	**Elika**	Variant of Elijah
Efrat	Hebrew – honoured, distinguished	**Eliot**	Alternative spelling of Elliot
Efrem	Alternative spelling of Ephraim	**Eliott**	Alternative spelling of Elliot
Egan	Phonetic spelling of the Gaelic name Aodhagan meaning 'fiery', 'ardent'	**Elis**	Variant of Elisha
		Elisha	Variant of Elijah
Egbert	Anglo-Saxon – eminently bright, sword-edge bright. Short/pet forms: Bert, Bertie	**Eljah**	Variant of Elijah
Egmont	Old German – sword protector, patriot		
Einar	Old Norse – warrior, leader		
Eiran	Irish – peace		
Eitan	Variant of Ethan		
Elan	Native American – friendly		
Elber	Anglo-Saxon – elf grove		
Elden	Alternative spelling of Eldon		
Eldon	Anglo-Saxon – Ella's hill (*Elden*)		

Elkan	Hebrew – he belongs to God
Ellery	Old German/Anglo-Saxon. A surname meaning 'one who lives near the elder tree', now used as a first name for both boys and girls
Elliot	Diminutive form of Ellis, derived from the Hebrew name Elias *(Eliot, Eliott, Elliott)*
Elliott	Alternative spelling of Elliot
Ellis	Old French form of the Hebrew name Elias
Elmer	Anglo-Saxon – noble, famous
Elmo	Greek – amiable
Elmore	Anglo-Saxon – dweller by the elm tree moor
Elroy	French name taken from the Latin word, meaning 'regal'. A name derived from the title 'the king'
Elsdon	Anglo-Saxon place name meaning 'Ella's valley'
Elton	Anglo-Saxon place name meaning 'Ella's enclosure/settlement' or 'from the old estate/town'. The name has recently been boosted in its popularity by the singer Elton John
Elvan	Unknown origin – quick willed
Elvert	Unknown origin – variable
Elvin	Anglo-Saxon – friend of elves

Elvis	American name possibly adapted from Elvin, or from the trade name for cars, Alvis. Made fashionable by rock 'n' roll star Elvis Presley
Elwin	Anglo-Saxon – old friend *(Elwyn)*
Elwood	Anglo-Saxon – elf woods
Elwyn	Alternative spelling of Elwin
Ely	Alternative spelling of Eli
Emanuel	Alternative spelling of Emmanuel
Emanuele	Alternative spelling of Emmanuel
Emerson	Variant of Emery
Emery	Old German – powerful, rich, strong, wealthy. Anglicized form of the German name Emmerich, it was given to both sexes until confined to boys in the 19th century *(Emmery)*
Emil	German – striving, industrious *(Emile)*

ENOCH

EMMANUEL

ERNEST

Emile	Alternative spelling of Emil
Emilio	Italian form of Emil
Emlyn	Welsh name possibly derived from the Latin *aemulus* for 'rival'
Emmanuel	Hebrew – God is here. The biblical name for Christ – a popular Jewish name. Short/pet form: Manny *(Emanuel, Emanuele, Imanuel)*
Emmery	Alternative spelling of Emery
Emmet	Anglo-Saxon – industrious *(Emmett)*
Emmett	Alternative spelling of Emmet
Emrys	Variant of Ambrose
Emyr	Welsh – ruler, lord
Enan	Celtic – anvil, firm
Engelbert	Old German – bright messenger. Short/pet forms: Bert, Bertie
Ennis	Derived from Dennis
Enoch	Hebrew – dedicated, trained, teacher. Name of Cain's son in the Bible
Enold	Unknown origin – anointed
Enos	Hebrew – mankind
Enrico	Spanish form of Henry
Enrique	Basque form of Henry
Enyon	Cornish – anvil
Ephraim	Hebrew – very fruitful *(Efrem)*
Erasmus	Greek – to love. Name of the well-known 15th/16th-century Dutch humanist

Erastus	Greek – amiable
Erbert	Variant of Ebert
Erek	Polish – lovable
Erhard	Old German, meaning 'intelligent resolution'
Eric	Possibly Old Norse – ever ruling, island ruler, kingly, powerful. An ancient name in Scandinavian countries, it seems to have been brought to England by the Danes – there is an Iricus mentioned in the Domesday Book
Erik	German form of Eric
Erland	Old Norse – honourable
Erle	Alternative spelling of Earl
Erlon	Unknown origin – elfish
Ernest	Anglicized form of the German name Ernst. Short/pet forms: Ernie, Erno *(Earnest)*

ERWIN

EVANDER

EZEKIEL

Ernst	German – serious, earnest *(Earnst)*	**Evan**	Welsh form of John
Erol	Alternative spelling of Errol	**Evander**	Greek – good man
Eros	God of love in Greek mythology, equivalent to the Roman god Cupid	**Evar**	Unknown origin – life
Errol	Originally a Sottish surname derived from a place name. Made famous by the Hollywood actor Errol Flynn *(Erol, Erroll)*	**Evelyn**	Originally an Anglo-Saxon surname. Used for both boys and girls
		Everard	Old German – boar, brave, strong. The Normans brought the name to England
Erroll	Alternative spelling of Errol	**Everett**	Variant of Everard
Erskine	Gaelic – dweller situated at the top of the cliff	**Everhart**	Dutch form of Everard
Ervand	Scandinavian –sea warrior	**Ewald**	Anglo-Saxon – always powerful
Ervin	Variant of Irving. Short/pet form: Erv	**Ewan**	Gaelic – born of the yew tree, or possibly derived from the Gaelic for 'youth' *(Euan, Ewen)*
Erevu	Swahili – clever, talented		
Erwin	Alternative spelling of Irwin. Also a variant of Irving	**Ewart**	Possibly a Norman French form of Edward
Eryx	Name of the son of Aphrodite and Poseidon in Greek mythology	**Ewen**	Alternative spelling of Ewan
		Ezar	Unknown origin – treasure
Esmond	Anglo-Saxon – protected by the gods	**Ezekiel**	Hebrew – God strengthens. An old biblical name often chosen by the Puritans in the 17th century. Short/pet form: Zeke
Esteban	Spanish – crown		
Etan	Variant of Ethan		
Ethan	Hebrew – firm, constant		
Euan	Alternative spelling of Ewan	**Ezra**	Hebrew – helper. Another fine old biblical name approved by the 17th-century Puritans.
Eugene	Greek – born lucky. A popular name in the 19th century inspired by Napoleon's wife – the female form is Eugenie. Short/pet form: Gene		
Eustace	Greek – bountiful, fruitful *(Eustis)*		
Eustis	Alternative spelling of Eustace		

ESMOND

FERGUSON

FABIEN

FELIX

F

Fabian	Latin – grower of beans. Name of an illustrious old Roman family, who listed among their members a historian and a general whose tactics against Hannibal inspired the naming of the Fabien society *(Fabien)*
Fabien	Alternative spelling of Fabian
Fabio	Variant of Fabian
Fabron	French – he who works with his hands
Fagan	Gaelic – little fiery one
Fairburn	Old German/Anglo-Saxon – comely child
Fairfax	Anglo-Saxon – fair-haired
Faisal	Arabic – resolute *(Faizel, Faysal)*
Faizel	Alternative spelling of Faisal
Falkener	Anglo-Saxon – trainer of hawks, falconer *(Falkner, Faulkner)*
Falkner	Alternative spelling of Falkener
Fane	Anglo-Saxon – joyful
Farman	Anglo-Saxon – traveller
Farquhar	Friendly man
Farrell	Celtic – courageous
Faulkner	Alternative spelling of Falkener
Faxon	Old German – long-haired

Faysal	Alternative spelling of Faisal
Felix	Latin – happy, lucky
Fenn	Variant and short/pet form of Fenton
Fenton	Anglo-Saxon – marshland dweller. Short/pet form: Fenn
Fenuku	Egyptian – born late
Ferdinand	Old German – peace + readiness. A royal name found in medieval Europe, it was brought to Britain by the Normans. Short/pet form: Ferdi
Fergal	Anglicized form of the Gaelic name, Fearghal, meaning 'man of valour'. Short/pet form: Fergie
Fergus	Anglicized form of the Gaelic name, Fearghus, meaning 'best choice', 'strong', 'man of vigour'. Short/pet forms: Fergie, Gus
Ferguson	Son of Fergus

BRITISH
MONARCHS

Take a look at the history of Britain if you decide you would like a name with regal associations for your child.

The following list of monarchs starts in 1066, a turning point in English history that saw not only the arrival of William the Conqueror and his knights, but the introduction of Norman French into the English language. From this time on, names with Old French and Old German origins mingled with, and sometimes replaced, existing Anglo-Saxon names to initiate the wide heritage of names that we have today.

Examples of the names of rulers before 1066 include Egbert, Ethelred and Canute – names that are unlikely to appeal to parents today.

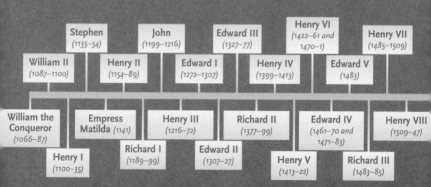

Stephen (1135–54)

John (1199–1216)

Edward III (1327–77)

Henry VI (1422–61 and 1470–1)

Henry VII (1485–1509)

William II (1087–1100)

Henry II (1154–89)

Edward I (1272–1307)

Henry IV (1399–1413)

Edward V (1483)

William the Conqueror (1066–87)

Empress Matilda (1141)

Henry III (1216–72)

Richard II (1377–99)

Edward IV (1461–70 and 1471–83)

Henry VIII (1509–47)

Henry I (1100–35)

Richard I (1189–99)

Edward II (1307–27)

Henry V (1413–22)

Richard III (1483–85)

Names of English monarchs and their spouses

Boys		**Girls**		
Aethelbald	Edward	Adelaide	Ecgwyn	Joan
Aethelbert	Egbert	Aelfgifu	Edith (Eadgyth)	Judith
Aethelred	Geoffrey	Aelfgiva	Eleanor	Margaret
Aethelstan	George	Aethelflaeda	Elfreda	Maria
Aethelwulf	Harold	Alexandra	(Aelfgifu)	Mary
Albert	Henry	Anne	Elgiva	Matilda
Alfred	James	Berengia	Elizabeth	Osburga
Canute	John	Caroline	Emma	Philippa
Charles	Philip	Catherine	Gunhilda	Redberga
Eadred	Richard	Charlotte	Henrietta	Sophia
Eadwig	Stephen	Eadgifu	Maria	Victoria
Edgar	Svein	Eahlswith	Isabel	Wulfthryth
Edmund	William	Ealdgyth	Isabella	
			Jane	

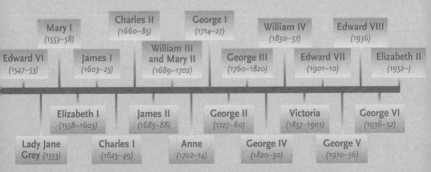

Edward VI (1547–53)

Mary I (1553–58)

Lady Jane Grey (1553)

James I (1603–25)

Elizabeth I (1558–1603)

Charles II (1660–85)

James II (1685–88)

Charles I (1625–49)

William III and Mary II (1689–1702)

George I (1714–27)

George II (1727–60)

Anne (1702–14)

George III (1760–1820)

William IV (1830–37)

Victoria (1837–1901)

George IV (1820–30)

Edward VII (1901–10)

Edward VIII (1936)

George VI (1936–52)

George V (1910–36)

Elizabeth II (1952–)

6 1

FLOYD

FILIBERT

FORTESCUE

Fernand	Variant of Ferdinand	**Flannan**	Gaelic – ruddy, red-haired
Ferran	Arabic – baker	**Flavian**	Latin – yellow, blonde
Ferris	Gaelic – man of iron	**Fletcher**	French – maker of arrows
Ferrol	Variant of Ferris	**Flinn**	Celtic – son of the red-haired
Feste	Name invented by Shakespeare		one *(Flynn)*
	for a character in *Twelfth Night*	**Flint**	Anglo-Saxon – stone *(Flynt)*
Fico	Unknown origin – fig	**Florean**	Alternative spelling of Florian
Fidel	Latin – faithful	**Florian**	Latin – floral beauty *(Florean)*
Fife	Scottish place name *(Fyfe)*	**Floyd**	Probably derived from the Celtic
Filibert	Old German – flashing will.		surname Lloyd meaning 'grey' or
	Short/pet forms: Bert, Bertie		'dark', when the English tried to
Finbar	Phonetic spelling of the Gaelic		pronounce the difficult 'll' sound
	name Fionnbharr, meaning 'fair-	**Flynn**	Alternative spelling of Flinn
	haired', 'white-haired'. Short/pet	**Flynt**	Alternative spelling of Flint
	forms: Finn, Fynn *(Finnbarr)*	**Forbes**	Gaelic – grazing grass, field. A
Findal	Unknown origin – inventive		Scottish place now a first name
Findlay	Alternative spelling of Finlay	**Ford**	Anglo-Saxon – river crossing
Fingar	Breton form of Egan	**Forest**	Alternative spelling of Forrest.
Finlay	Phonetic spelling of the Gaelic name		Also a colour name
	Fionnlagh, 'fair-warrior'. Short/pet	**Forrest**	Latin – of the woods, a forester *(Forest)*
	forms: Finn *(Findlay, Finley)*	**Forrester**	Variant of Forrest
Finley	Alternative spelling of Finlay	**Forster**	Variant of Forrester
Finn	Short/pet form of Finbar and Finlay,	**Fortescue**	Old French – strong shield
	also an independent name *(Fynn)*	**Foster**	Variant of Forrester
Finnbarr	Alternative spelling of Finbar	**Fox**	Anglo-Saxon – fox
Finnegan	Gaelic – fair, handsome		
Finnian	Variant of Finnegan		
Fisk	Old Norse – fisherman		
Flann	Variant of Flannan		

FREDERICK
FRANKLYN
FULLER

Francis	Derived from the Latin word *Franciscus*, meaning 'Frenchman'. A name kept popular by saints and royals, notably St Francis of Assisi. Short/pet forms: Frank, Frankie
Francisco	Variant of Francis
Frank	Short/pet form of Francis, now also an independent name. Short/pet form: Frankie
Franklin	Norman French – freeholder, free man. Short/pet forms: Frank, Frankie *(Franklyn)*
Franklyn	Alternative spelling of Franklin
Franz	German form of Francis
Fraser	An old Highland surname with uncertain origins, now used as a first name *(Frasier, Frazer)*
Frasier	Alternative spelling of Fraser
Frayne	Old French – ash tree. Also Anglo-Saxon – stranger
Frazer	Alternative spelling of Fraser
Fred	Short/pet form of Alfred and Frederick, it is now also an independent name
Freddie	Alternative spelling of Freddy
Freddy	Short/pet form of Alfred and Frederick, now also an independent name *(Freddie)*
Frederic	Alternative spelling of Frederick

Frederick	Old German – peaceful ruler. Short/pet forms: Fred, Freddie, Freddy *(Frederic, Fredric, Fredrick)*
Fredric	Alternative spelling of Frederick
Fredrick	Alternative spelling of Frederick
Freed	Derived from Frederick
Freeman	Anglo-Saxon – free man
Fremont	Old German – freedom mountain
Frewen	Anglo-Saxon – free friend
Fritz	German form of Frederick
Fritzi	Variant of Fritz
Frost	Anglo-Saxon – frost
Fry	Anglo-Saxon – free man
Fulbert	Old German – bright, shining. Short/pet forms: Bert, Bertie
Fuller	Anglo-Saxon – clothing presser
Fyfe	Alternative spelling of Fife
Fynn	Alternative spelling of Finn

GARRETT

GALAHAD

GASTON

G

Gabriel	Hebrew – man of God. In the Bible, it was the name of the Archangel who told the Virgin Mary that she was to give birth to Christ. Short/pet form: Gabe *(Gabryel)*
Gabryel	Alternative spelling of Gabriel
Gage	French – pledge
Gaius	Latin – one who rejoices
Galahad	Name of one of King Arthur's legendary knights
Galen	Greek – healer
Galeno	Spanish – little bright one
Gallagher	Celtic – eager helper
Galvin	Gaelic – shining, fair, or sparrow
Gamba	Shona – warrior
Gannon	Gaelic – fair-complexioned
Gardner	Old German/Anglo-Saxon – gardener
Gareth	Possibly derived from the Welsh word *gwaredd*, meaning 'gentle'. Short/pet forms: Gary, Garry
Garfield	Anglo-Saxon – field of spears, battlefield. Popularized by the cricketer Sir Garfield Sobers
Garland	Derived from an Anglo-Saxon
	surname meaning 'owner of triangle-shaped piece of land'
Garner	Old French – granary protector
Garret	Phonetic spelling of the Gaelic name Gearóid *(Gerard)*, meaning 'brave with the spear'. Short/pet forms: Gary, Garry *(Garrett)*
Garrett	Alternative spelling of Garret
Garrick	Variant of Garret
Garrison	Hebrew – column of conquest
Garry	Alternative spelling of Gary
Garson	Variant of Garrison
Garth	Variant of Gareth
Garvey	Anglo-Saxon – spear bearer
Gary	Short/pet form of Gareth and Garret, now also an independent name *(Garry)*
Gaspar	Alternative spelling of Gasper

GERMAIN
GEMMEL
GIFFORD

Gasper	Variant of Casper *(Gaspar)*	**Gerard**	Variant of Gerald
Gaston	French – man from Gascony	**Gerhard**	Alternative spelling of Gerard
Gavan	Alternative spelling of Gavin	**Gerhart**	Alternative spelling of Gerard
Gaven	Alternative spelling of Gavin	**Gerik**	Polish variant of Gerard
Gavin	Scottish form of Gawain	**Gerius**	Unknown origin – steadfast
	(Gavan, Gaven, Gavyn)	**Germain**	Latin – akin, belonging,
Gavrie	Russian – man of God		brother *(Jermaine)*
Gavyn	Alternative spelling of Gavin	**Gerrold**	Alternative spelling of Gerald
Gawain	Welsh – little hawk. Name of one	**Gersham**	Hebrew – exiled *(Gershom)*
	of King Arthur's legendary knights	**Gershom**	Alternative spelling of Gersham
Gaylord	French – brave	**Gervaise**	German – servant of the spear
Gemmel	Scandinavian – old	**Gerwen**	Alternative spelling of Gerwyn
Gene	Short/pet form of Eugene, now	**Gerwyn**	Welsh – fair *(Gerwen)*
	also an independent name	**Ghalib**	Swahili – winner
Gentilis	Unknown origin – of kindness	**Gibson**	Anglo-Saxon – son of Gilbert.
Geoffrey	More modern spelling of Jeffrey.		Short/pet form: Gib
	Short/pet form: Geoff		
George	Greek – farmer. Although St George		
	is the patron saint of England,		
	it was the four Hanoverian King		
	Georges who popularized the name.		
	Short/pet form: Georgie *(Jorge)*		
Geraint	Welsh – old, venerable. Medieval		
	name derived from Gerontius,		
	pronounced 'gher-aynt'		
Gerald	Old German – spear + rule.		
	Short/pet form: Gerry		
	(Gerrold, Jerald, Jerold)		
Geraldo	Spanish form of Gerald		

GEORGE

GODFREY

 GILDAS

GRAHAM

Gideon	Hebrew – one-handed. Biblical name adopted by the Puritans
Gifford	Old German – brave giver
Gilbert	Old German – bright pledge. An old name that, in medieval times, gave rise to surnames such as Gibbs, Gilbertson and Gilson. Short/pet forms: Bert, Bertie, Gib, Gil
Giles	Derived from the Greek *Aegidius*, meaning 'young goat', or possibly from *aegis*, the shield of Zeus, father of the gods in Greek mythology *(Gyles)*
Gilman	Old German – big man. Short/pet form: Gil
Gilroy	Gaelic – red-haired boy. Short/pet form: Gil
Glen	Welsh – from the valley *(Glenn)*
Glenn	Alternative spelling of Glen
Glyn	Variant of Glen
Godfrey	Old German – God's peace. The name came to Britain with the Normans and was common in medieval times. In the past it was often confused with Geoffrey but the two names are now quite distinct from one another
Godwin	Anglo-Saxon – good friend, God's friend

Goldwin	Variant of Godwin *(Goldwyn)*
Goldwyn	Alternative spelling of Goldwin
Gomer	Hebrew – to complete
Goodard	Anglo-Saxon – gesolute, pious
Gordon	Anglo-Saxon – wooded dell, great hill, spacious fort. A Berwickshire place name from which the Scottish clan took its name. General Gordon of Khartoum brought it into use as a Christian name at the end of the 19th century. Short/pet form: Gordy
Gorham	Anglo-Saxon – dweller at the mud house
Gorman	Old German/Gaelic – blue-eyed
Grady	Gaelic – noble, illustrious
Graeme	Alternative spelling of Graham
Graham	Possibly derived from the Lincolnshire place name, Grantham, meaning 'gravelly place'. Short/pet form: Gray *(Graeme, Grahame)*

GRENVILLE
GRASHAM
GWYNN

Grahame	Alternative spelling of Graham
Granger	Anglo-Saxon – grainstore, farm labourer
Grant	Old French – great. Originally a surname only, but, like many Scottish surnames, adopted in recent years into use as a first name
Granville	French – from the big town
Grasham	Alternative spelling of Gresham
Gray	Grey – may have once referred to grey hair or to the cloaks of the Franciscan and Cistercian monks, known as the Greyfriars (*Grey*)
Grayson	Alternative spelling of Greyson
Greger	Old Norse – vigilant
Gregor	Variant of Gregory
Gregory	Greek – watchful, vigilant. There were two Eastern saints of this name and 16 popes, including Gregory the Great who sent St Augustine out to convert the English to Christianity. Short/pet forms: Greg, Gregg
Grenville	Variant of Granville. An aristocratic surname, now used as a first name
Gresham	Anglo-Saxon – dweller on the grassland (*Grasham*)
Grey	Alternative spelling of Gray
Greyson	Variant of Gray (*Grayson*)

Griffin	Welsh mythological beast
Grigori	Russian form of Gregory
Griswold	Old German – from the wild/grey forest
Grover	Anglo-Saxon – from the grove
Gruffydd	Welsh – strong warrior
Gunnar	Old German – bold warrior
Gunther	Old Norse – battle army, warrior
Gus	Short/pet form of names ending with 'gus', such as Angus, Argus and Augustus, now also an independent name
Guy	Possibly Old German – wood or wide. Commonly used before the exploits of Guy Fawkes put it out of favour
Gwyn	Welsh – white, blessed (*Gwynn, Gwynne*)
Gwynn	Alternative spelling of Gwyn
Gwynne	Alternative spelling of Gwyn
Gyles	Alternative spelling of Giles

NAMING
TWINS

It can be hard enough deciding on a name for one child at a time, but when you have two or more names to find you may really struggle. Whether you need to find names for babies of the same sex, or one for each sex, there are a few paths you can take if you want to narrow your choices.

Letters in common

A good starting point adopted by some parents is to choose names with the same initial, for example Laura and Lewis, or Antony and Anna. If you take this route your children will definitely need middle names with different initials to avoid confusion when it comes to family matters like making dental appointments and receiving mail. Alternatively you could choose names that end in the same letter(s) or the same sound, for example Keeley and Gary, Kyle and Michael or Lucy and Chloe.

Clever combinations

Another option is to be clever with letters and words. You could either come up with names that are anagrams of each other, or choose names that are almost the reverse of each other like Dorothea and Theodore.

There is undoubtedly more scope if you play around with words and different languages. You could pick a word, such as star, and look at it in different languages. Alternatively you could choose some opposites, like sun and moon or fair and dark, and pick names that equate to these. Similarly you could limit your choice of available names by picking a theme such as place names, flower names or colours (see pages 50, 194 and 214 for inspiration).

Use your common sense

However much fun it may be to pick names for your twins that have some clever connection, never forget that your children have to endure their names through their school days at least, so don't pick unsuitable names for the sake of being clever. As always, it is more important that the first name goes well with the surname and that the initials are acceptable (see page 12).

Ideas for naming twins

Joe and Janet *(alliteration)*

Dawn and Sean *(rhyming names)*

Alan and Lana *(anagram of each other)*

Keri and Erik *(anagram of each other)*

Leon and Noel *(each reads backwards to create the other)*

Jonas and Paloma *(both mean 'dove' – Jonas in Hebrew and Paloma in Spanish)*

Enid and Zoe *(both mean 'life' – Enid in Welsh and Zoe in Greek)*

Brendan and Tiana *(Brendan means 'prince' in Irish, Tiana means 'princess' in Greek)*

Margaret and Pearl *(Margaret means 'pearl' in Greek)*

Evan and Ian *(both derived from John)*

Bianca and Nigella *(white and black)*

Magnus and Paul *(large and small)*

Brent and Dale *(hill and valley)*

Tyne and Jordan *(English place names)*

Acacia and Rowan *(tree names)*

HAMISH

HADWIN

HAMILTON

H

Habib	Syriac – beloved one
Hackett	German – little woodsman
Hadden	Anglo-Saxon – of the moors, heathland *(Haddon)*
Haddon	Alternative spelling of Hadden
Hadley	Variant of Hadden
Hadrian	Old Norse – dark one
Hadwin	Anglo-Saxon – family friend
Hagan	Old German – strong defence
Hagbert	Old German – skilful. Short/pet forms: Bert, Bertie
Haima	Unknown origin – made of gold
Haines	Old German/Anglo-Saxon – from a fenced area/cottage
Hakan	Native American – fiery
Halbert	Variant of Albert. Short/pet forms: Bert, Bertie
Hale	Anglo-Saxon – hero
Hallam	Anglo-Saxon – hill-dweller
Halsey	Anglo-Saxon – from Hal's island
Ham	Hebrew – hot, south
Hamal	Arabic – lamb
Hamilton	Old French/Anglo-Saxon. A place name and aristocratic surname; possibly means 'beautiful mountain'

Hamis	Variant of James
Hamish	A pseudo-Gaelic form of James, it is a 19th-century variant frowned on by some purists as an attempt to emulate the Gaelic Seamus. It has come to be used and pronounced as spelt and it remains a popular version in Scotland
Hamlet	German – home
Hamlin	Alternative spelling of Hamlyn
Hamlyn	French – home lover *(Hamlin)*
Hammond	Variant of Hamo. A surname, sometimes used as a first name, as in the case of writer Hammond Innes
Hamo	Derived from the Old German *haimi*, meaning 'house' or 'home'. The name came to England with the Normans *(Haymo)*

HARVEY
HARDING
HAYWOOD

H

Hank	American form of Henry derived from the Dutch name, Henk
Hanley	Anglo-Saxon – of the meadow
Hans	German and Dutch short form for Johannes, the equivalent of John
Harald	Alternative spelling of Harold
Harden	Anglo-Saxon – from the hare valley
Harding	Old German/Anglo-Saxon – brave, resolute, strong, hardy, tough
Hardwin	Variant of Harding
Hardy	Variant of Harding
Hari	Sanskrit – he who removes evil
Harlan	Old German – battle country
Harley	Anglo-Saxon – wood with hares, deer hunter
Harman	Variant of Herman (*Harmon*)
Harmon	Alternative spelling of Harman
Harold	Anglo-Saxon – ruler of the army, brave leader (*Harald, Harrold*)
Harper	Anglo-Saxon – harpist
Harrison	Anglo-Saxon – son of Harry
Harrold	Alternative spelling of Harold
Harry	Short/pet form of Henry and Harold, now also an independent name. Short/pet form: Hal
Hart	Anglo-Saxon – deer, stag
Hartley	Anglo-Saxon – stag wood
Hartman	Old German – firm
Harve	Alternative spelling of Harvey

Harvey	Old Breton – battle-worthy, warrior (*Harve, Herve*)
Hasaka	Unknown origin – jester
Hassan	Arabic – handsome
Hastin	Hindi – elephant
Hastings	German – swift
Havelock	Old Norse – sea battle (*Havlock*)
Havilah	Hebrew – sandy land
Havlock	Alternative spelling of Havelock
Hayden	Anglo-Saxon – pastureland
Haydn	Celtic – fire
Haymo	Alternative spelling of Hamo
Hayward	Alternative spelling of Haywood
Haywood	Anglo-Saxon – guardian/dweller by the dark forest (*Hayward, Heyward*)
Heath	Anglo-Saxon – high plain, wasteland
Heathcliff	From the heath cliff

HERCULES
HOGAN

 HEDLEY

Hector	Greek – anchor, steadfast. The name of the Trojan hero who led the fight against the Greeks for ten years. In Scotland, it is a form of the Gaelic Eachdoin, meaning 'horse lord'
Hedley	Anglo-Saxon – meadow for sheep. A place name adopted as a first name during the 19th century
Heilyn	Welsh – cup bearer, pronounced 'hay-lin'
Heinrich	German form of Henry
Helios	Greek – sun. Charioteer god of the sun in Greek mythology, equivalent to the Roman god Sol
Hendrick	Variant of Henry
Hendry	Unknown origin – manly
Henley	Anglo-Saxon – from the high clearing
Henri	French form of Henry
Henrik	Variant of Heinrich
Henry	Old German – ruler of the home. This old name has remained in fashion for centuries and was given to eight kings of England. Harry, now a pet form or an independent name, was the original English version of the name; Henry took over in the 17th century. Short/pet forms: Hal, Harry

Herbert	Old German – bright army. Short/pet forms: Bert, Bertie, Herb, Herbi, Herbie
Hercules	Derived from the Greek name Herakles, meaning 'glory of Hera' (queen of the Greek gods)
Heremon	Variant of Irving
Heriot	Variant of Henry
Herman	Old German – army + man *(Hermann)*
Hermann	Alternative spelling of Herman
Hermes	Messenger of the gods in Greek mythology, equivalent to the Roman god Mercury
Herschel	Hebrew – deer
Herve	Alternative spelling of Harvey
Hew	Alternative spelling of Hugh
Heyward	Alternative spelling of Haywood
Hick	Variant of Richard
Hilton	Anglo-Saxon – manor on the hill
Hiram	Hebrew – exalted brother
Hisham	Swahili – generous
Hoel	Alternative spelling of Howell
Hogan	Gaelic/Anglo-Saxon – youthful
Holden	Old German – kindly, gracious
Hollace	Alternative spelling of Hollis
Hollis	Anglo-Saxon – hero *(Hollace)*
Holt	Anglo-Saxon – son of the unspoiled forest

Homer	Greek – unknown meaning. Name of ancient Greek poet and popular cartoon character Homer Simpson
Horace	French form of Horatio
Horatio	Latin – time. Originated from a renowned old Roman family, Horatius
Houston	Anglo-Saxon – hill town
Howard	Comes from a surname with an aristocratic pedigree as the family name of the Dukes of Norfolk, but its origins are uncertain. It may mean either 'protection' or 'heart'. Short/pet form: Howie
Howe	Variant of Howe
Howel	Alternative spelling of Howell
Howell	Anglicized form of the Welsh name Hywel, meaning 'eminent'. May also come from the English place name meaning 'hill for swine' (Hoel, Howel)
Hu	A nature god in Egyptian mythology
Hubbard	Variant of Hubert
Hubert	See Hugh. Short/pet forms: Bert, Bertie, Hugh
Hudd	Variant of Richard
Hudson	Old German/Anglo-Saxon – son of Hudd, or Hugh. Also a river name
Huey	Alternative spelling of Hughie
Hugh	Old German – mindful, thinker. The name came to England with the Normans in the form Hugo, and was made popular by the learned 11th-century bishop St Hugh of Lincoln. Both Hugo and Hubert are Latin versions, meaning 'bright mind'. Short/pet forms: Huey, Hughie (Hew, Huw)
Hugo	See Hugh
Humbert	Old German – bright warrior. Short/pet forms: Bert, Bertie
Hume	Unknown origin – home lover
Humfrey	Alternative spelling of Humphrey
Humphrey	Possibly Old German – giant peace, or Anglo-Saxon – honey + another word (Humfrey)
Hunter	Anglo-Saxon – huntsman
Huntley	Anglo-Saxon – hunter's meadow
Hussein	Arabic – handsome one
Huw	Welsh form of Hugh
Huya	Unknown origin – fighting eagle
Hyman	Hebrew – he who lives in a high place. Short/pet forms: Hy

IAN ISAIAH IVOR

I

Iain	Alternative spelling of Ian
Ian	Modern form of John, meaning 'God is gracious' *(Iain, Ion)*
Ibrahim	Islamic form of Abraham
Idogbe	Egyptian – brother of twins
Idris	Old Welsh – fiery lord
Ifor	*See* Ivor
Iggi	Alternative spelling of Iggy
Iggy	Greek – only son *(Iggi)*
Ignatius	Latin – fiery
Igor	Russian form of Ivor
Ike	Variant of Isaac
Illaris	Unknown origin – merry
Imanuel	Alternative spelling of Emmanuel
Indra	Name of a Hindu god
Ingmar	Old Norse – famous son
Ingram	Old German – raven
Inigo	Spanish form of Ignatius
Inir	Unknown origin – honour
Ion	Alternative spelling of Ian
Irfon	Unknown origin – anointed one
Irvin	Alternative spelling of Irving
Irvine	Variant of Irving
Irving	Anglo-Saxon – boar-friend *(Irvin)*
Irwin	Variant of Irving *(Erwin)*

Isa	Old German – strong willed
Isaac	Hebrew – laughter, laughing one. Appears in the Old Testament as the name of the son of Abraham and Sarah. Now regarded as a chiefly Jewish name *(Izaak)*
Isaiah	Hebrew – salvation of the Lord
Isard	Old German – tough as iron
Ismael	Hebrew – God heareth
Israel	Hebrew – may God reign
Itzak	Variant of Isaac
Ivan	Russian form of John
Ivar	Old Norse – archer, a Norse god
Ives	Variant of Ivo
Ivo	German – yew wood. A popular name in Normandy, it arrived in England during the Norman Conquest
Ivor	An old-established Celtic name although its meaning is uncertain. It gave rise to Scottish surnames such as MacIvor and MacIver. Welsh parents use Ifor, which means 'lord'
Izaak	Alternative spelling of Isaac

JAMES

JACOB

JAGGER

Jaime	Spanish form of James
Jaimie	Alternative spelling of Jamie
Jake	Derived from Jack/John and Jacob
James	Developed from the name Jacob, meaning 'supplanter'. Although there were two apostles called James, it only became popular once James Stuart became King of England in 1603. Short/pet forms: Jaimie, Jamie, Jas, Jay, Jim, Jimmy
Jabriel	Unknown origin – God's health
Jack	A form of John, and not derived from the French Jacques (James) as is sometimes thought. The name went through an interesting process of evolution from Johannes through to Jehan, Jan (the popular form of John in the Low Countries) and Jankin (with the Flemish suffix). The French pronunciation of Jankin sounded like Jackin and led to the shortened form, Jack
Jamie	Short/pet form of James, now also an independent name for both boys and girls (*Jaimie*)
Jamieson	Alternative spelling of Jamison
Jamison	Anglo-Saxon – son of James (*Jamieson*)
Jackson	Son of Jack
Jacob	Hebrew – supplanter. In the Old Testament Jacob tricked his brother Esau out of his inheritance. It came into general use after the Reformation, though is now mainly used by Jewish families. Short/pet forms: Jake, Jeb
Jamil	Swahili – handsome
Jamsheed	Persian – from Persia
Jacques	French form of James, itself derived from Jacob
Jagger	Anglo-Saxon – a teamster
Jago	Cornish form of James, itself derived from Jacob

JEDIDIAH
JERMAINE

JARED

Jan	Variant of John	**Jedidiah**	Hebrew – friend of Jehovah, beloved of the Lord. Short/pet form: Jed
Janus	Latin – archway. God of gateways and beginnings in Roman mythology, after whom the month of January is named		
		Jedrek	Polish – strong and manly
Jared	Hebrew – descendant. A biblical name (*Jarod*)	**Jefferson**	Derived from the surname meaning 'son of Godffrey'. Short/pet form: Jeff
Jareth	Variant of Jared	**Jeffrey**	Old German – God, or district, + peace. Short/pet form: Jeff (*Geoffrey*)
Jarod	An alternative spelling of the name Jared		
Jarrah	Aborigine – species of Australian Eucalyptus tree	**Jerald**	Alternative spelling of Gerald. Short/pet forms: Jerry, Jerrie
Jarratt	Alternative spelling of Jarrett	**Jered**	Variant of Jared (*Jerod*)
Jarrett	Variant of Jared, Garrett and Gerard (*Jarratt*)	**Jeremiah**	Hebrew – God exalts. Short/pet forms: Jerry, Jerrie
Jarvis	Variant of Gervaise	**Jeremy**	Modern variant of Jeremiah. Short/pet forms: Jerry, Jerrie
Jason	Greek – healer		
Jasper	Anglicized form of the German name, Casper, meaning 'imperial', 'precious', 'treasurer'	**Jermaine**	Alternative spelling, and more popular version, of Germain
		Jermyn	Hebrew – bright
		Jerod	Alternative spelling of Jered
Javas	Unknown origin – swift	**Jerold**	Alternative spelling of Gerald
Javier	French – January	**Jerome**	Greek – of holy name. St Jerome (AD340–420) was the translator of the Latin version of the Bible, accepted as the authorized version of the Roman Catholic Church. Short/pet forms: Jerry, Jerrie
Jay	Derived from the bird name, which in Anglo-Saxon and Old French meant 'chattering'. Also short/pet form of James		
Jecha	Swahili – sunrise		
Jed	Arabic – the hand. Also short/pet form of Jedidiah	**Jerrard**	Variant of Gerard. Short/pet forms: Jerry, Jerrie

JOCELYN
JETHRO
JOHANN J

Jerrie	Alternative spelling of Jerry
Jerry	Short/pet form of Jerald, Jeremiah, Jeremy, Jerome and Jerrard, now also an independent name (*Jerrie*)
Jerwais	Variant of Gervaise
Jess	Alternative spelling of Jesse
Jesse	Hebrew – the Lord exists. In the Old Testament Jesse is the name of King David's father. It was popularized in the 20th century by the athlete Jesse Owens (*Jess*)
Jesus	Hebrew – God will help
Jethro	Hebrew – abundance. A biblical name and that of the English inventor and agriculturalist Jethro Tull (1647–1741). Short/pet forms: Jeth, Jett
Joachim	Hebrew – may Jehovah exult. Legend gives this name to the father of the Blessed Virgin Mary
Job	Hebrew – persecuted. In the Old Testament he endured great suffering with exemplary patience
Jobey	Variant of Job

Jocelyn	Old French – of the Goths. Referring to the German people, the name was introduced by the Normans and originally given only to boys, but now more commonly to girls. Short/pet form: Joss
Jock	Variant of Jacob or John
Joda	Unknown origin – playful
Joe	Short/pet form of Joseph and Jonathan, it is now also an independent name
Joel	Hebrew – Jehovah is the Lord. Name of one of the minor prophets of the Old Testament, brought to Britain as a personal name by the Normans
Johan	Alternative spelling of Johann
Johann	German variant of John, pronounced 'yo-hann' (*Johan*)
John	Comes from the Hebrew Jochanaan (*Johanan*), which means 'God is gracious'. The Latin form Johannes was brought from the East by the Crusaders. Short/pet form: Johnny (*Jon*)
Jolin	Variant of Julian
Jolyon	Variant of Julian
Jon	Alternative spelling of John, and short/pet form of Jonathan
Jonah	*See* Jonas

BIBLICAL
NAMES

For more than 2,000 years, Christian parents have been naming their children after people in the Bible. Biblical names were particularly popular with the 17th-century English Puritans who, following the Reformation, favoured names such as Boaz, Cyrus, Gideon, Eli and Naomi, among many others. Most of the biblical names are of Hebrew or Greek origin. There are plenty of names to choose from throughout the Bible – the main listings given opposite are only a small sample of those that can be found in the Old Testament.

New Testament names

Boys		Girls
Andrew	Nathaniel	Chloe
Gabriel	Paul	Elizabeth
James	Peter	Lois
John	Philip	Lydia
Joseph	Saul	Martha
Jude	Silas	Mary
Luke	Simon	Phoebe
Mark	Stephen	Rhoda
Matthew	Thomas	Susanna
	Timothy	

Boys

Aaron Older brother of Moses and the first Israelite high priest

Adam First man, who lived with Eve in the Garden of Eden

Benjamin The 12th and youngest son of Jacob

Cyrus King of Persia who freed the captive Jews and allowed them to return to Israel

Daniel Biblical prophet who was thrown into the lion's den

David As a boy he killed the giant Goliath and later became king of Israel and father of the wise King Solomon

Emmanuel Means Christ

Ethan A wise man and also a musician

Gideon Hero who led the Israelites against the Midianites

Isaac Son of Abraham and Sarah; father of Esau and Jacob

Jacob Tricked his brother Esau out of his inheritance

Jared Father of Enoch

Jesse Father of King David

Joel Minor prophet

Jonah Prophet who was swallowed by a whale

Jonathan Eldest son of Saul and close friend of King David

Joseph The 11th son of Jacob, who owned the famous multi-coloured coat

Moses Hidden among bulrushes as a baby to save his life. Led the Israelites out of Egypt and received the Ten Commandments from God

Nathan Prophet and son of King David

Noah Builder of the ark and survivor of the Great Flood

Reuben Eldest son of Jacob and Leah, ancestor of one of the 12 tribes of Israel

Samson Long-haired hero of exceptional strength, who was betrayed by Delilah

Samuel Ruling judge who anointed Saul as king of Israel

Saul The first king of Israel

Seth The third son of Adam and Eve

Girls

Abigail Wife of King David

Deborah Prophetess who successfully led the Israelites against the Canaanites

Delilah Lover of Samson whom she betrayed to the Philistines by cutting his hair – that was the source of his power

Dinah The daughter of Jacob and Leah

Esther Wife of the King of Persia who saved many Jews from persecution

Eve First woman; lived with Adam in the Garden of Eden

Hannah Mother of Samuel

Jemima Oldest daughter of Job

Judith Wife of Esau

Leah Wife of Jacob and mother of seven

Miriam Elder sister of Moses and Aaron

Naomi Mother-in-law of Ruth

Rachel Favourite wife of Jacob

Rebecca Wife of Isaac and mother of Esau and Jacob

Ruth Central character in the Book of Ruth

Sarah Abraham's wife. Elderly mother of Isaac

JOVE

JONATHAN

JUNIUS

Jonas	Hebrew – dove. Favoured form of Jonah, the name of the Old Testament prophet that became associated with bad luck	**Josiah**	Hebrew – God heals, praised, faith
		Jove	Latin. Another name for Jupiter, the father of the gods in Roman mythology, equivalent to the Greek god Zeus
Jonathan	Hebrew – gift of God. The name of King David's close friend in the Old Testament. Short/pet forms: Joe, Johnny, Jon (*Jonathon, Jonothon*)		
		Jovian	Latin – of Jupiter
		Jovita	Variant of Jove
		Juan	Spanish form of John
Jonathon	Alternative spelling of Jonathan	**Jubalus**	Unknown origin – lute player
Jonothon	Alternative spelling of Jonathan	**Judas**	Hebrew – praised. Unpopular name thanks to its association with Judas Iscariot, the disciple who betrayed Jesus. Short/pet form: Jude
Jonty	Scottish form of John		
Jordan	Name of the principal river in Israel,where Christ was baptised by John the Baptist		
		Judd	Variant of Jude
Jorge	Alternative spelling of George	**Jude**	Short/pet form of Judas, now also an independent name. St Jude is the patron saint of lost causes. The name was promoted by Thomas Hardy's 1895 novel *Jude the Obscure*
Jorgen	Variant of Jorge		
Josef	Alternative spelling of Joseph		
Joseph	Hebrew – may the Lord add. The name in the New Testament for the husband of the Virgin Mary and Joseph of Arimathea. Short/pet forms: Joe, Joey (*Josef*)		
		Julian	Greek/Latin. Derived from the old Roman name Julius, meaning 'soft-haired', 'downy-bearded'. Short/pet form: Jules
Josepth	Variant of Joseph		
Josh	Short/pet form of Joshua, now also an independent name		
		Juma	Swahili – born on a Friday
		Junior	Young, child. Popular US pet name
Joshua	Hebrew – God saves. Another form of the name Jesus. Short/pet form: Josh	**Junius**	Latin – born in June
		Justin	Latin – righteous, just
		Justus	Variant of Justin

K

Kacy	Alternative spelling of Casey
Kai	Hawaiian – sea
Kaie	Celtic – combat
Kain	Alternative spelling of Kane
Kalil	Arabic – good friend
Kalman	Hungarian – strong and manly
Kalo	Unknown origin – royal
Kalon	Alternative spelling of Kalo
Kamau	Kikuyu – quiet warrior
Kamil	Arabic – perfect
Kane	Welsh – beautiful. Manx – warrior *(Kain)*
Kaniel	Hebrew – stalk, reed
Kareem	Arabic – noble, exalted *(Karlm)*
Karim	Alternative spelling of Kareem
Karl	Alternative spelling of Carl
Karle	Alternative spelling of Carl
Karsten	Variant of Christian
Kasey	Alternative spelling of Casey
Kaspar	Alternative spelling of Casper
Kean	Alternative spelling of Keane
Keane	Anglo-Saxon – sharp, bold *(Kean)*
Keanu	Hawaiian – cool breeze from the mountains. Popularized by the actor Keanu Reeves

Keaton	Anglo-Saxon – where hawks fly
Keefe	Gaelic – handsome, well
Keefer	Variant of Keefe
Keegan	Derived from a Gaelic surname
Keena	Unknown origin – brave
Keenan	Derived from a Gaelic surname
Keene	Gaelic – wise, learned
Kegan	Gaelic form of Hugh, meaning 'little fiery one'
Keir	Derived from a Scottish surname. Also a variant of Kerr
Keith	Derived originally from a Scottish place name, meaning 'wood'
Kelby	Old German – from a farm
Kelcey	Alternative spelling of Kelsey
Kell	Anglo-Saxon – from the spring
Kellen	German – swamp
Kelsey	Anglo-Saxon – ship + victory *(Kelcey, Kelsie)*
Kelsie	Alternative spelling of Kelsey
Kelvin	Originally the name of a Scottish river, possibly meaning 'narrow stream' *(Kelvyn)*
Kelvyn	Alternative spelling of Kelvin

K

KENNAN

KERMIT

KIERAN

Kelwin	Variant of Kelvin
Kemble	Variant of Kimball
Kemp	Anglo-Saxon – champion, warrior
Kenaz	Unknown origin – hunter
Kendale	Variant of Kendall
Kendall	Anglo-Saxon – valley of the River Kent. Also Celtic – chief of the dale
Kendrick	Derived from a Gaelic surname
Kenelm	Anglo-Saxon – bold + helmet/ protection
Kenley	Anglo-Saxon – dweller at the king's meadow
Kennan	Variant of Keene
Kennard	Anglo-Saxon – strong
Kennedy	Phonetic spelling of the Gaelic name Cinneide, meaning 'helmet head', 'helmeted chief'
Kenneth	Gaelic – handsome. Popular name with Scottish parents from the time of Kenneth MacAlpin, the first king of Scotland, but has now lost its strong Scottish associations. Short/pet forms: Ken, Kenny
Kenny	Short/pet form of Kenneth, now also an independent name
Kenrick	Variant of Kendrick
Kent	Celtic – chief, or possibly brilliant white, bright. Also a place name and surname

Kenton	Anglo-Saxon place name
Kenward	Variant of Kenneth
Kenway	Anglo-Saxon – valiant soldier
Kenyon	Gaelic – blond-haired
Kerel	Afrikaans – young
Kermit	Celtic – son of Diarmad/Dermot
Kern	Gaelic – dark
Kerr	Old Norse – marshland
Kerrin	Variant of Kieran *(Kerryn)*
Kerry	Irish place name used for both boys and girls
Kerryn	Alternative spelling of Kerrin
Kester	Variant of Christopher
Ketan	Sanskrit – home
Kevan	Alternative spelling of Kevin
Kevin	Gaelic – comely at birth, handsome *(Kevan, Kevyn)*
Kevyn	Alternative spelling of Kevin
Kiefer	German – barrel maker
Kieran	Phonetic spelling of the Gaelic name Ciaran, meaning 'black', 'dark-skinned', 'dark-haired' *(Kieren, Kieron, Kyran)*
Kieren	Alternative spelling of Kieran
Kieron	Alternative spelling of Kieran
Kile	Alternative spelling of Kyle
Kilroy	Derived from a surname, itself derived from the name Gilroy

Kim	Short/pet form of Kimball, now also an independent name but more usually used for girls than for boys – as the short/pet form of the girl's name Kimberley
Kimball	Anglo-Saxon – bold. Short/pet form: Kim
King	Anglo-Saxon – king, chief
Kingley	Variant of Kingsley
Kingsley	Anglo-Saxon – king's wood or meadow. A name promoted in modern times by the novelist Kingsley Amis (Kingslie)
Kingslie	Alternative spelling of Kingsley
Kingston	Anglo-Saxon – of the king's town. Also a place name
Kinton	Hindi – crowned
Kiran	Sanskrit – a ray of light
Kirby	Anglo-Saxon – from the church town
Kirin	Unknown origin – spearman
Kirk	Old Norse – church, house of worship
Kirkland	Anglo-Saxon/Gaelic – dweller on church land
Kirkwood	Anglo-Saxon/Gaelic – dweller in the wood by the church
Kit	Short/pet form of Christopher, now also an independent name
Kito	Swahili – jewel

Klaus	Derived from Nicholas
Koi	Native American – panther
Konrad	Old German – brave counsel, bold
Korben	Unknown origin (Corban, Korbyn)
Korbyn	Alternative spelling of Korben
Korey	Alternative spelling of Corey
Kory	Alternative spelling of Corey
Krishna	Sanskrit – black, dark. Name of a Hindu god
Krispin	Variant of Christian
Krister	Variant of Christian
Kristian	Alternative spelling of Christian
Kristoffer	Alternative spelling of Christopher
Krystof	Alternative spelling of Christoph
Kumar	Sanskrit – prince, boy
Kurt	Variant of the German name, Konrad (Curt)
Kurtwood	Old German – enclosed wood
Kyle	Derived from a Scottish place name. Occasionally used for girls (Kile)
Kyler	Dutch – archer
Kyran	Alternative spelling of Kieran

LANGSTON
LAMBERT
LAURENCE

L

Lachlan	Gaelic – a viking, man from the land of the lochs
Laird	Scottish – lord
Lajuan	Variant of John, pronounced 'la-hwawn'
Lamar	Latin – of the sea/lake
Lambert	Old German – bright as the land. Short/pet forms: Bert, Bertie
Lamont	Old Norse – lawyer
Lance	Old German – land. Also the short/pet form of Lancelot
Lancelot	Name of one of King Arthur's legendary knights. Short/pet form: Lance
Lander	Variant of Leander
Landers	Variant of Landry
Landis	Variant of Landry
Landon	Anglo-Saxon – long hill
Landor	Anglo-Saxon – country dweller
Landry	Anglo-Saxon – rough land
Lane	Anglo-Saxon – narrow road, passageway
Lang	Old Norse – tall man
Langdon	Variant of Landon
Langer	Variant of Lang

Langley	Anglo-Saxon – dweller at the long meadow
Langston	Anglo-Saxon – long, narrow town
Lankston	Variant of Langston
Lansing	English place name
Laris	Latin – cheerful
Larken	Alternative spelling of Larkin
Larkin	Variant of Laurence (Larken)
Larry	Short/pet form of Laurence, now also an independent name
Lars	Swedish form of Laurence
Larsen	Son of Lars (Larson)
Larson	Alternative spelling of Larsen
Laszlo	Variant of Lazarus
Latimer	Anglo-Saxon – interpreter
Laurel	Variant of Laurence
Laurence	Latin. Anglicized form of the old Roman Laurentus, probably derived from *laurus*, 'bay tree', or from the place name Laurentium. The third-century martyr St Laurence, the Archdeacon of Rome, later gave his name to the St Laurence River in Canada. Short/pet forms: Larry, Laurie (*Lawrence, Lorence*)

LEIGH
LEANDER
LENNON L

Lawler	Gaelic – soft-spoken
Lawrence	Alternative spelling of Laurence
Lawrencia	Variant of Laurence
Lawson	Anglo-Saxon – son of Laurence
Lawton	Anglo-Saxon – from the village on the hill
Lazar	Variant of Lazarus
Lazarus	Hebrew – God has helped
Leabua	Sotho – one who speaks
Leander	Greek – lion-like, brave
Leaf	Alternative spelling of Leif
Lear	Variant of Lee
Leary	Phonetic spelling of the Gaelic name Laoghaire, meaning 'calf herd'
Lee	Anglo-Saxon – meadow. Sometimes used for girls (Leigh)
Leif	Old Norse – beloved, descendant (Leaf)
Leigh	Alternative spelling of Lee
Leighton	Anglo-Saxon – herb garden
Leland	Anglo-Saxon – meadow dweller
Len	Native American – flute. Also short/pet form of Leonard
Lennan	Gaelic – sweetheart
Lennard	Alternative spelling of Leonard
Lennart	Scandinavian form of Leonard
Lennon	Gaelic – little cape
Lennox	Derived from a Scottish surname (Lenox)

Lenox	Alternative spelling of Lennox
Lensar	Anglo-Saxon – with his parents
Leo	Latin – lion. Thirteen popes have taken the name so it has always been favoured by Roman Catholic parents, while Jewish families prefer the form Leon
Leon	See Leo
Leonard	Derived from the Old German name, Leonhard, meaning 'lion' and 'brave'. Short/pet forms: Len, Lennie, Lenny (Lennard)
Leonardo	Italian and Spanish form of Leonard
Leonidas	Greek – lion-like
Leopold	Old German – bold people
Leroy	Old French – the king

LEONARDO

LINDSAY
LESTER
LLEWELLYN

Leslie
A Scottish surname originally derived from an Aberdeenshire place name, probably meaning 'little meadow', it is now used as a first name for both boys and girls. The usual masculine form is Leslie and the feminine Lesley, but the spellings are interchangeable. Short/pet form: Les

Lester
Originally a surname, now a first name derived from the place name Leicester. Short/pet form: Les

Levi
Hebrew – joined to, associated

Levon
Variant of Levi

Lewie
Alternative spelling of Louis

Lewis
Anglicized form of the French name Louis. Brought to public attention in England by Lewis Carroll, author of *Alice in Wonderland*. Short/pet forms: Lew, Lou

Lex
Variant of Alex

Lexi
Variant of Alex

Liam
Gaelic form of William

Lian
Chinese – the graceful willow

Lienard
French form of Leonard

Lincoln
Anglo-Saxon – settlement by the lake/pool *(Lyncoln)*

Lindell
Alternative spelling of Lyndell

Linden
Alternative spelling of Lyndon

Lindley
Anglo-Saxon – lime tree field *(Lyndley)*

Lindo
Old German – gentle man

Lindsay
Ancient Scottish surname taken from a place name, Lindon's Isle. Now more commonly used for girls than for boys

Linford
Anglo-Saxon – ford by the linden

Linfred
Old German – gentle grace

Lingard
Old German – gentle/sea guard

Linton
Alternative spelling of Lynton

Linus
Greek – flaxen-coloured

Lionel
French diminutive of Leon, meaning 'young lion', 'little lion'

Lisle
Old French – of the island *(Lyall, Lyle)*

Liu
Nguni – voice

Livvy
Derived from Oliver

Llew
Celtic – lion. Also a short/pet form of Llewellyn

Llewellyn
Celtic – like a lion. Short/pet forms: Llew, Lyn *(Llywelyn)*

Lloyd
Welsh – grey. A common surname and popular as a first name, having spread to families without Welsh connections during the early part of the 20th century

Llywelyn
Alternative spelling of Llewellyn

Logan
Gaelic – small hollow

Lomas
Anglo-Saxon – by the stream

LUCIAN
LORENZO
LYNDELL L

Lomax	Variant of Lomas		meaning 'man of Luciana', the name
Lombard	Old German – long beard		of St Luke the Evangelist. Lucas is
London	Place name		the Latinized form that reached
Lonnie	Variant of Lenny, a short/pet		England about the 12th century *(Lukas)*
	form of Leonard. Popularized	**Luce**	Variant of Lucius
	by the singer Lonnie Donnegan	**Lucian**	Alternative spelling of Lucien
Lorcan	Gaelic – fierce	**Lucien**	Variant of Lucius *(Lucian)*
Lorence	Alternative spelling of Laurence	**Lucius**	Latin – bringer of light
Lorenzo	Italian and Spanish form of Laurence	**Ludovic**	Variant of Louis. Short/pet form: Ludo
Lorimer	Latin – maker of bridles	**Ludwig**	Variant of Louis
Loring	Unknown origin – instructive	**Luigi**	Italian form of Louis
Lorne	Derived from Scottish place	**Luis**	Spanish form of Louis
	name Lorn, and equivalent	**Lukas**	Alternative spelling of Lucas
	to the girl's name Lorna	**Luke**	Variant of Lucas
Lorus	Variant of Laurence	**Lumumba**	Swahili – talented
Lothar	German form of Louis	**Luther**	Old German – famous army,
Louie	Alternative spelling of Louis		illustrious warrior
Louis	French – famous warrior, glorious		
	in battle. Short/pet forms: Lew,	**Lyall**	Alternative spelling of Lisle
	Lou *(Lewie, Louie)*	**Lyle**	Alternative spelling of Lisle
Lovelace	Possibly Anglo-Saxon – love token	**Lyncoln**	Alternative spelling of Lincoln
Lovell	Norman French – wolf cub	**Lynde**	Variant of Lyndon
Lowell	Variant of Lovell	**Lyndell**	Anglo-Saxon – (dweller in the)
Loy	Unknown origin – open		valley of lime trees *(Lindell)*
Loyal	Old French – legal	**Lyndley**	Alternative spelling of Lindley
Lubin	Unknown origin – beloved friend	**Lyndon**	Anglo-Saxon – (dweller on the
Luc	Welsh form of Lucas		hill by the) lime tree *(Linden)*
Luca	Variant of Lucas	**Lynton**	Anglo-Saxon – place by the
Lucas	Derived from the Greek, Loukas,		lime tree *(Linton)*
		Lysander	Greek – liberator

AND COLOUR

This is another fun way of deciding on a name for your new baby. It's a slightly risky one, however, in that it is quite usual for the colour of a baby's hair to bear little or no resemblance to the colouring it will have as it grows older. This is down to the pigmentation in hair, which changes throughout our lives. Those babies actually born with hair will probably lose it quite quickly, and then experience gradual regrowth. The new hair is often different in appearance from the original, both in colour and type.

Hair colour is, however, a fun category from which to choose a name and if both parents have the same hair colour you have a good idea of what your child's will be like when he/she is older.

Many of the names relating to hair colour are of Celtic origin, thanks to the Celts' habit of naming people by their appearance (see page 113 for those listings).

CALVINA XANTHE
DUFF

RUFUS

Boys

Alroy (red-haired)
Banning (blond child)
Bayard (reddish-brown hair)
Bialy (white-haired boy)
Blaine (yellow-haired)
Bowie (yellow-haired)
Boyd (yellow-haired)
Colley (swarthy, black-haired)
Crispin (curly-haired)
Dewitt (blond, fair-haired)

Dolan (dark-haired)
Dory (golden-haired boy)
Dow (black-haired)
Duff (dark-haired)
Fairfax (fair-haired)
Faxon (long-haired)
Flannan (red-haired)
Finbar (fair-/white-haired)
Flavian (blonde)
Flinn (son of the red-haired one)

Gilroy (red-haired boy)
Julian (soft-haired, downy-bearded)
Kenyon (blond-haired)
Reid (red-haired)
Rooney (red-haired)
Roth (red-haired)
Rufus (red-haired)
Ruskin (red-haired one)
Rusty (red-headed)

Girls

Brenna (raven-haired maiden)
Bruna (dark-haired)
Burnetta (little brown-haired one)
Calvina (bright-haired)
Chrysilla (golden-haired)
Crispina (curly-haired)
Duana (little dark-haired maiden)

Flanna (red-haired)
Flavia (blonde)
Fresa (curly-haired)
Gillian (soft-haired, downy)
Ginger (red-haired)
Juliana (soft-haired, downy)
Julie (soft-haired, downy)

Kiera (dark-haired)
Leila (dark-haired)
Rhonwen (white-haired)
Rufina (red-haired)
Tawny (with yellowish-brown hair colour)
Xanthe (golden yellow)

FLAVIAN
TAWNY
JULIANA
BLAINE
BRENNA

MANUEL

MADDOX

MARCUS

M

Maarten	Dutch form of Martin
Mack	Originally a nickname for anyone whose surname began with 'Mc' or 'Mac', it is now also an independent name in its own right
Maddock	Variant of Maddox (Madoc)
Maddox	Celtic – beneficent, kind
Madigan	Gaelic – a bear
Madison	Anglo-Saxon – mighty warrior
Madoc	Alternative spelling of Maddock
Magnus	Latin – great, noble, regal, large
Maitland	Anglo-Saxon – dweller in the meadow
Malachi	Hebrew – God's messenger
Malachy	Traditional Gaelic name
Malcolm	Gaelic – servant of St Columba, devotee of the dove (Columba means 'dove'). A favourite in Scotland, with four Scottish kings bearing the name
Maldwyn	Welsh form of Baldwin
Malik	Arabic – master
Malin	Anglo-Saxon – little warrior
Mallard	Probably old German – strong in counsel

Mallory	Old French – unhappy person
Manfred	Old German – man of peace
Manley	Anglo-Saxon – shared wood
Manning	Anglo-Saxon – son of the hero
Manton	Anglo-Saxon – hero's village
Manuel	Variant of Emmanuel. Short/pet form: Manny
Manus	Variant of Magnus
Marc	French form of Mark
Marcel	Variant of Marc
Marcello	Italian form of Marc
Marcellus	Diminutive of Marcus
March	Variant of Marcus
Marcius	Variant of Marcus
Marco	Italian form of Mark
Marcus	Original Latin form of Mark, derived from Mars, the god of war in Roman mythology, meaning 'war-like' (Markus)

MARTIN
MARKUS
MATTHIAS

Marden	Anglo-Saxon – from the valley with the pool
Marek	Polish form of Mark
Mario	Variant of Marcus
Marion	Variant of Marcus
Marius	Variant of Marcus
Mark	Derived from Marcus, itself derived from Mars, the Roman god of war *(Marc)*
Markos	Greek form of Mark
Markus	Alternative spelling of Marcus
Marley	Anglo-Saxon – pleasant wood
Marlin	Variant of Merlin
Marlon	Uncertain origin, possibly French, popularized by the American actor Marlon Brando
Marsden	Anglo-Saxon – valley of combat
Marshall	French/German – farrier
Marston	Variant of Marsden
Martel	Unknown origin – war hammer
Marten	Alternative spelling of Martin
Martin	Derived, like Mark, from Mars, the god of war in Roman mythology. Short/pet forms: Mart, Marty *(Marten, Martyn)*
Martyn	Alternative spelling of Martin
Marvin	A variant of Merlin. Short/pet form: Marv
Maska	Unknown origin – powerful

Mason	Anglo-Saxon – stone worker
Mateo	Spanish – gift of God
Mateus	Portuguese form of Matthew
Mather	Anglo-Saxon – strong army
Matheus	Dutch form of Matthew
Mathew	Alternative spelling of Matthew
Mathias	Variant of Matthew *(Matthias)*
Matias	Spanish form of Matthew
Matt	Short/pet form of Matthew, now also an independent name
Matteo	Italian form of Matthew
Matthew	Hebrew – gift of God. Common name in the Middle Ages, producing surnames such as Macey, Matthews and Mayhew. Short/pet forms: Matt, Mattie, Matty *(Mathew, Matthieu)*
Matthias	Alternative spelling of Mathias
Matthieu	French form of Matthew

MAXIM
MEREDITH
MICHAEL

Maurice	Derived from the Latin *mauritius*, meaning 'a moor', 'swarthy', 'dark-skinned'. Short/pet forms: Maurie, Maury, Mo *(Morris)*
Max	Short/pet form of Maximilian and Maxwell, it is now also an independent name
Maxim	Variant of Maximilian *(Maxime)*
Maxime	Alternative spelling of Maxim
Maximilian	Latin – greatest. A favourite name in Germany before spreading to Britain. Short/pet forms: Macks, Max
Maxwel	Alternative spelling of Maxwell
Maxwell	Anglo-Saxon/Scottish – large spring. Short/pet form: Max *(Maxwel)*
Maynard	Old German – strong, hardy, powerful
Mayo	Gaelic – plain of yew trees
Mbizi	Egyptian – water
Mckale	Alternative spelling of Michael
Mead	Anglo-Saxon – meadow *(Meade)*
Meade	Alternative spelling of Mead
Medwin	Anglo-Saxon – strong, worthy companion, friend
Mehrdad	Persian – gift of the sun
Melchior	Persian – king of light
Melville	Celtic – Old French – bad land. Short/pet form: Mel
Melvin	Uncertain origin, possibly Gaelic. Short/pet form: Mel *(Melvyn)*
Melvyn	Alternative spelling of Melvin
Memphis	US place name, used for both boys and girls
Mensah	Egyptian – born third
Mercer	Latin – merchant
Meredith	Welsh – sea protector/lord
Mergus	Unknown origin – diver
Merlin	Old Welsh – sea hill, hill by the sea. Name of King Arthur's magician
Merrick	Welsh form of Maurice
Merrill	Masculine form of Merle, a girl's name that means 'blackbird' *(Meryle)*
Merton	Anglo-Saxon – from or near the sea
Mervin	Variant of Merlin. Short/pet form: Merv *(Mervyn)*
Mervyn	Alternative spelling of Mervin
Meryle	Alternative spelling of Merrill
Meurig	Welsh form of Maurice
Meyer	German – a farmer
Michael	Hebrew – God-like. Short/pet forms: Mick, Micky, Mike *(Mckale, Mikael, Mikkel)*
Mick	Short/pet form of Michael. So common in Ireland it is now a nickname for any Irishman
Miguel	Spanish form of Michael, pronounced 'mee-gell'

Mikael	Alternative spelling of Michael
Mikhail	Slavonic form of Michael
Mikkel	Alternative spelling of Michael
Milan	Latin – warrior, graceful one. Also an Italian place name
Miles	Uncertain origin but may mean 'beloved'. An old name brought to England by the Normans (*Myles*)
Milford	Anglo-Saxon – from the ford by the mill. A Welsh and New Zealand place name
Millard	Variant of Miller
Miller	Anglo-Saxon – miller
Milo	Variant of Miles
Milt	Variant of Milton
Milton	Anglo-Saxon – mill enclosure, mill keeper, from the mill town
Minco	Native American – chief
Miroslav	Slavonic – beautiful slave
Misha	Russian pet form of Michael
Mishka	Variant of Misha
Mitchel	Alternative spelling of Mitchell
Mitchell	Surname derived from the medieval French form of Michael, now used as a first name. Short/pet form: Mitch (*Mitchel*)
Mohamed	Alternative spelling of Muhammad
Mohammad	Alternative spelling of Muhammad
Mohammed	Alternative spelling of Muhammad

Moke	Variant of Moses
Monroe	Gaelic – from the red swamp
Montague	Originally from a French place name meaning 'pointed hill', it came to Britain as a surname with the Norman invasion. Short/pet forms: Monte, Monty (*Montagu*)
Montagu	Alternative spelling of Montague
Montana	Latin – mountain
Montgomery	Old French – of the hill. Also a place name. Short/pet forms: Monte, Monty
Monti	Aborigine – stork
Monty	Short/pet form of Montague and Montgomery, it is now also an independent name
Moray	Alternative spelling of Murray
Mordecai	Hebrew – warrior, war-like

MURDO

MORTIMER

MYCROFT

Mordred	Anglo-Saxon – bold adviser
Morgan	Welsh name of uncertain meaning. Used for both boys and girls *(Morgen)*
Morgen	Alternative spelling of Morgan
Morley	Anglo-Saxon – meadow
Morrell	Variant of Morris
Morris	More modern spelling of Maurice, meaning dark-skinned. Short/pet forms: Mo, Morey, Morrie
Morrison	Latin – son of Morris
Morten	Danish form of Martin
Mortimer	French place name and surname, now used as a first name. Short/pet forms: Mort, Morty
Morton	Anglo-Saxon – from the farm on the fen, town near the moor. Short/pet forms: Mort, Morty
Morven	Anglo-Saxon – seaman
Moses	Hebrew – saved, saviour. Hidden among bulrushes as a baby to save his life, this biblical hero led the Israelites out of Egypt and received the Ten Commandments from God. The name has always been popular with Jewish families
Moshe	Egyptian variant of Moses
Moss	Egyptian variant of Moses
Moy	Variant of Moses
Msanaa	Swahili – talented man

Muhammad	Arabic – praised *(Mohamed, Mohammad, Mohammed)*
Mungo	Celtic nickname meaning 'most dear' for St Kentigern, founder of the church in Glasgow
Munro	Scottish surname, now used as a first name *(Munroe)*
Munroe	Alternative spelling of Munro
Murdo	Variant of Murdoch
Murdoch	Gaelic – sailor *(Murdock)*
Murdock	Alternative spelling of Murdoch
Murphy	Celtic – of the sea. An Irish favourite, even though Murphy's Law states that if anything can go wrong, it will!
Murray	Celtic clan name, possibly taken from the Moray Firth, which is sometimes used as a personal name. Possibly meaning 'seaman' *(Moray)*
Myall	Aborigine – acacia tree
Mycroft	Anglo-Saxon – marsh homestead
Myles	Alternative spelling of Miles
Myron	Greek – fragrant

NELSON

NATHAN

NICANDER

N

Nando	Old German – prepared traveller
Napoleon	Italian name of uncertain meaning – possibly derived from Naples
Nardo	Derived from Bernard
Narok	Kenyan place name
Nasim	Persian – breeze
Nathan	Derived from Nathaniel. The name of a prophet in the Old Testament. Short/pet forms: Nat, Nate, Natty
Nathanael	Alternative spelling of Nathaniel
Nathaniel	Hebrew – God has given. One of the biblical names that came into use after the Reformation. Short/pet forms: Nat, Nate, Natty *(Nathanael)*
Neal	Alternative spelling of Neil
Neely	Variant of Neil
Neil	Gaelic – champion *(Neill, Neal)*
Neill	Alternative spelling of Neil
Nelson	Originally a surname meaning 'Nell's son', which came into fashion as a first name in honour of the hero of Trafalgar, Lord Nelson
Nero	Latin – unknown meaning. Name of notoriously cruel Roman Emperor
Nestor	Greek – homecoming

Netis	Unknown origin – trusted friend
Nevil	Alternative spelling of Neville
Neville	A Norman surname taken from a place name, Neuville (meaning 'new town'), in France. The Nevilles were a powerful family in the Middle Ages. The name appears as a first name in the 17th century *(Nevil)*
Nevin	Gaelic – nephew
Nevlin	Unknown origin – seaman, sailor
Newton	Anglo-Saxon – of the new town
Nial	Alternative spelling of Niall
Niall	Gaelic form of Neil *(Nial, Niull)*
Nicander	Variant of Nicholas
Nicanor	Variant of Nicholas
Nichol	A variant of Nicholas *(Nicholl, Nicol, Nicoll)*

NEVILLE

NOAH
NICOLAS
NORWOOD

Nicholas	Greek – the people's victory. Short/pet forms: Nic, Nick, Nicky *(Nickolas, Nicolas)*
Nicholl	Alternative spelling of Nichol
Nickolas	Alternative spelling of Nicholas
Nico	Italian form of Nicholas
Nicol	Alternative spelling of Nichol
Nicolas	Alternative spelling of Nicholas
Nicoll	Alternative spelling of Nichol
Niel	Derived from Nathaniel
Niels	Danish form of Nicholas
Nigel	Latin – black, dark
Nika	Variant of Nicholas
Nikita	Greek – unconquered
Nikko	Unknown origin – daylight
Nikolos	Modern Greek form of Nicholas
Nikos	Variant of Nikolos
Niles	Variant of Neil
Nils	Variant of Neil
Ninian	Uncertain origin. Possibly of Celtic origin or, less likely, perhaps a corruption of Vivian, from the Latin *vivus*, meaning 'alive'
Niran	Thai – eternal
Niull	Alternative spelling of Niall
Noah	Hebrew – long lived, peace, long rest
Noam	Hebrew – pleasant, delight
Noe	Spanish – peace, rest
Noel	French – Christmas. Used since the Middle Ages as a name for both boys and girls born at Christmas time. Nowadays Noel is more usually the version used for boys and Noelle for girls *(Nowell)*
Nolan	Gaelic – descendant of a noble
Noland	Variant of Nolan
Norbert	Old German – famous in the north. Short/pet forms: Bert, Bertie
Norman	Anglo-Saxon – man from the north (ie Norseman). Short/pet form: Norm
Norris	Old French – northerner
Norton	Anglo-Saxon – north town
Norvin	Variant of Norman
Norwood	Anglo-Saxon – (from the) north wood
Notus	South wind
Nowell	Alternative spelling of Noel

OMARI

ODYSSEUS

ORLANDO

O

Oakes	Anglo-Saxon – from the oak-tree grove
Oakley	Anglo-Saxon – field of oak trees
Obadiah	Hebrew – servant of God
Oberon	Variant of Auberon
Octavus	Latin – eighth
Odin	Father of the gods in Norse mythology
Odo	Variant of Otto
Odon	Hungarian – wealthy protector
Odysseus	Hero in Greek mythology, equivalent to Ulysses in Roman mythology
Ogden	Anglo-Saxon – from the oak valley
Ola	Unknown origin – eternity
Olaf	Old Norse – ancestral relic, descendant *(Olav, Olave)*
Olav	Alternative spelling of Olaf
Olave	Alternative spelling of Olaf
Olin	Old Norse – holly
Oliver	Latin – olive tree (signifying peace). An old-established name that went out of favour with Oliver Cromwell, only returning to regular use during the 20th century. Short/pet forms: Ollie, Olly
Olivier	French form of Oliver
Omar	Arabic – first-born son
Omari	Swahili form of Oliver
Oran	Phonetic spelling of the Gaelic name Odhran, meaning 'green'
Orban	Latin – the world, globe
Orel	Unknown origin – listener
Oren	Hebrew – ash-tree
Orion	Name of a great hunter in Greek mythology, and of a stellarconstellation
Orlando	Variant of Roland. Also a US place name
Orman	Anglo-Saxon – spear man
Ormond	Old German – famous protector
Orsen	Alternative spelling of Orson
Orsin	Alternative spelling of Orson
Orsino	Variant of Orson
Orso	Latin – bear
Orson	Anglicized form of the Italian name, Orso, which was popularized by the actor and film-maker Orson Wells, *(Orsen, Orsin)*
Ortensio	Italian – gardener
Orville	Derived from a French place name meaning 'gold town'. Best known as the name of the pioneer aviator Orville Wright
Orwin	Anglo-Saxon – golden friend

OTTO

O OSBERT

OSWALD

Os	Short/pet form for names beginning with 'Os', for example Oscar
Osbert	Old German/Anglo-Saxon – shining god. Originally confined to the north of England where 'Os' had been the prefix of the Northumbrian rulers
Osborne	Old German/Anglo-Saxon – warrior, soldier of God. Also old German – sacred bear
Oscar	Anglo-Saxon – God + spear. Short/pet forms: Os, Ossie, Ossy, Oz, Ozzie *(Oskar)*
Oskar	Alternative spelling of Oscar
Osmond	Old German/Anglo-Saxon – divine protector. A name made popular by St Osmund, William the Conqueror's Chancellor and Bishop of Salisbury. Short/pet forms: Os, Ossie, Ossy, Oz, Ozzie *(Osmund)*
Osmund	Alternative spelling of Osmond
Ostin	Alternative spelling of Austin
Oswald	Anglo-Saxon – god of the woods, god of power. Short/pet forms: Os, Ossie, Ossy, Oz, Ozzie

Othello	Variant of Otto
Otis	Greek – keen of hearing, or possibly a variant of Otto
Ottah	Egyptian – third born
Otto	Old German – wealthy, prosperous. A German royal name that has never been popular in Britain
Ouray	Native American – arrow
Owain	Alternative spelling of Owen
Owen	Believed to derive from the Latin *Eugenius*, meaning 'well-born', though it is sometimes thought to derive from the Welsh word *oen*, meaning 'lamb' *(Owain)*
Oxford	Anglo-Saxon – of the oxen farm/crossing. Also a place name

OSCAR

OSBORNE

OWEN

PATRICK

PALMER

PAULOS

P

Pabla	Variant of Pablo
Pablo	Spanish form of Paul
Paco	Native American – bald eagle
Padraig	Gaelic form of Patrick, pronounced 'paw-drig'
Paget	Anglo-Saxon – little page. Used for both boys and girls
Paine	Latin – of the country
Pallas	Greek – understanding
Palma	Masculine form of the girl's name Pamela, meaning 'honey- like sweetness'
Palmer	Anglo-Saxon – pilgrim to the Holy Land
Pancho	Spanish – tuft, plume
Paolo	Latin – little
Paris	French and US place name and name of the romantic hero in Greek mythology whose elopement with Helen caused the Trojan War. Used for both boys and girls
Parker	Anglo-Saxon – keeper of the estate
Parri	Aborigine – a stream
Parry	Welsh – son of Harry
Parson	Anglo-Saxon – minister, clergy

Pascal	French – Easter *(Pascale)*
Pascale	Alternative spelling of Pascal
Pascoe	Variant of Pascal *(Pascow)*
Pascow	Alternative spelling of Pascoe
Patrice	French form of Patrick
Patrick	Derived from the Latin word *patricius*, meaning 'nobleman' and made famous by the fifth-century patron saint of Ireland. So popular that 'Paddy' has become a general nickname for any Irishman. Short/pet forms: Paddy, Pat, Patch
Pattison	Variant of Patrick
Patton	Anglo-Saxon – from the castle of the warrior
Paul	Latin – small
Paulo	Italian form of Paul
Paulos	Greek form of Paul

LITERARY
LEANINGS

If you or your partner are a bookworm you might need look no further than a favourite book, play or poem for a suitable name for your child. You might decide to name your baby after a literary character like RD Blackmore's Lorna Doone, Margaret Mitchell's Scarlett O'Hara from *Gone with the Wind* or Charles Dickens's Oliver Twist. Or, if you have a favourite author or playwright, try picking one of their works and browse through it for ideas. From James Joyce and Mark Twain to VS Naipaul and JK Rowling, it doesn't matter whether your chosen author wrote classic novels or modern fiction, the fact is you like their work and it may provide a suitable name for your child.

Classics

Shakespeare was such a prolific writer that it shouldn't be too difficult to find a Shakespearean name that you like. Look at *Romeo and Juliet* and consider names like Sampson, Gregory and Tybalt for a boy or Juliet for a girl. In *As You Like It* you will find Audrey, Celia, Rosalind and Phebe for girls' names while *Macbeth* includes Malcolm and Ross for boys.

Alternatively, peruse the works of Jane Austen, the Brontë sisters or Charles Dickens for some traditional names, browse through Beatrix Potter or turn to JRR Tolkein's *Lord of the Rings* for some unusual names – such as Aragorn and Legolas for boys and Eowyn and Galadriel for girls.

Harry Potter

For up-to-date literary inspiration, why not look at the series of Harry Potter books? An apprentice wizard at Hogwart's School of Witchcraft and Wizardry, this popular fictional character probably helped account for the inclusion of Harry in the UK's Top 10 baby names for boys in 2000 and 2001. There are plenty of other characters in the books, whose names might appeal to you (see box, right). If you go down this route you are probably best advised to choose names of good or popular characters like the Weasley family rather than evil or nasty ones like Uncle Vernon and Harry's cousin Dudley. Of course there are plenty of more unusual names to be found here, too, like Rubeus and Albus, but they might not necessarily be kind options for your child!

SEAMUS
MINERVA
GEORGE
ANGELINA

Names from the Harry Potter books

Boys		Girls
Alastor	James	Alicia
Arthur	Lee	Angelina
Bill	Marcus	Bertha
Charlie	Neville	Gabrielle
Colin	Nicolas	Ginny
Cornelius	Oliver	Hedwig
Dean	Percy	Hermione
Dennis	Ron	Minerva
Fred	Seamus	Molly
George	Severus	Penelope
Harry	Sirius	Rita
	Trevor	

PHILANDER

P

PERCIVAL

PERTH

Pavel	Russian form of Paul
Pawl	Welsh form of Paul
Pawley	Variant of Paul
Paxton	Latin – peaceful town
Payton	Scottish – pastor, guardian *(Peyton)*
Pearce	Alternative spelling of Pierce
Peder	Variant of Peter
Pedro	Spanish form of Peter
Peers	Alternative spelling of Piers
Pellegrino	Italian form of Peregrine
Pembroke	Celtic/Anglo-Saxon – broken hill
Penn	Anglo-Saxon – enclosure
Percival	Medieval French name, given to one of King Arthur's legendary knights. Short/pet form: Percy
Percy	Derived from a Norman place name. The Northumbrian family of that name were associates of William the Conqueror. Also short/pet form of Percival
Peregrine	Latin – traveller, pilgrim. Short/pet form: Perry
Peridot	Arabic – name of a green gemstone
Perkin	Variant of Peter
Perrin	Variant of Perry
Perry	Short/pet form of Peregrine, now also an independent name. Also, possibly derived from the Anglo-Saxon word for pear tree

Perth	Celtic – thornbush thicket. Scottish and Australian place name
Peru	Basque form of Peter. Also a place
Peter	Greek – a rock. The name given to Jesus's disciple, Simon. Short/pet form: Pete
Petiri	Shona – here we are
Peyton	Variant of Patrick. Also alternative spelling of Payton
Philander	Greek – he who loves mankind
Philemon	Greek – kiss, loving
Philibert	Old German – brilliant. Short/pet forms: Bert, Bertie
Philip	Greek – lover of horses. Short/pet forms: Phil, Phip, Pip *(Phillip, Phylip)*
Phillip	Alternative spelling of Philip
Philo	Greek – love
Phineas	Egyptian – black, swarthy

PRESTON

PLATON

QUINTUS

Phoenix	Latin – phoenix (mythological bird that rises from the ashes). A US place name. Used for boys and girls
Phylip	Alternative spelling of Philip
Pier	Variant of Pierre
Pierce	Variant of Piers *(Pearce)*
Pierre	More modern French form of Piers
Piers	Old French form of Peter, which came to England with the Normans *(Peers)*
Pierson	Anglo-Saxon – son of Peter
Pieter	Dutch form of Peter
Pitt	Anglo-Saxon – dweller by a claypit
Placido	Latin – calm, quiet
Platon	Spanish – broad-shouldered
Porter	Latin – keeper of the gate
Potter	Anglo-Saxon – a potter
Prentice	Latin – beginner, learner
Prescott	Anglo-Saxon – priest's cottage
Presley	Anglo-Saxon – priest's meadow
Preston	Anglo-Saxon – priest's farm. Also an English place name
Price	Celtic – son of Rhys
Prince	Latin – chief, first. Old Roman name first adopted as a British surname
Purvis	Old French – provider of sustenance
Pyralis	Greek – of fire
Pythias	Friend of Damon in Greek mythology. According to legend the friends were rewarded for their mutual loyalty

Qeb	Egyptian – father of the earth
Quentin	Derived from the Latin *quinctus*, meaning 'fifth', and from the name of an old Roman clan
Quillan	Gaelic – cub
Quinby	Old Norse – from the queen's estate
Quincy	French – (estate owned by) fifth son
Quinlan	Gaelic – well shaped, athletic
Quinn	Gaelic – counsel
Quintin	Variant of Quentin
Quinton	Variant of Quentin
Quintus	Latin – fifth-born child

QUINCY

RANALD

RAIDON

RANDOLPH

R

Rab	Scottish short/pet form of Robert, now also an independent name
Radburn	Anglo-Saxon – red stream/brook
Radcliffe	Anglo-Saxon – red cliff
Rafael	Alternative spelling of Raphael
Rafe	Variant of Ralph
Raffaello	Variant of Raphael
Ragmar	Old German – wise warrior
Raidon	Japanese – thunder god
Rainer	Old German – prudent warrior
Raleigh	Anglo-Saxon – deer pasture. A name honouring Sir Walter Raleigh, a favourite of Queen Elizabeth I
Ralf	Alternative spelling of Ralph
Ralph	Anglo-Saxon – courageous adviser, wise hero *(Ralf)*
Ralston	Variant of Ralph. A place name and surname, used as a first name since the 19th century
Ramiro	Basque – great judge
Ramon	Spanish form of Raymond
Ramsay	Gaelic – (from the) sheep's or raven's island. An ancient Scottish surname that became a first name and was made better known by James Ramsay MacDonald (1866–1937), Britain's first Labour Prime Minister *(Ramsey)*
Ramsey	Alternative spelling of Ramsay
Ranald	Variant of Ronald
Randal	Anglo-Saxon – shield + wolf, ie courageous protector, which gave rise in the Middle Ages to surnames like Randal, Randle and Rason *(Randall)*
Randall	Alternative spelling of Randal
Randolf	Alternative spelling of Randolph
Randolph	Derived from the earlier name, Randal. The name of Winston Churchill's father, the statesman Randolph Churchill (1849–95). Short/pet forms: Dolf, Dolph *(Randolf)*
Randy	Variant of Randal/Randolph
Ranen	Hebrew – joyous
Ranger	French – guardian of the forest
Ranjit	Sanskrit – the delighted one
Ranulf	Variant of Randal/Randolph *(Ranulph)*
Ranulph	Alternative spelling of Ranulf

RALPH

REGINALD

RAYNOR

REUBEN

R

Raoul	French form of Ralph
Raphael	Hebrew – God has healed. Short/pet form: Raffi *(Rafael)*
Rauri	Gaelic form of Rory
Ravelin	Unknown origin – rampart
Raven	Anglo-Saxon – like the raven
Ravid	Hebrew – wander
Raymond	Old German – counsel + protection. The name came to England with the Normans. Short/pet form: Ray *(Raymund)*
Raymund	Alternative spelling of Raymond
Raynauld	Alternative spelling of Reynold
Rayner	Alternative spelling of Raynor
Raynor	Old German – advising, discreet warrior *(Rayner)*
Razi	Hebrew – secret
Read	Alternative spelling of Reid
Reade	Alternative spelling of Reid
Reagan	Alternative spelling of Regan
Rearden	Alternative spelling of Riordan
Redford	Anglo-Saxon – from the red river crossing
Redmond	German – protecting counsellor
Reece	Alternative spelling of Rhys
Reed	Alternative spelling of Reid
Rees	Alternative spelling of Rhys
Reese	Alternative spelling of Rhys
Reeve	Anglo-Saxon – high official, steward

Reeves	Variant of Reeve
Regan	Celtic – royal *(Reagan)*
Reginald	Anglo-Saxon – power + force. Short/pet forms: Reg, Reggie
Regis	Latin – kingly, regal. This name is derived from Reginald
Reid	Anglo-Saxon – red, ruddy, red-haired. A surname that has come into use as a first name *(Read, Reade, Reed)*
Reilly	Alternative spelling of Riley
Remus	One of the founders of Rome
Renard	Variant of Reynard
Renauld	Latin – reborn
René	French – reborn
Renfred	Old German – wise, peaceful judgement
Reuben	Hebrew – behold a son. One of the biblical names adopted by the Puritans in the 17th century. In Britain it has come to be regarded as a mainly Jewish name. Short/pet form: Rube *(Ruben)*
Revelin	Gaelic form of Roland
Rex	Latin – king. Originally a short form of Reginald, but in modern usage is regarded as a separate name and has almost lost its earlier associations
Rey	Variant of Rex

RILEY

RICHARD

ROBERT

Name	Meaning	Name	Meaning
Reynard	Old German/Old French – advice + brave, strong. Has become the generic term for a fox thanks to a sly character in medieval French tales	**Rico**	Spanish form of Rick
		Rider	Anglo-Saxon – horseman
		Ridgley	Anglo-Saxon – by the meadow's edge
Reyner	Variant of Rex	**Ridley**	Anglo-Saxon - reed clearing
Reynold	Earlier form of Reginald *(Raynauld)*	**Rigby**	Anglo-Saxon – ruler's valley
Rhett	Welsh – enthusiastic. Popularized by the character Rhett Butler in *Gone with the Wind*	**Riley**	Anglo-Saxon – rye meadow *(Reilly, Ryley, Rylie)*
		Ringo	Japanese – apple
Rhodrhi	Alternative spelling of Rhodri	**Rio**	Spanish – river. Also a place name
Rhodri	Welsh – wheel + ruler *(Rhodhri)*	**Riordan**	Phonetic spelling of the Gaelic name Rioghbhardan, meaning 'the king's poet' *(Rearden)*
Rhys	Welsh – rash, impetuous, swift, ardent *(Reece, Rees, Reese)*		
Rian	Alternative spelling of Ryan	**Roald**	Variant of Ronald
Riane	Gaelic – little king	**Roan**	Variant of Rowan
Ricardo	Spanish form of Richard	**Robert**	Derived from the Old German name, Hrodebert, from *hrothi*, 'fame', and *berhta*, 'bright'. There was an Anglo-Saxon name, Hreodbeorht, already in existence when the Normans brought Robert, the French derivation, from Germany, to England. Short/pet forms: Bob, Bobbie, Bobby, Rob, Robbie, Robby
Richard	Thought to derive from the Old German name, Ricohard, although there had been an Anglo-Saxon name, Ricehard, meaning 'rule hard', 'strong ruler'. It seems to have always been one of the most commonplace names in English life. Dick, the favourite abbreviation, was used, like Jack, to stand for Everyman. Short/pet forms: Dick, Dickie, Dickon, Dicky, Rich, Richie, Rick, Ricky		
		Robin	Diminutive of Rob, the short form of Robert, but now an independent name. Used for both boys and girls
Richmond	Variant of Richard. A place name	**Rocco**	Variant of Richard and Rockne

ROLAND

RODERICK

RONALD

Rock	Variant of Rockne		aristocratic surname, now used
Rockne	Anglo-Saxon – a rock		as a first name
Rocky	Variant of Rockne. Also the	**Roland**	Derived from the Old German
	name of a mountain range		name, Hrodland, from *hrothi*,
Rod	Short/pet form of Roderick and		'fame', and *landa*, 'land'.
	Rodney. Now an independent name		Roland has always been a name
Roderic	Alternative spelling of Roderick		with romantic associations
Roderick	Derived from the Old German		*(Rowland, Rolland)*
	name, Hrodric, from *hrothi*,	**Rolando**	Italian form of Roland
	'fame', and *ricja*, 'rule'. In Scotland	**Roldan**	Variant of Roland
	it became confused with the Gaelic	**Rolf**	Old German – famous for bravery.
	name Rharidh, 'red', which then		The Normans introduced this form
	became Anglicized as Roderick.		of the German name, Hrodult, but
	Short/pet forms: Rod, Rodd,		it was revived in its full form,
	Roddie, Roddy *(Roderic)*		Rudolph, last century
Roderigo	Variant of Roderick	**Rolland**	Alternative spelling of Roland
Rodger	Alternative spelling of Roger	**Rollo**	Variant of Rolf
Rodman	Variant of Roderick	**Roman**	Latin – of Rome
Rodney	Anglo-Saxon – reed island.	**Romeo**	Latin – of the Romans, pilgrim
	Short/pet forms: Rod, Rodd,		to Rome, romantic lover
	Roddie, Roddy	**Romero**	Latin – wanderer
Rogan	Variant of Rory	**Ronald**	Derived from an Old Norse name,
Roger	Derived from the Anglo-Saxon		Rögnvaldrand meaning 'power' +
	name, Hrothgar, from *hrothi*,		'force', 'ruler'. This is the Scottish
	'fame', and *ger*, 'spear', which		equivalent of Reynold, the old
	merged with the French name,		form of Reginald, but no longer
	Roger, brought over by the		considered only a Scottish name.
	Normans *(Rodger)*		Short/pet forms: Ron, Ronnie
Rohan	A French place name and	**Ronan**	Gaelic – a seal (the mammal)

RUDOLPH

R

ROSS

RYAN

Rooney	Gaelic – red-haired	**Rudolf**	Alternative spelling of Rudolph
Roosevelt	German – field of roses	**Rudolph**	*See* Rolf. Short/pet forms:
Rory	Phonetic spelling of the Gaelic		Dolf, Dolph Rudi, Rudy *(Rudolf)*
	name, Ruairidh, meaning 'red'	**Rudyard**	Anglo-Saxon – red yard
Roscoe	Old Norse – from the deer forest	**Rufus**	Latin – red-haired
Ross	Probably Celtic – promontory.	**Rune**	German – secret
	Other possible origins are from	**Runako**	Shona – handsome
	the Germanic 'fame', French 'red',	**Rupert**	Derived from the Old German,
	or from the Anglo-Saxon 'horse'.		Hrodebert, meaning 'fame bright',
	Originally a Scottish surname, it		the same root as for Robert.
	was brought into general use as		Short/pet form: Roo
	a first name in the 20th century	**Ruskin**	French – red-haired one
Roth	German – red-haired	**Russ**	Short/pet form of Russell, now
Rowan	Gaelic – little red one. Also a		also an independent name.
	species of tree. (The rowan tree is	**Russel**	Alternative spelling of Russell
	believed to have the power to drive	**Russell**	Derived from the French, *roux*,
	away evil.) Used for boys and girls		meaning 'red'. Short/pet form:
Rowdy	Spirited		Russ *(Russel)*
Rowland	Alternative spelling of Roland	**Rusti**	Alternative spelling of Rusty
Roy	Derived from the Gaelic *ruahd*,	**Rusty**	Anglo-Saxon – red-headed *(Rusti)*
	meaning 'red', although it is often	**Ryan**	Gaelic – little king. A modern
	believed to come from the French		first name taken from an Irish
	roi, meaning 'king'		surname *(Rian)*
Royce	Anglo-Saxon – chief, son of the king	**Ryder**	Anglo-Saxon – knight, rider
Royle	Anglo-Saxon – rye hill	**Rye**	Anglo-Saxon – rye grass. Also
Royston	English place name meaning		an English place name
	'Rory's town'. Short/pet form: Roy	**Rylan**	Anglo-Saxon – dweller at the rye land
Ruben	Alternative spelling of Reuben	**Ryley**	Alternative spelling of Riley
Rudd	Anglo-Saxon – ruddy	**Rylie**	Alternative spelling of Riley

SAVERO

SAMUEL

SEAN

S

Saku	Variant of Zachary
Salman	Arabic – safe
Saloman	Hebrew – peaceful
Salvador	Latin – saviour. Short/pet form: Sal
Salvatore	Variant of Salvador
Sampson	Alternative spelling of Samson
Samson	Hebrew – sun. Short/pet forms: Sam, Sammie, Sammy *(Sampson)*
Samuel	Hebrew – heard by God, name of God. Short/pet forms: Sam, Sami, Sammie, Sammy
Sanat	Unknown origin – ancient
Sancho	Latin – holy
Sanders	Anglo-Saxon – son of Alexander
Sandford	Anglo-Saxon – sandy ford or crossing *(Sanford)*
Sandon	Anglo-Saxon – from the sandy hill
Sandor	Variant of Alexander
Sandy	Short/pet form of Alexander, now also an independent name. Also a colour name
Sanford	Alternative spelling of Sandford
Sanfred	Old German – peaceful counsel
Santa	Seasonal name given to boys born at Christmastime

Santo	Spanish – a saint
Santos	Variant of Santo
Sargent	French – to serve
Sasha	Slavonic pet form of Alexander
Sashenka	Slavonic form of Alexander
Saul	Hebrew – asked for. The name appears in the Bible as the first king of Israel and Saul of Tarsus, who became St Paul
Saunders	Variant/son of Alexander
Savero	Arabic – bright
Saxon	Anglo-Saxon – swordsman
Scholem	Derived from the Hebrew word *shalom*, meaning 'peace'
Scot	Alternative spelling of Scott
Scott	Anglo-Saxon – a Scotsman. Short/pet forms: Scottie, Scotty *(Scot)*
Seadon	Alternative spelling of Seaton
Seaforth	Unknown origin – peaceful conqueror
Seamus	Gaelic form of James, pronounced 'shay-mus' *(Seumas, Seumus, Shamus)*
Sean	Gaelic form of John, pronounced 'shawn'. It evolved through the Old French name Jehan, modern French Jean, and is equivalent to the Irish Gaelic name Eoin *(Shaughan, Shaun, Shawn)*
Searle	Old German – armed warrior, wearer of armour *(Searles)*

SEYMOUR

S SEBASTIAN

SHERLOCK

Seaton	Anglo-Saxon – dweller by the sea *(Seadon)*
Sebastian	Greek – majestic, revered. Latin – man of Sebatia. Short/pet form: Seb *(Sebastien)*
Sebastien	Alternative spelling of Sebastian
Sebert	Old German – famous victory
Sekani	Nguni – laughter
Selby	Old German – manor house
Selmar	Unknown origin – rolling sea
Selwyn	Anglo-Saxon – close friend. Welsh – fair zeal
Serge	French – servant. French form of an old Roman family name
Sergei	Russian form of Serge
Sergio	Italian – attendant
Serlo	Variant of Searle
Seth	Hebrew – appointed. The name of Adam and Eve's third son
Seumas	Alternative spelling of Seamus
Seumus	Alternative spelling of Seamus
Severin	Anglo-Saxon – river in England
Seward	Anglo-Saxon – warden of the sea coast
Sewell	Unknown origin – winner
Seymour	A French place name and aristocratic surname, now used as a first name
Shale	Type of sedimentary rock
Shamus	Alternative spelling of Seamus

Shanahan	Gaelic – sagacious, wise
Shane	Variant of Sean
Shanley	Gaelic – child of the old hero
Shaughan	Alternative spelling of Sean
Shaun	Alternative spelling of Sean
Shaw	Anglo-Saxon – a grove
Shawn	Alternative spelling of Sean
Shawnee	Native American – southern people. Used for both boys and girls
Sheean	Celtic – courteous
Sheldon	Anglo-Saxon – from the hill ledge, protected hill. Short/pet form: Shel
Sheridan	Gaelic – searcher
Sherlock	Anglo-Saxon name of uncertain meaning. A name made popular by Sir Arthur Conan Doyle's fictional detective, Sherlock Holmes
Sherman	Anglo-Saxon – wool shearer

SIVAN
SIGMUND
SPENCER

S

Sherwin	Anglo-Saxon – true friend	**Simpson**	Variant of Simon
Sherwood	Anglo-Saxon – from the bright forest	**Sims**	Variant of Simon
Sholto	Gaelic – sower	**Sinclair**	French – shining brightly, saintly,
Sidney	Believed to be a contraction of the		illustrious. Anglicized form of the
	French 'St Denis', it is the surname		French name St Clair *(Synclair)*
	of a famous English family.	**Sivan**	Hebrew – the ninth month
	Short/pet forms: Sid, Syd *(Sydney)*	**Skipper**	Old Norse – shipmaster.
Siegfried	Old German – peaceful victory,		Short/pet form: Skip
	victorious peace. Short/pet forms:	**Slade**	Anglo-Saxon – child of the valley
	Sig, Siggy, Ziggy	**Slate**	Type of rock. Also a colour name
Sigmund	Old German – protector, victorious.	**Slevin**	Gaelic – mountaineer
	Short/pet forms: Sig, Siggy, Ziggy	**Sloane**	Gaelic – warrior
Silas	Derived from Silvanus	**Smith**	Anglo-Saxon – blacksmith
Silva	Latin – of the forest/wood	**Sofian**	Arabic – devoted
Silvanus	Variant of Silva. Name of the god	**Sol**	Latin – sun. Also the short/pet
	of forests in Roman mythology		form of Solomon
Silvester	Latin – wood/forest dweller. Three	**Solomon**	Hebrew – little man of peace,
	popes ensured the popularity of this		worshipper of Shalman. Regarded
	name in medieval Europe. Short/pet		chiefly as a Jewish name.
	form: Sly *(Sylvester)*		Short/pet forms: Sol, Solly
Simeon	Variant of Simon	**Sorley**	Anglicized form of the Gaelic
Simon	Derived from the Hebrew Shimeon,		name, Somhairle, meaning
	meaning 'hearkening', this is the		'traveller', 'Viking'
	Greek form, which literally means	**Spalding**	Anglo-Saxon – divided field
	'snub nose'. It occurs in the New	**Spencer**	Anglo-Saxon – dispenser, provider.
	Testament and was popular in		Short/pet form: Spence
	England in the Middle Ages as the	**Spike**	Anglo-Saxon – point, ear of corn
	name of the Apostle, Simon Peter.	**Stacy**	Latin – stable, reliable
	Short/pet forms: Si, Sim	**Stamford**	Alternative spelling of Stanford

CELTIC
NAMES

Celtic names are often popular among parents seeking an unusual name for their baby. 'Celtic' describes the branch of languages spoken by the Indo-European people who spread out to the westernmost regions of Europe in ancient times and settled in what we now know as Brittany (in France), Cornwall, Ireland, Scotland and Wales. Breton, Cornish, Gaelic (Irish and Scottish versions) and Welsh are all Celtic languages, and so the number of Celtic names is enormous. Indeed, many common English personal names are of Celtic origin as they were derived from the Anglicization of true Celtic names, some of which date back to pre-Christian times.

Origins

Like the Anglo-Saxons, the Celts took their names from many aspects of everyday life. These included myths and pagan gods (for example Brighid after the Celtic goddess of fire, light and poetry), place names (like Creighton - 'border settlement') and their warring way of life (for example Bevan – 'youthful warrior'). In addition, many Celtic names were used to describe someone's appearance, for example Cameron ('crooked nose') and Brenna ('maiden with raven hair').

The following names comprise just a small sample of the thousands of Celtic names, or Anglicized names derived from a Celtic dialect, that are available.

Boys

Angus (unique choice, chosen one)
Artur (bear, or stone)
Bevan (youthful warrior)
Brian (hill, or strong)
Brice (speckled/freckled one)
Calhoun (warrior)
Callum (dove)
Cameron (crooked nose)
Campbell (crooked mouth)
Caradoc (friendly, loving)
Carrick (dweller on the rocky headland)
Colm (dove – pronounced 'coll-um')

Conan (wolf, hound)
Conlan (hero, mighty)
Creighton (border settlement)
Dillon (faithful)
Donaghan (of dark complexion)
Donal (world ruler)
Duane (black)
Eamon (form of Edmund)
Egan (fiery, ardent)
Fergal (man of valour)
Fergus (man of vigour)
Finn (fair/white-haired)
Finnegan (fair, handsome)
Ifor (Welsh – 'lord')

Keefe (handsome, well)
Kennedy (helmet head, helmeted chief)
Kieran (black, dark-skinned, dark-haired)
Liam (form of William)
Niall (champion)
Padraig (form of Patrick – pronounced 'paw-drig')
Ronan (a seal)
Ryan (little king)
Seamus (form of James – pronounced 'shay-mus')
Sean (form of John – pronounced 'shawn')

Girls

Aislinn (dream, inspiration – pronounced 'ash-ling')
Angharad (much loved)
Aoife (beauty – 'ee-vah')
Blodwen (flowers)
Brighid (the exalted/august one – pronounced 'breed')
Bronwen (white-breasted)
Cairrean (form of Karen)
Caitlin (form of Catherine/ Katherine – pronounced 'kat-leen')
Carys (loved one)

Delyth (pretty)
Dilys (sincere, genuine)
Erin (Ireland)
Fionnhuala (white-shouldered – pronounced 'finn-nu-lah')
Glynis (little/from the valley)
Maire (form of Mary)
Mairead (form of Margaret)
Mairin (form of Mary – pronounced 'more-een')
Meadhbh (intoxicating – pronounced 'mayv')

Morna (beloved)
Nerys (lady)
Niamh (bright, beautiful – pronounced 'neeve')
Nuala (derived from Fionnhuala – pronounced 'noo-ah-lah')
Rhiannon (nymph, goddess)
Sian (form of Jane – 'sharn')
Sinead (form of Janet – pronounced 'shin-aid')
Siobhan (form of Joan – pronounced 'shah-vawne')

SULLY

 S STEPHEN

SYLVESTER

Stanford	Anglo-Saxon – stony meadow, stony crossing. Short/pet form: Stan *(Stamford)*	**Strom**	German – stream
		Stuart	Famous Scottish clan name, which originally meant 'steward', or 'sty ward', the keeper of the animals. It was the name of the royal house of Scotland, which gave us four kings of England as well as two queens. It was brought into use as a first name towards the end of the 19th century, which is when many Scottish surnames became fashionable. Short/pet forms: Stew, Stewie, Stu *(Stewart)*
Stanislaus	Slavonic – glory of the camp		
Stanislav	Variant of Stanislaus		
Stanislaw	Variant of Stanislaus		
Stanley	Variant of Stanford		
Steafan	Alternative spelling of Stephen		
Stefan	Russian and German form of Stephen *(Steffan)*		
Steffan	Alternative spelling of Stefan		
Stepan	Russian form of Stephen		
Stephan	Alternative spelling of Stephen		
Stephen	Greek – garland, crown. A common name in the Middle Ages leading to surnames such as Stephens, Stevenson and Stimpson. Short/pet forms: Steve, Stevie *(Steafan, Stefan, Steffan, Stephan, Steven)*	**Sully**	Anglo-Saxon – to stain
		Suman	Sanskrit – cheerful and wise
		Sumner	French – one who summons
		Sutherland	Old Norse – from the southern land
		Sutton	Anglo-Saxon – the town that is to the south
Sterling	Anglo-Saxon – little star *(Stirling)*	**Swain**	Old German – youthful
Steven	Alternative spelling of Stephen	**Sydney**	Alternative spelling of Sidney. Also an Australian place name
Stewart	Alternative spelling of Stuart		
Stig	Old Norse – wanderer		
Stirling	Alternative spelling of Sterling. Also a place name	**Sylvester**	Alternative spelling of Silvester
		Synclair	Alternative spelling of Sinclair
Stoke	Anglo-Saxon – village/village dweller. Also a place name	**Syshe**	Hebrew – street
Storm	A modern 'vocabulary name' used for both girls and boys		

TAYLOR

TALIESIN

THADEUS

T

Teague	Phonetic spelling of the Gaelic name Tadhg, meaning 'poet'
Tedman	Unknown origin – patriot
Templeton	Anglo-Saxon – town of sanctuary
Terence	Latin. Derived from an old Roman clan name, Terentius, the origin of which is not known, but possibly means 'tender', 'gracious'. Short/pet form: Terry *(Terrance, Terrence)*
Tabor	Turkish – fortified encampment
Taffy	Welsh pet form of David
Tai	Vietnamese – the talented one
Taite	Alternative spelling of Tate
Talbot	An aristocratic surname of Norman French/Old German origin, now used as a first name. Richard Talbot came to England with William the Conqueror
Terrance	Alternative spelling of Terence
Terrel	Variant of Terence
Terrence	Alternative spelling of Terence
Terris	Variant of Terence
Taliesin	Welsh – shining brow, pronounced 'tal-yes-in'
Thaddeus	Possibly derived from Theodore meaning 'gift of God'. Short/pet forms: Tad, Thad, Thady *(Thadeus)*
Tameron	Variant of Cameron
Taree	Aborigine – wild fig tree
Thadeus	Alternative spelling of Thaddeus
Tarik	Arabic – conqueror *(Tariq)*
Tariq	Alternative spelling of Tarik
Tarquin	Uncertain origin but family name of the legendary line of early Roman kings. Lucius Tarquinius Superbus, the seventh and last king of Rome, was sent with his family into exile in 510BC and a republic established
Tate	Anglo-Saxon – cheerful, great talker *(Taite)*
Taylor	Anglo-Saxon – tailor. A surname turned first name

TIMON

 THEODORE

TITUS

Thane	Anglo-Saxon – servant. A thane held land given by the king and ranked with an earl's son. It was the title of a clan chief in Scotland
Thanos	Greek – noble
Thatcher	Anglo-Saxon – roof fixer
Thayer	Old German – of the nation's army
Theobald	Old German – bold people. Along with Tybalt, this is a variant of the ancient name Theobeald. Short/pet form: Theo
Theodore	Greek – divine gift, gift of God. There were several saints of this name. Short/pet forms: Ted, Teddie, Teddy, Telly, Theo
Theophilus	Greek – beloved of God
Theron	Greek – hunter
Thierry	Old German – people's ruler
Thomas	Aramaic – twin. Name of one of Jesus' disciples. Short/pet forms: Tom, Tommie, Tommy (Tomas)
Thorburn	Derived from an Old Norse name meaning 'Thor's bear'
Thornton	Anglo-Saxon – village near thorns
Thurstan	Alternative spelling of Thurston
Thurston	Old Norse – Thor's stone (Thurstan)
Tibalt	Greek – people's prince
Tiernan	Phonetic spelling of the Gaelic name Tiarnan, meaning 'kingly' 'lordly'

Tierney	Variant of Tiernan
Tilden	Anglo-Saxon – fertile valley. Short/pet form: Tilly
Timon	Variant of Timothy. Name of the hero of Shakespeare's *Timon of Athens*, who is a rich Athenian so generous that he becomes penniless and goes to live in a cave where he finds a pile of gold
Timothy	Derived from the Greek, Timotheos, meaning 'honouring God', 'respect'. Short/pet forms: Tim, Timmie, Timmy
Tino	Unknown origin – small
Titus	Latin – sun, day. The Roman Emperor Titus Flavius Vespasianus (AD9–79) began building the Coliseum in Rome

TRISTAN

TORBERT

TYRONE

Tobey	Alternative spelling of Toby	**Tristan**	Variant of Drystan. Also thought to be associated with *triste*, the French for 'sad'
Tobias	Hebrew – the Lord is good		
Tobit	Variant of Tobias		
Toby	Modern variant of Tobias *(Tobey)*	**Tristram**	Less popular variant of Tristan
Tod	Alternative spelling of Todd	**Troy**	Probably derived from the French place name, Troyes, meaning 'from the place of the people with curly hair'
Todd	Anglo-Saxon – fox *(Tod)*		
Tom	Short/pet form of Thomas, now also an independent name		
Tomas	Alternative spelling of Thomas	**Truman**	Anglo-Saxon – faithful man/servant
Tony	Short/pet form of Anthony, now also an independent name	**Tuart**	Aborigine – type of Eucalyptus
		Tulivu	Swahili – peace and tranquillity
Torbert	Old German – bright eminence	**Tully**	Latin – a little hill
Torin	Gaelic – chief	**Ty**	Latin – house
Torn	Derived from Torrance	**Tybalt**	Like Theobald, a variant of the ancient name Theobeald
Torquil	Old Norse – Thor's cauldron. Brought to England by the Danes before the Norman Conquest		
		Tyee	Native American – chief
Torrance	Variant of Terence	**Tymon**	Variant of Timon
Townsend	Anglo-Saxon – end of the town	**Tyne**	English place and river name
Travers	Variant of Travis	**Tyrol**	Austrian place name
Travis	Latin/French – from the road crossing, crossroads, toll keeper	**Tyrone**	Derived from the Irish place name meaning 'Owen's country' and publicized by the actor Tyrone Power
Trefor	Welsh form of Trevor		
Trent	English place and river name	**Tyson**	Old German – son of Ty
Trevor	Anglicization of the Welsh name, Trefor, from *tref*, 'homestead', and *mawr*, 'great'. Short/pet form: Trev		
Trey	Anglo-Saxon – three		
Trini	Spanish – the Trinity		

URIAH

ULRICH

VALENTINE

UV

Uberto	Italian form of Hubert
Udo	Japanese – ginseng. Also Old German – prosperity
Ugo	Italian form of Hugh
Ulf	Old Norse – wolf
Ulises	Spanish form of Ulyses
Ulric	Anglo-Saxon – wolf power. The name has been the name of three saints *(Ulrich, Ulrik)*
Ulrich	Alternative spelling of Ulric
Ulrik	Alternative spelling of Ulric
Ulton	Gaelic – Ulsterman
Ulysses	Hero in Roman mythology, equivalent to the Greek form Odysseus *(Ulises)*
Umberto	Italian – colour of earth

Unni	Old Norse – modest. Used for both boys and girls
Unwin	Anglo-Saxon – non-friend, ie enemy
Upton	Anglo-Saxon – from the upper town
Urban	Latin – of the town
Uri	Variant of Uriah
Uriah	Hebrew – God is my light. A biblical name taken up during the Reformation, then made notorious by Charles Dickens' cunning villain, Uriah Heep, in *David Copperfield*
Uriel	Variant of Uriah
Urlwin	Anglo-Saxon – noble friend
Usiku	Nguni – night
Vadin	Hindi – talker
Vadim	Derived from Vladimir
Vail	Anglo-Saxon – valley
Valdis	Old German – spirited warrior
Valentine	Derived from the Latin *valens*, meaning 'strong' or 'healthy'. Name of a third-century Roman saint martyred on 13 February, the eve of the pagan festival for lovers, now remembered on St Valentine's Day. Short/pet form: Val
Valentino	Italian form of Valentine
Valiant	Unknown origin – brave
Valter	Scandinavian and Portuguese form of Walter

VIRGIL

VAUGHAN

VASILY

Van	Dutch – of, from. Usually seen as the prefix to a surname, but sometimes treated as an independent first name
Vance	Anglo-Saxon – very high places, marshes
Vangelis	Greek – Variant of Evangelos
Vanya	Russian pet form of Ivan
Varden	Old French – from the green hills
Varg	Old Norse – wolf
Vasili	Greek – royal *(Vasily)*
Vasily	Alternative spelling of Vasili
Vaughan	Welsh – little, small, modest *(Vaughn)*
Vaughn	Alternative spelling of Vaughan
Veli	Finnish – brother
Vere	A French place name and aristocratic surname, used as a first name since the 17th century
Vergil	Alternative spelling of Virgil
Vern	Variant of Vernon
Vernon	French – alder tree, springtime. Brought to Britain initially as a Norman surname
Vicente	Spanish form of Vincent
Victor	Latin – conqueror, victorious. Short/pet forms: Vic, Vick *(Viktor)*
Vijay	Sanskrit – victory
Viktor	Russian form of Victor

Vimal	Sanskrit – pure
Vincent	Latin – conquering. Short/pet forms: Vin, Vince, Vinnie, Vinny
Vincenzo	Italian form of Vincent
Virgil	Latin – strong *(Vergil)*
Vito	Variant of Victor
Vittore	Italian form of Victor
Vivian	Derived from the Latin word *vivianus* meaning 'alive', 'lively' *(Vyvyan)*
Vladimir	Russian – prince. Short/pet form: Vlad
Von	Variant of Van
Vyvyan	Alternative spelling of Vivian

VICTOR

WARNER

WALLACE

WESLEY

W

Wade	Anglo-Saxon – dweller by the ford, river crossing
Wagner	Dutch – wagon driver
Walden	Old German – mighty
Waldo	Variant of Walden
Walker	Anglo-Saxon – one who thickens cloth
Wallace	French/Anglo-Saxon – foreigner, stranger. Originally a Scottish surname, before being given as a first name. Short/pet forms: Wal, Wally
Walter	Derived from two Old German words, *vald* meaning 'rule' and *harja* meaning 'folk'. Brought to England with the Norman Conquest and common enough to give rise to surnames like Walters, Watson and Waters. Short/pet forms: Wal, Wally, Walt
Wanekia	Native American – he who makes life
Ward	Anglo-Saxon – watchman, guardian
Warner	Variant of Warren
Warrain	Aborigine – belonging to the sea

Warren	Derived from the Old Germanic Varin, a folk name, meaning 'defender' or 'protection'. Brought to England by the Normans
Warrun	Aborigine – sky
Warui	Kikuyu – comes from the river
Warwick	Anglo-Saxon – farm beside a weir
Wayne	Derived from Anglo-Saxon occupational surname, meaning 'wagoner', 'wagon-maker', 'cartwright'
Webster	Anglo-Saxon – one who weaves
Wendell	Old German – wanderer
Werner	Variant of Warren
Wesley	Anglo-Saxon – west meadow. Parents used it in honour of John Wesley, the 18th-century founder of the Methodists. Short/pet form: Wes (Wesley)

WILMOT

WILHELM

WINTHROP

Westley	Alternative spelling of Wesley
Wheeler	Anglo-Saxon – driver
Whitby	Old Norse – farm with white walls. Also a place name
Whitfield	Anglo-Saxon – from the small field
Whitley	Variant of Whitfield
Wilbur	Believed to derive from Old German words, *wil*, 'will', and *burh*, 'defence'
Wiley	Anglo-Saxon – of the willows
Wilford	Variant of Wilfred. Also Anglo-Saxon – willow tree near ford
Wilfred	Old German/Anglo-Saxon – *will* (will) + *frith* (peace). Short/pet form: Wilf
Wilhelm	German form of William
Will	Short/pet form of William, now also an independent name
Willard	Variant of William
Willem	Variant of William
William	Derived from two Old German words: *vilja*, meaning 'will' and *helma*, meaning 'helmet'. It became famous in Britain through William the Conqueror. Many surnames came from it, including Williams, Wilkes and Willis. Popularized in modern times by the birth of Prince William in 1982. Short/pet forms: Bill, Billy, Will, Willie, Wills Willy

Willis	Variant of William
Willoughby	Anglo-Saxon – farm beside the willow trees
Wilmot	Variant of William
Wilson	German – son of William
Windsor	Old German/Anglo-Saxon – from the river's bend
Winslow	Anglo-Saxon – from the friendly hill, dweller in a friendly town
Winston	Anglo-Saxon. A place name that may mean 'wine settlement' or 'town of victory', or is possibly connected with an Anglo-Saxon name Winestan, 'friend stone'
Winthrop	Anglo-Saxon – from the friendly village
Wolfgang	Old German – path of a wolf
Wood	Variant of Woods
Woodrow	Anglo-Saxon – path through the woods, houses by the wood
Woods	Anglo-Saxon – of the woods, woods dweller, woodsman
Woody	Variant of Sherwood and Woods
Wyatt	Anglo-Saxon – war brave
Wyndham	Anglo-Saxon – windy settlement
Wynn	Welsh – light-complexioned
Wystan	Anglo-Saxon – stony battleground

WYATT

YOSEFU

YANCEY

YVON

XY

Xanthus	Greek – yellow, pronounced 'zan-thus'
Xavier	Arabic – bright, shining. A place name in the Basque region of Spain, and the surname of a 16th-century Spanish Jesuit, St Francis Xavier. Pronounced 'zay-vee-ur'
Xenos	Greek – stranger, pronounced 'zee-nos'
Xerxes	Persian – ruler, king. Name of the Persian king (519–465BC) who defeated the Greeks at Thermopylaoe, pronounced 'zerk-seez'
Yakov	Russian form of Jacob
Yale	Welsh – fertile upland
Yancey	Alternative spelling of Yancy
Yancy	Dutch – son of John *(Yancey)*
Yanni	Variant of Yannis
Yang	Chinese – model, pattern
Yannis	Hebrew – gift of God
Yardley	Anglo-Saxon – from the pasture, enclosed meadow
Yehudi	Hebrew – praise. Made famous by the violinist Yehudi Menuhin
Yogi	Sanskrit – one who practises yoga

Yorick	Variant of George
York	Anglo-Saxon – boar farm. English place name
Yosef	Variant of Joseph
Yosefu	Variant of Joseph
Yuan	Variant of John
Yuji	Japanese – second son
Yule	Norse name whose origins are either a 12-day long heathen festival, or a winter month that began mid-November
Yuma	Native American – son of the chief
Yuri	Russian form of George
Yusef	Arabic form of Joseph *(Yusuf)*
Yusuf	Alternative spelling of Yusef
Yve	Alternative spelling of Yves
Yves	French – archer, yew tree *(Yve)*
Yvon	Variant of Yves

YUSEF

ZEPHANIAH

ZACHARY

ZURIAL

Z

Zac	Alternative spelling of Zak
Zacaria	Variant of Zacharias
Zaccheus	Aramaic – innocent, pure
Zach	Alternative spelling of Zak
Zacharias	Hebrew – God has remembered, the Lord is renowned. Short/pet forms: Zac, Zach, Zack, Zak
Zachary	Variant of Zacharias (Zachery)
Zachery	Alternative spelling of Zachary
Zack	Alternative spelling of Zak
Zadok	Hebrew – just
Zak	Short/pet, most common, form of Zacharias, now also an independent name (Zac, Zach, Zack)
Zamir	Arabic – thought
Zared	Hebrew – brook
Zebedee	Greek – gift of God. Short/pet form: Zeb
Zebulon	Hebrew – exalted/honoured (Zebulun)
Zebulun	Alternative spelling of Zebulon
Zedekiah	Hebrew – God is fair. Short/pet form: Zed
Zeke	Short/pet form of Ezekiel. Also Arabic – the memory of the Lord

Zelig	Old German – blessed
Zenon	Spanish – living
Zephaniah	Hebrew – hidden by God. Short/pet form: Zeph
Zephyr	Greek – west wind. Name of the god of the west wind in Greek mythology
Zerah	Unknown origin – rising light
Zetan	Hebrew – olive tree
Ziggy	Slavonic – to get rid of anger. A common Polish name
Zion	Hebrew – a sign, excellent
Zircon	Persian – type of mineral
Zivan	Slavonic – lively (Zyvan)
Zoltan	Arabic – ruler
Zorba	Greek – live life to the full
Zurial	Hebrew – God is my rock
Zyvan	Alternative spelling of Zivan

RIDGETTE
YASMIN WARRAH IRIS SARA
CRESSIA THALIA
OPHELIA KYLIE
CHANTE
SERAFINA NELLY
ANNABEL FILOMINA
JACARTA
HOLLY
CHERALYN XANTHE
VANESSA LOURDES
URSALA DIDO
PRIMRO
GARDENIA ELKIE
MEGAN ZAHAR
ROBYN
GWYNNETH

A-Z DIRECTORY OF
GIRLS' NAMES

You will find that there is a far greater range of names to choose from for girls than there is for boys. This is explained by the fact that, whereas boys tend to be named more conservatively – perhaps according to family tradition, there is a much more imaginative use of names when it comes to girls. They are often given boys' names, made-up names, names created from two other names (for example Heloise from Helen and Lois), vocabulary words such as names of plants, colours and jewels or simply traditional names that have been given modern, fanciful spellings. So you can be as creative and original as you want to be when you are putting together your list of possible names...

A

Aamor	Breton – sunbeam
Aba	Fanti – born on a Thursday
Abigail	Hebrew – my father's joy. Short/pet forms: Abbey, Abbie, Abby, Abi
Acacia	Greek – species of tree, it is also known as wattle
Acadia	Native American – place of plenty
Acantha	Greek – thorny
Ada	Uncertain origin – possibly derived from Old German meaning 'noble'. Also a short/pet form of Adelaide and Adele
Adah	Hebrew – beautiful addition
Adalia	Variant of Adelaide (*Adelia*)
Adaline	Alternative spelling of Adeline
Adamina	Hebrew – daughter of the earth
Adela	Variant of Adelaide (*Adella*)
Adelaide	German – noble and of kind spirit. Also Australian place name.Short/pet forms: Ada, Ady
Adèle	French form of Adele
Adele	Variant of Adelaide. Short/pet forms: Ada, Ady (*Adell, Adelle*)
Adelia	Alternative spelling of Adalia
Adelina	Variant of Adeline, itself a variant of Adelaide
Adeline	Variant of Adelaide (*Adaline*)
Adell	Alternative spelling of Adele
Adella	Alternative spelling of Adela
Adelle	Alternative spelling of Adele
Adiel	Hebrew – ornament of the Lord
Adione	Latin – traveller's friend
Adoncia	Spanish – sweet
Adonia	Greek – beautiful
Adora	French – beloved
Adria	Variant of Adrienne
Adriana	Italian form of Adrienne
Adriane	Alternative spelling of Adrienne
Adrianne	Alternative spelling of Adrienne
Adriene	Alternative spelling of Adrienne
Adrienne	French feminine form of Adrian meaning 'dark one' and 'from the town of Adria' (*Adriane, Adrianne, Adriene*)
Aenea	Hebrew – praiseworthy
Aeron	Celtic – bright queen
Affrica	Celtic – pleasant. Also continent name (*Africa, Afrika*)
Afric	Variant of Africa
Africa	Alternative spelling of Affrica
Afrika	Alternative spelling of Affrica
Agate	Variant of Agatha. It is also the name of a gemstone

AGNES

ALABAMA

Agatha — Greek – good. A third-century martyr, St Agatha is regarded as a protector against fire. Short/pet forms: Aggie, Aggy

Agila — Latin – active mind and body

Agnes — Greek – chaste, pure, holy

Agneta — Variant of Agnes

Agnola — Variant of Agnes

Agrippina — Latin – born feet first

Aida — Variant of Ida

Aila — Gaelic – light bearer

Aileen — Gaelic form of Eileen

Ailish — Variant of Elizabeth

Ailsa — Alternative spelling of Elsa. Also chosen by Scottish parents after the Ailsa Craig, an island rock in the Firth of Clyde

Aimée — Alternative spelling of Amy

Ainsley — Gaelic – one's own meadow

Aisleen — Alternative spelling of Aislinn

Aislin — Alternative spelling of Aislinn

Aisling — Alternative spelling of Aislinn

Aislinn — Gaelic – dream, vision, inspiration; pronounced 'ash-ling' *(Aisleen, Aislin, Aisling)*

Akela — Hawaiian – noble

Akili — Tanzanian – wisdom

Alabama — Native American – thicket clearers. Also a US place name

Alaine — Variant of Alana

Alana — Feminine form of the boy's name Alan, meaning 'peaceful harmony' or 'fair one'. Also Hawaiian – offering *(Alanna, Allanah)*

Alanna — Alternative spelling of Alana

Alaura — Variant of Laura

Alberta — Feminine form of Albert, from Old German meaning 'noble and bright'

Albertina — Variant of Alberta

Albertine — Variant of Alberta

Albina — Latin – feminine form of Alban meaning 'white', 'blonde'

Alcyone — Possibly Greek – calm. Name of a woman in Greek mythology who was turned into a kingfisher

Alda — Feminine form of the boy's name Alden, meaning 'old friend' or 'wise protector'

Aleandria — Variant of Alexandra

Aleka — Variant of Alex

Aleksandra — Alternative spelling of Alexandra

Alena — Greek – form of Helen

Alessandra — Italian form of Alexandra. Short/pet forms: Sandy, Sandie

Alessia — Variant of Alessandra

Aleta — Variant of Alethea

Alethea — Greek name – truth. Short/pet form: Thea

ALEXANDRA ALMA

ALISON

Aletta	Latin – winged one	**Alina**	Old German – used in the Middle
Alex	Short/pet form of Alexandra, now		Ages as a pet form of Adeline,
	also an independent name *(Alix)*		it is now an independent name
Alexa	Short/pet form of Alexandra,	**Aline**	Variant of Alana
	now also an independent name	**Alise**	Alternative spelling of Alice
Alexandra	Feminine form of Alexander,	**Alisha**	Variant of Alice
	meaning 'helper and defender of	**Alison**	Derived from Ailis, the true
	men'; particularly popular in Eastern		Gaelic form of Alice. Short/pet
	Europe and Scandinavia. Short/pet		forms: Ailie, Ali, Allie, Ally
	forms: Alex, Alix, Sandy, Sandie		*(Allison, Allyson, Alyson)*
	(Aleksandra, Alexandria)	**Alissa**	Alternative spelling of Alicia
Alexandria	Alternative spelling of Alexandra.	**Alix**	Alternative spelling of Alex
	Also Egyptian place name		and variant of Alice
Alexandrina	Variant of Alexandra	**Aliza**	Hebrew – joyous
Alexei	Variant of Alex	**Allanah**	Alternative spelling of Alana
Alexina	Variant of Alexandra	**Allegra**	Latin – joyful, merry, cheerful,
Alexis	Variant of Alex		comforter
Alfreda	Feminine form of Alfred,	**Allison**	Alternative spelling of Alison
	meaning 'intelligent and	**Allyson**	Alternative spelling of Alison
	wise advice'. Short/pet forms:	**Alma**	Probably derived from the Latin
	Freda and Freddy		word meaning 'kind' but may be
Alice	Like Adelaide, derived from		from the Celtic for 'all good', the
	the Old German *adalheidis*,		Hebrew for 'maiden' or the Spanish
	meaning 'noble one', an ancient		and Italian for 'soul' or 'spirit'.
	title for German princesses		The term 'Alma Mater', meaning
	(Alise, Alyce, Alys, Alyse)		foster mother, was an affectionate
Alicia	Variant of Alice *(Alissa)*		nickname coined by the Romans for
Alima	Arabic – wise		several of their favourite goddesses
Alina	Polish – bright, beautiful	**Almira**	Arabic – the exalted one

ALTHEA

AMETHYST

AMAZONIA

Aloysia	Old German – war maid
Alphonsine	Old German – ready for combat
Althea	Greek – healing, healthy. Also the botanical family name for the hollyhock. Short/pet form: Thea
Alvina	Old German – elfin friend
Alyce	Alternative spelling of Alice
Alyn	Variant of Alana
Alys	Alternative spelling of Alice
Alyse	Alternative spelling of Alice
Alysia	Greek – unbroken bond
Alyson	Alternative spelling of Alison
Alyssa	Greek – logical
Amabel	Latin – lovable, fortune, beautiful
Amabella	Variant of Amabel. Short/pet form: Bella
Amalea	Alternative spelling of Amelia
Amalia	Alternative spelling of Amelia
Amana	Hebrew – faithful
Amanda	Latin – lovable. Short/pet forms: Manda, Mandi, Mandy
Amanta	Variant of Amanda
Amarina	Aborigine – rain
Amarinda	Greek/Latin – unfading, everlasting. A name given by poets to an imaginary ever-flowering, ever-beautiful blossom
Amaris	Anglo-Saxon – child of the moon
Amaryllis	Greek – fresh, new. Species of flower

Amata	Spanish – beloved
Amazonia	Greek – warlike. Also derived from the river name
Amber	Arabic – reddish-yellow precious jewel, resin (of the sun)
Ambrosia	Greek – food of life, immortality. The name given to the food eaten by the mythological gods to perpetuate their immortality, later used for any food or smell fit for the gods
Ameerah	Arabic – princess
Amelia	German – industrious, hardworking, eager, striving. Short/pet forms: Millie, Milly *(Amalea, Amalia)*
Ameline	Variant of Amelia *(Ammeline)*
Amena	Celtic – honest woman
Amery	Hardworking in power. Originally a German name, Almeric, it was introduced to Britain by the Normans
Amethyst	Greek – a semi-precious stone. Also a colour name
Amey	Alternative spelling of Amy
Amie	Alternative spelling of Amy
Amina	Swahili – trustworthy, faithful
Amity	Latin – friendship
Ammeline	Alternative spelling of Ameline
Amorette	Latin – little love, sweetheart. One of several names made up by writers to describe a character

ANASTASIA

ANGELA

ANKE

Amy	Latin – beloved. This name has been used in Britain since the Middle Ages, becoming especially popular since the 19th century (*Aimée, Amey, Amie*)
Ana	Alternative spelling of Anna, and short/pet form of Anastasia
Anabel	Alternative spelling of Annabel Possibly French or Greek – fruitful
Anastasia	Greek – resurrection, awakening. Short/pet form: Ana
Ancelin	Latin – handmaiden
Andea	Unknown origin – woman of the Andes
Andorra	Name of a country
Andra	Variant of Andrea
Andralyn	From Andra + Lynn
Andrea	Probably derived from Aindrea, the Gaelic form of Andrew (*Andria*)
Andreana	Variant of Andrea (*Andrianna*)
Andrée	French form of Andrea
Andria	Alternative spelling of Andrea
Andrianna	Alternative spelling of Andreana
Andrina	Variant of Andrea
Andromeda	Name of beautiful maiden rescued by Perseus in Greek mythology
Anemone	Greek – wind flower
Anezka	Slavonic – pure
Angel	Variant of Angela

Angela	Greek – heavenly messenger, bringer of good tidings, angelic. Feminine form of the now rarely used boy's name Angel. Short/pet form: Angie (*Anjela*)
Angelica	Latin – angelic one. Also a species of plant
Angelina	Variant of Angela
Angelique	French form of Angelica
Angharad	Welsh – much loved
Anica	Alternative spelling of Anneka
Aniela	Variant of Angela
Anika	Alternative spelling of Anneka
Anina	Variant of Ann
Anis	Alternative spelling of Annice
Anisa	Arabic – friendly
Anise	Alternative spelling of Annice. Also a species of plant
Anita	Spanish form of Ann. Short/pet form: Nita
Anjela	Alternative spelling of Angela
Anke	Variant of Ann
Ann	Comes from the Hebrew name Hannah, meaning 'full of grace', 'favoured'. Ann was originally the French form, but has long been common in Britain. Short/pet form: Annie (*Anne*)
Anna	Variant of Ann (*Ana, Annah*)

ANNEMARIE
APHRODITE
ANTOINETTE

Annabel	Variant of Amabel. Short/pet forms: Anna, Annie, Belle (*Anabel, Annabelle*)
Annabella	Variant of Annabel. Short/pet forms: Anna, Annie, Bella
Annabelle	Alternative spelling of Annabel
Annah	Alternative spelling of Anna
Anne	Alternative spelling of Ann
Anneka	Scandinavian form of Ann (*Anica, Anika, Annika*)
Annemarie	From Anne + Maria. Annamari is a variation and both can be used with or without a hyphen
Annette	Diminutive of Ann
Annice	Variant of Agnes (*Anis, Anise, Annis*)
Annie	Short/pet form of Ann and Annabel, now also an independent name
Annika	Alternative spelling of Anneka
Annis	Alternative spelling of Annice
Annissa	Variant of Anna
Annora	Latin – honour
Annunciata	Latin – bringer of news; derived from its association with the Annunciation, which is when the angel from God told Mary she would give birth to Christ. This is therefore an apt name for a Christmas baby
Anouska	Variant of Anushka

Antares	Name of the brightest star in the constellation of Scorpio, derived from a Greek word meaning 'like Mars'
Anthea	Greek – lady of flowers. Short/pet form: Thea
Anthelia	Greek – opposite the sun
Antje	German – grace
Antoinette	Variant of Antonia. Short/pet forms: Tania, Tanya, Toni, Tonia, Tonya (*Antonette*)
Antonette	Alternative spelling of Antoinette
Antonia	Feminine form of the boy's name Anthony. Short/pet forms: Tania, Tanya, Toni, Tonia, Tonya
Antonica	Variant of Antonia
Antonie	Variant of Antonia
Anushka	Russian form of Ann
Anya	Russian form of Anna
Aoife	Gaelic – beauty; pronounced 'ee-vah'
Aphrodite	Greek – goddess of love and beauty in Greek mythology
Apollonia	Greek – feminine form of Apollo, the god of truth, light and poetry
April	Latin – the name of the month that means 'ready for the sun'. The use of this month as a first name, with its springtime association of new life, began only in the 20th century

Aquila   Latin – eagle. Aquilina means 'little eagle'

Arabella   Uncertain origin. Possibly derived from the Latin *orabilis* meaning 'yielding to prayer'. First known in Scotland, appearing in different forms – Arabel, Orable and Orabell in the 13th century, and later as Arbell and Arbella. Short/pet form: Bella

Arabelle   Variant of Arabella

Araminta   Uncertain origin – possibly Hebrew, Greek or Latin

Arbor   Latin – herb gardener

Arcacia   Variant of Acacia

Arcadia   Latin – derived from Arcady, which is a Greek mountain range

Ardelia   Latin – ardent, zealous

Ardis   Variant of Ardelia

Ardra   Variant of Ardelia

Aretha   Greek – best

Aria   Old German – melody

Ariadne   Greek – meaning most divine, very holy one

Ariana   Variant of Ariadne *(Arianna)*

Arianna   Alternative spelling of Ariana

Ariel   Hebrew – lioness of God

Arleen   An alternative spelling of the name Arlene

Arlena   Variant of Arlene

Arlene   Possibly derived from a Gaelic word meaning 'pledge', 'promise', or perhaps derived from Charlene or Marlene *(Arleen, Arline)*

Arlette   French, of obscure origin – possibly derived from the Old German *arn*, meaning 'eagle'.

Arline   Alternative spelling of Arlene

Arlyne   Variant of Arlene

Armani   Persian – desire

Arnhilda   Old German – battle maid

Artema   Variant of Artemis

Artemesia   Variant of Artemis *(Artemisa, Artimisia)*

Artemis   Goddess of the moon, animals and hunting, and lover of music in Greek mythology, equivalent to the Roman goddess Diana

Artemisa   Alternative spelling of Artemesia

Artimisia   Alternative spelling of Artemesia

Asenath   Egyptian – daughter

Ash   Short/pet form of Ashleigh, now also an independent name

Ashleigh   Anglo-Saxon – ash field/wood. Used for both girls and boys, although the spelling Ashley is usually preferred for boys. Short/pet form: Ash *(Ashley)*

Ashley   Alternative spelling of Ashleigh

AUGUSTINE

Ashling	Phonetic spelling of Aislinn
Ashlyn	Gaelic – from Ashleigh + Lyn
Asia	Greek – east. Also a place name
Asmara	Ethiopian place name
Aspen	Old German – species of tree
Aster	Greek – species of flower
Astra	Greek – star-like
Astrea	Greek – goddess of justice found in Greek mythology
Astrid	Old Norse – divine beauty
Atalanta	Greek – of equal weight
Athena	Goddess of wisdom, civilization and practical skills in Greek mythology. Also derived from the city of Athens
Athene	Variant of Athena
Auberta	Variant of Alberta
Audra	Variant of Audrey
Audree	Alternative spelling of Audrey
Audrey	Began as a pet form of Ethelreda, which came from the Anglo-Saxon meaning 'noble strength' (Audree)
Audria	Variant of Audrey
Augusta	Feminine form of the boy's name Augustus, meaning 'great', 'venerable'. A royal favourite introduced by the Hanoverians. Also a US place name
Auguste	Variant of Augusta
Augustina	Variant of Augusta

Augustine	Variant of Augusta
Aurea	Variant of Aurelia
Aurelia	Latin – golden one
Aureola	Variant of Aurelia
Auriel	Variant of Aurelia (Oriel, Oriole)
Aurilia	Variant of Aurelia
Aurora	Latin – golden dawn. Goddess of the dawn in Roman mythology, equivalent to the Greek goddess Eos
Aurore	Variant of Aurora
Autumn	Anglo-Saxon – name of a season
Ava	Variant of Eve
Avara	Sanskrit – the youngest
Aveline	Variant of Evelyn
Aveza	Variant of Avis
Avice	Alternative spelling of Avis
Avis	Norman French – refuge in war (Avice)
Aviva	Hebrew – joyful spring
Avril	French word for the month of April
Awel	Welsh – breeze
Ayiana	Native American – eternal bloom
Azalea	Latin – dry earth. Also a species of flower
Azura	Italian/Old French – blue skies

MODERN
TRENDS

There have always been trends in the way names have been chosen. In the 17th century the Puritans were keen on so-called 'virtue' names for girls, such as Charity, Constance, Faith, Grace, Joy and Mercy. Then in the 19th century the Victorians favoured flower names (see page 194). Today, the choice of names has increased dramatically and there are many more adventurous names – particularly for girls.

Modern namesakes

These days parents are likely to be inspired by showbiz and sports celebrities. Kylie and Madonna are girls' names clearly inspired by current pop stars. Mia is staking a claim in the popularity stakes for girls thanks to its use by actress Kate Winslett for her daughter in 2000, just as the birth of the prime minister's son, Leo Blair, (in the same year) has increased the popularity of the name Leo for boys.

Made-up names and new, unusual spellings

In the search for a totally individual name, some parents turn to complete invention. This is a trend evident among celebrity parents, some of whom have created wild and wacky names that are unlikely to be copied by other parents (see box, right).

If you are seeking a name that is just a little bit out of the ordinary then try

BETTY KITTEN
PIPER MARU
LARK SONG

altering the spelling of a standard name. For example, spell Michele with one 'l'. This makes your child's name more unusual but can lead to frustration if the name is constantly misspelt.

Celebrity creations

Betty Kitten, daughter of Jonathan Ross and Jane Goldman

Dweezil, son of Frank Zappa

Fifi Trixibelle, daughter of Bob Geldof and Paula Yates

Heavenly Hiraani Tiger Lily, daughter of Michael Hutchence and Paula Yates

Lark Song, adopted daughter of Mia Farrow and Andre Previn

Lourdes Maria, daughter of Madonna

Moon Unit, daughter of Frank Zappa

Piper Maru, daughter of Gillian Anderson and Clyde Klotz

Pixie, daughter of Bob Geldof and Paula Yates

Rocco John, son of Madonna and Guy Ritchie

Rolan Bolan, son of Marc Bolan and Gloria Jones

Sage Moonblood, son of Sylvester Stallone and Sasha Czack

Other influences

Choosing names from other cultures (see page 204) is a popular option, as is using place names (see page 50). Another practice is to take the surname of an admired person and use it as a first name. For example, Liam Gallagher and Patsy Kensit named their son Lennon Francis after John Lennon, while Pamela Anderson and Tommy Lee named their son Dylan Jagger.

LOURDES MARIE
DWEEZIL

B

Babetta — Variant of Babette

Babette — French form of Elizabeth

Bambi — Italian – child

Baptista — Greek – baptised one

Barbara — Greek – foreigner, stranger. Short/pet forms: Babs, Barb, Barbi, Barbie, Barby, Bobbie, Bobby (Barbra)

Barbi — Alternative spelling of Barbie

Barbie — Short/pet form of Barbara, now also an independent name (Barbi, Barby)

Barbra — Alternative spelling of Barbara

Barby — Alternative spelling of Barbie

Barina — Aborigine – summit

Basha — Greek – the stranger

Basma — Swahili – a smile

Bassania — Greek – of the deep sea

Bathsheba — Hebrew – seventh daughter, daughter of the oath

Bathshua — Variant of Bathsheba

Beata — Variant of Beatrice/Beatrix

Beathag — Variant of Beth

Beatrice — Latin – bringer of joy/blessings. Short/pet forms: Bea, Bee

Beatrix — Earlier form of Beatrice, derived from the Latin word beatrix, meaning 'bringer of joy/blessings. Short/pet forms: Bea, Bee, Beattie, Beatty

Bebe — French – baby

Bel — Alternative spelling of Belle

Bela — Slavonic – bright, white

Belinda — Linked with the Old German word for 'serpent' but its origin is uncertain. Most likely to mean 'beautiful snake'. In ancient Scandinavia, snakes symbolized wisdom and immortality (Belynda)

Bella — Variant of Belle. Also short/pet form of names ending in 'bella' like Arabella and Isabella

Belle — Latin – beautiful (Bel)

BENICE

BETH

B

Bellini	Variant of Belle
Bellona	Latin – to fight
Belynda	Alternative spelling of Belinda
Benedetta	Variant of Benedicta
Benedicta	Feminine form of Benedict, meaning 'blessed' in Latin
Benice	Variant of Benedicta
Benita	Variant of Benedicta. Short/pet form: Nita
Bente	Variant of Benedicta
Berenice	Greek – bringer of victory. Short/pet forms: Bernie, Berny
Bernadette	French feminine form of Bernard meaning 'brave as a bear'. Short/pet forms: Bernie, Berny
Bernadine	Variant of Bernadette
Bernadot	Variant of Bernadette
Bernessa	Variant of Bernadette
Bernetta	Variant of Bernadette
Bernette	Variant of Bernadette
Bernice	Variant of Berenice
Bertana	Aborigine – day
Bertha	Anglo-Saxon – bright, shining, famous. Short/pet form: Bert
Bertille	Old German – heroine
Bertina	Variant of Bertha

Beryl	Sanskrit – precious stone. It is an ancient word meaning a jewel with the qualities of clarity, preciousness and the power to bring good luck
Beth	Short/pet form of Elizabeth and Old Hebrew name Bethia, meaning 'breath of life', now also an independent name
Bethan	Variant of Bethany
Bethanie	Alternative spelling of Bethany
Bethany	Hebrew – worshipper of God. Short/pet form: Beth *(Bethanie)*
Bethia	Variant of Beth
Betsy	Variant of Elizabeth
Bettie	Alternative spelling of Betty
Bettina	Variant of Elizabeth
Bettine	Variant of Bettina, itself a variant of Elizabeth
Betty	Short/pet form of Elizabeth, now also an independent name *(Bettie)*
Beulah	Hebrew – married
Beverley	Anglo-Saxon – beaver's meadow. Short/pet form: Bev *(Beverly)*
Beverly	Alternative spelling of Beverley
Bianca	Latin – white, purity
Biancha	Variant of Bianca
Bibi	French – lady
Billie	Feminine form of Bill, which derives from William – *see* Wilhelmina

BERNETTA

BLISS BRIDGETTE

BRANDY

Birgitta	Variant of Bridget
Blackberry	Name of a fruit
Blanca	Variant of Bianca
Blanche	French form of Bianca
Blandina	Variant of Bianca
Blinda	Variant of Belinda
Bliss	Anglo-Saxon – joy
Blithe	Alternative spelling of Blythe
Blodwen	Welsh – flowers
Blossom	Blossom
Bluma	German – a flower, bloom
Bly	Native American – tall
Blythe	Old Norse/Anglo-Saxon – joyous, blithe *(Blithe)*
Bonita	Latin – good, pretty, beautiful. Short/pet forms: Bonnie, Bonny and Nita
Bonnie	Short/pet form of Bonita, now also an independent name, particularly in Scotland *(Bonny)*
Bonny	Alternative spelling of Bonnie
Bramble	Anglo-Saxon – thorny bush
Brandi	Alternative spelling of Brandy
Brandie	Alternative spelling of Brandy
Brandy	Uncertain origin, possibly from the alcoholic spirit, or the feminine form of Brandon, meaning 'gorse hill' *(Brandi, Brandie)*
Brangwirin	Variant of Branwen
Branwen	Variant of Bronwen

Brenda	Old Norse – sword. It is also regarded as the feminine form of Brendan
Brenna	Celtic – raven-haired maiden
Briana	Alternative spelling of Brianna
Brianna	Feminine form of the boy's name Brian, which means 'strong' or 'hill' *(Briana)*
Brianne	Variant of Brianna
Briar	Alternative spelling of Brier, also means thorny, wild rose bush
Bridget	Celtic – the exalted/august one. The name also belongs to the Celtic goddess of fire, light and poetry. Short/pet forms: Biddy, Bridey, Bridie, Brit *(Bridgette, Bridgid, Bridgit, Brigit, Brigitte)*
Bridgette	Alternative spelling of Bridget

BRIETTA

BRITTANY

BURNETTA

Bridgid	Alternative spelling of Bridget
Bridgit	Alternative spelling of Bridget
Brie	Short/pet form of Sabrina. Also a region in France
Brier	French – heather *(Briar)*
Brietta	Variant of Bridget
Brighid	Gaelic form of Bridget; pronounced 'breed' *(Brigid)*
Brigid	Alternative spelling of Brighid
Brigit	Alternative spelling of Bridget
Brigitte	Alternative spelling of Bridget
Brina	Derived from Sabrina
Briony	Species of plant *(Bryony)*
Brita	Variant of Britannia
Britney	Alternative spelling of Brittany
Britta	Variant of Brietta
Brittania	Latin – from Britain, British. Short/pet form: Brit
Brittany	Variant of Brittania. Also a French place name *(Britney, Brittnee)*
Brittnee	Alternative spelling of Brittany
Bronwen	Welsh – white-breasted *(Bronwyn)*
Bronwyn	Alternative spelling of Bronwen
Bronya	Slavonic – armour, protection
Brooke	Anglo-Saxon – reward, pleasure. This was adopted as a surname before it became a first name for both sexes (the spelling for a boy is usually Brook)

Brooklyn	US place name, used rarely for boys
Bruna	The feminine form of the boy's name Bruno, meaning 'brown' or 'dark-haired'
Brunella	Variant of Bruna
Brunhilde	Old German – battle maid *(Brynhild)*
Brynhild	Alternative spelling of Brunhilde
Bryony	Alternative spelling of Briony
Buffy	Variant of Beverley
Bunny	Derived from Bernice
Bunty	Variant of Bunny
Burnetta	Old French – little brown-haired one
Buttercup	Species of flower

BROOKE

CAMILLE

CAITLIN

CALISTA

C

Cady	Anglo-Saxon – simple happiness
Caelia	Latin – heavenly, starry sky
Caileigh	Alternative spelling of Kayley
Cairrean	Gaelic form of Karen
Caitlin	Gaelic form of Catherine/Katherine; pronounced 'kat-leen' *(Caitlyn, Kaitlin Kaitlyn, Katelin, Katelyn)*
Caitlyn	Alternative spelling of Caitlin
Caitrin	Variant of Caitriona *(Caitrine, Catrin, Catrine)*
Caitrine	Alternative spelling of Caitrin
Caitriona	Gaelic form of Catherine/Katherine; pronounced 'ka-tree-nah'. Short/pet form: Trina
Calandra	Greek – lark. Short/pet form: Callie
Calantha	Greek – as beautiful as the flowers. Short/pet form: Callie
Caledonia	Latin – woman from Scotland. Short/pet form: Callie
Caleigh	Alternative spelling of Kayley
Calista	Greek – fairer than all other women. Short/pet form: Callie *(Callista)*
Calla	Greek – beautiful. Also a species of lily

Callista	Alternative spelling of Calista
Caltha	Latin – marigold
Calvina	Latin – bright-haired
Calypso	Greek – she who conceals
Camelia	Alternative spelling of Camellia
Camellia	Latin – species of flower *(Camelia)*
Cameo	Italian – engraved jewel
Camilla	Latin – noble, righteous, witness at a ritual. Name of the noble attendant of the goddess Diana in Roman mythology. Short/pet forms: Cammie, Millie, Milly
Camille	French form of Camilla
Camira	Aborigine – of the wind
Canda	Variant of Candice
Candace	Alternative spelling of Candice

CALYPSO

CAPRICE

CARNELIAN

CARLOTA

Candice	Greek – glowing. Derived from the title of Ethiopian queens. Short/pet form: Candy *(Candace)*
Candida	Latin – white hot, pure. Short/pet form: Candy
Candide	Variant of Candida
Candy	Short/pet form of Candice and Candida, but now also an independent name
Caoilinn	Alternative spelling of Keelin
Capri	Italian place name
Caprice	Italian – fanciful, unpredictable
Cara	Italian – friend, beloved
Cardinia	Aborigine – dawn
Caresse	French form of Cara
Carey	Alternative spelling of Cary
Carina	Variant of Cara
Carine	Variant of Carina
Carissa	Variant of Carina
Carla	Feminine form of Carl or Carlo, the Italian version of Charles, meaning 'free man', 'farmer' *(Karla)*
Carleen	Variant of Caroline or Charlene
Carletta	Variant of Carlotta
Carlota	Alternative spelling of Carlotta

Carlotta	Italian form of Charlotte (being the feminine form of Carlo, the Italian equivalent of Charles, meaning 'free man', 'farmer'). Short/pet forms: Lotta, Lottie, Lotty *(Carlota)*
Carly	Modern variation of Carla *(Karly)*
Carmel	Hebrew – vineyard or garden. Also a US place name
Carmela	Variant of Carmel
Carmelita	Variant of Carmel
Carmen	Latin – song. Familiar from the name of the heroine of Bizet's opera
Carmine	Variant of Carmen. It is also a colour name
Carnelian	Latin – a red gemstone
Carol	Feminine form of Charles, meaning 'free man', 'farmer'. The name is now best associated with Christmas songs. Short/pet form: Carrie *(Carole, Carroll, Caryl)*
Carole	Alternative spelling of Carol
Carolina	Variant of Caroline
Caroline	Began as the feminine form of Carlo, the Italian form of Charles. Meaning 'woman' or 'housewife', the name came to Britain in the 18th century with George II's bride and was instantly fashionable. Short/pet form: Carrie *(Carolyne)*

C CARRIE

CATTIMA

Carolyn	Variant of Caroline *(Karolyn)*
Carolyne	Alternative spelling of Caroline
Carrie	Short/pet form of Carol and Caroline, but now also an independent name
Carroll	Alternative spelling of Carol
Cary	A surname that has occasionally been adopted in recent times as a first name *(Carey)*
Caryl	Alternative spelling of Carol
Carys	Welsh – loved one
Casey	Gaelic – watchful, brave. Used for both girls and boys
Casimira	Latin – bearer of peace
Cassandara	Alternative spelling of Cassandra
Cassandra	Possibly Greek – shining upon man. Short/pet forms: Cass, Cassie *(Cassandara)*
Cassia	Species of tree
Cassiopea	Alternative spelling of Cassiopeia
Cassiopeia	Possibly Latin – cassia juice. Also constellation near the Pole Star *(Cassiopea)*
Casta	Greek – purity
Catalin	Basque form of Catherine
Caterina	Italian form of Catherine
Cathay	Archaic name for China
Catherina	Variant of Catherine

Catherine	Originating from the Greek word meaning 'pure', this was the name of a 4th-century martyr, St Catherine, who was tortured on a spiked wheel (hence the name given to wheel-shaped fireworks). Catherine is the favourite spelling, although the older forms are Katherine or Katharine. Short/pet forms: Cath, Cathie, Cathy *(Cathryn)*
Cathleen	Alternative spelling of Kathleen
Cathryn	Alternative spelling of Catherine
Catrin	Alternative spelling of Caitrin
Catrine	Alternative spelling of Caitrin
Catriona	Scottish form of Catherine
Cattima	Latin – slender reed
Cayla	Variant of Catherine
Cecila	Alternative spelling of Cecilia
Cecile	French form of Cecilia

CHANDRA

CECILIA

CHARLOTTE C

Cecilia	Feminine form of the boy's name Cecil, meaning 'blind' The early spelling was Caelia, the form used in Ancient Rome *(Cecila)*
Cecily	Variant of Cecilia. Short/pet forms: Cissie, Cissy, Sissie, Sissy
Celandine	Greek – a swallow. Species of plant
Celesta	Variant of Celeste
Celeste	Latin – heavenly
Celestina	Variant of Celeste
Celestine	Variant of Celeste
Celia	Variant of Cecilia
Cerelia	Latin – of the spring
Cerise	French – cherry red
Cerys	Variant of Carys
Chaela	Variant of Michaela, the feminine form of Michael
Chaeli	Variant of Chaela
Chandra	Sanskrit. Goddess, brighter than stars
Chanel	French – canal
Chaniya	Nguni – rich
Channon	Alternative spelling of Shannon
Chantal	French – song, singer *(Chantel, Chantelle)*
Chantel	Alternative spelling of Chantal
Chantelle	Alternative spelling of Chantal
Charis	Greek – giver of graciousness, charity *(Charisse, Sherise)*
Charisa	Variant of Charis *(Charissa)*

Charissa	Alternative spelling of Charisa
Charisse	Alternative spelling of Charis
Charity	Latin – benevolent, charitable, brotherly love. One of the many 'virtue' names favoured by the Puritans in the 17th century
Charla	Variant of Charlotte
Charleen	Alternative spelling of Charlene
Charlene	A feminine form of Charles, meaning 'free man', 'farmer'. Short/pet forms: Charley, Charlie *(Charleen, Sharleen, Sharlene)*
Charlotte	French feminine form of the boy's name Charles. Short/pet forms: Charley, Charlie, Lotte, Lottie, Lotty
Charmain	Variant of Carmen *(Charmaine)*
Charmaine	Alternative spelling of Charmain

CHAELI

CHARLENE

NAMES AND
STAR SIGNS

If you are into astrology and enjoy reading your horoscope, then what better way to choose your baby's name than by his/her sign of the zodiac? Star signs, which are determined by date of birth, are a good means of choosing a name as they suit the personality of the child. If your child is born on the cusp – the date on which one star sign finishes and another is about to begin – then you should consider the subsequent sign as being equally important.

The profiles of each of the 12 signs below list their symbol, ruling planet, element (Fire, Air, Earth or Water), colours and personality characteristics, as well as giving a small selection of the names you could choose.

Aries: 21 Mar–20 Apr
Characteristics: Ram, Mars, Fire, red and orange, bold, brave, dynamic, possessing leadership qualities
Boys' names: Alex, Andrew, Cadogan, Martin, Neil, William
Girls' names: Alexandra, Athena, Elaine, Erica, Valda, Wilma

Taurus: 21 Apr–20 May
Characteristics: Bull, Venus, Earth, sky blue and green, gentle, steady, industrious, over of nature
Boys' names: Craig, Denham, George, Lee, Peter, Sholto,
Girls' names: Chloe, Fleur, Gaia, Georgina, Olivia, Petra

Gemini: 21 May–20 Jun
Characteristics: Twins, Mercury, Air, yellow and white, quick-witted, versatile, sociable, communicative
Boys' names: Dexter, Findlay, Hubbard, Hugh, Tate, Thomas
Girls' names: Blanche, Concetta, Eulalia, Hermione, Tammy, Vivienne

Cancer: 21 Jun–22 Jul
Characteristics: Crab, Moon, Water, sea colours, emotional, sensitive, home lover, affinity with the sea
Boys' names: Arlin, Dylan, Graham, Hamlyn, Murray, Terry
Girls' names: Amaris, Coral, Delia, Diana, Harriet, Selena

Leo: 23 Jul–22 Aug
Characteristics: Lion, Sun, Fire, orange, yellow and gold, attention seeking, aspirational, charismatic, proud, friendly
Boys' names: Aaron, Austin, Boyd, Leo, Max, Steven
Girls' names: Amber, Helen, Leonie, Lucy, Roberta, Topaz

Virgo: 23 Aug–22 Sep
Characteristics: Virgin, Mercury, Earth, grey, brown and white, discerning, loyal, reliable, sensible, meticulous
Boys' names: Constantine, Christopher, Dillon, Emil, Ernie, Hugo
Girls' names: Donna, Honesta, Katherine, Mary, Ola, Virginia

Libra: 23 Sep–23 Oct
Characteristics: Scales, Venus, Air, blue and pink, charming, handsome, sensual, peace loving, dispute settling
Boys' names: Conrad, Finnegan, Justin, Kevin, Oliver, Romeo
Girls' names: Amanda, Annabel, Cherry, Grace, Kevina, Venus

Scorpio: 24 Oct–22 Nov
Characteristics: Scorpion, Mars, Water, red and saffron, intense, single-minded, perceptive, passionate, loyal
Boys' names: Alexander, Archie, Ernest, Mark, Niall, Roy
Girls' names: Andrea, Briana, Hilda, Louisa, Maud, Sandra

Sagittarius: 23 Nov–21 Dec
Characteristics: Archer, Jupiter, Fire, green, blue and purple, sincere, joyful, thoughtful, big-hearted, larger than life
Boys' names: Aidan, Archibald, Chase, Fletcher, Hunter, Haydn
Girls' names: Charity, Emma, Hilary, Hope, Joy, Virida

Capricorn: 22 Dec–20 Jan
Characteristics: Goat, Saturn, Earth, black, steady, dependable, clever, dignified
Boys' names: Brian, Douglas, Duff, Ernst, Kieran, Richard
Girls' names: Amelia, Honor, Maxine, Melanie, Sonia, Sophie

Aquarius: 21 Jan–19 Feb
Characteristics: Water carrier, Saturn, Air, black, yellow and various fluorescent colours, inquisitive, charming, kind, a good communicator, quick-thinking
Boys' names: Alfie, David, Declan, Findal, Quinn, Sherwin
Girls' names: Amy, Charity, Consuela, Monica, Palmeda, Ruth

Pisces: 20 Feb–20 Mar
Characteristics: Fishes, Jupiter/Neptune, Water, green, coral and navy blue, dreamy, sensitive, modest, poetic
Boys' names: Dylan, Kelsey, Linford, Merlin, Murphy, Teague
Girls' names: Ann, Halcyon, Bridget, Jennifer, Marina, Nerissa

Charo	Variant of Carol	**Chimalis**	Native American – bluebird
Chastina	Variant of Chastity	**China**	Name of a country *(Chynna)*
Chastity	Latin – purity	**Chiquita**	Spanish – little one
Chelsea	London place name, meaning 'a landing place for limestone' *(Chelsey, Chelsie)*	**Chispa**	Spanish – spark
		Chloe	Greek – tender budding plant, green shoots *(Cloe)*
Chelsey	Alternative spelling of Chelsea	**Chloris**	Greek – green. A goddess from Greek mythology
Chelsie	Alternative spelling of Chelsea		
Chenoa	Native American – white dove	**Choden**	Tibetan/Sherpa – the devout one
Cher	French – beloved, darling	**Christabel**	Greek/Latin – fair follower of Christ, beautiful Christian. Short/pet forms: Chris, Chrissie, Chrissy, Christa, Christie *(Christabelle, Christobel)*
Cheralyn	From Cheryl + Linda *(Cherillynn, Cherlin, Sherilyn)*		
Cheri	Alternative spelling of Cherie		
Cherie	Variant of Cher. *See also* Sheree *(Cheri, Cherrie)*	**Christabella**	Variant of Christabel. Short/pet forms: Bella, Chris, Chrissie, Chrissy, Christa, Christie
Cherillynn	Alternative spelling of Cheralyn		
Cherlin	Variant of Cheralyn	**Christabelle**	Alternative spelling of Christabel
Cherrie	Alternative spelling of Cherie	**Christel**	Alternative spelling of Crystal
Cherry	Variant of Charity. It came into its own as an independent name along with the flower names favoured by the Victorians		
Cheryl	Anglicized form of Cher/Cherie *(Cheryll, Cheryle, Sheral, Sherill, Sherryl, Sheryl)*		
Cheryle	Alternative spelling of Cheryl		
Cheryll	Alternative spelling of Cheryl		
Chesna	Slavonic – peaceful		
Chiara	Latin – famous, light		

CLARETTE

Christiana	Variant of Christine. Short/pet forms: Chris, Chrissie, Chrissy, Christa, Christie
Christie	Gaelic feminine contraction of Christopher, stemming originally from the Latin, meaning 'fair follower of Christ'. It is also a short/pet form for many names beginning with 'Christ' (*Christy, Cristy*)
Christina	Variant of Christine (*Kristina, Krystyna*)
Christine	Latin – follower of Christ, Christian. Short/pet forms: Chris, Chrissie, Chrissy, Christie (*Cristine, Kristine*)
Christmas	Name used for both girls and boys born at Christmastime, the annual Christian festival that celebrates the birth of Christ
Christobel	Alternative spelling of Christabel
Christy	Alternative spelling of Christie
Chryseis	Greek – golden. Notable figure in Greek mythology
Chrysilla	Greek – golden-haired
Chrystal	Alternative spelling of Crystal
Chynna	Alternative spelling of China
Ciara	Gaelic – dark. *See also* Kiera (*Kiara, Kyara*)
Cicely	Variant of Cecily. Also short for sweet cicely, a species of herb (*Cicily, Sisley*)

Cicily	Alternative spelling of Cicely
Cilla	Short/pet form of Priscilla, now also an independent name
Cinderella	Humble, little cinder, derived from the French *Cendrillon*. Short/pet form: Cindy
Cindy	Short/pet form of Cinderella, Cynthia and Lucinda, now also an independent name (*Cyndi*)
Claire	French form of Clare
Clairine	Variant of Clare
Clara	Variant of Clare. Also short/pet form of Claribel (*Klara*)
Claral	Variant of Clare
Clare	Latin – famous or possibly clear, bright. Also Irish place name (*Claire*)
Clarette	Variant of Clare
Claribel	Variant of Clare. Short/pet form: Clara
Clarice	Variant of Clare (*Clarisse*)

CLAUDINE

CORAL

CLORINDA

Clarissa	Variant of Clare
Clarisse	Alternative spelling of Clarice
Claudette	French feminine form of Claudius, meaning 'lame'
Claudia	Feminine form of Claud/Claudius, meaning 'lame' (Clodia)
Claudine	Another French feminine form of Claudius
Clea	Variant of Chloe and Cleo
Clementina	Variant of Clementine
Clementine	Latin – merciful, gentle
Cleo	Greek – fame and glory. A short/pet form of Cleopatra, now also an independent name (Clio)
Cleodora	Greek – glorious gift
Cleopatra	Greek – from a famous father. Short/pet forms: Cleo, Clio
Cleosa	Variant of Cleo
Cleta	Variant of Cleo
Cliantha	Greek – flower of glory
Clio	Alternative spelling of Cleo
Clodia	Alternative spelling of Claudia
Cloe	Alternative spelling of Chloe
Clorinda	Persian – renowned
Clover	Anglo-Saxon – clover blossom
Colette	Variant of Nicolette
Colinette	Gaelic – little dove
Colleen	Gaelic – girl
Collice	Variant of Colleen

Columbe	Variant of Columbia
Columbia	Latin – dove
Columbine	Latin – species of flower
Comfort	Latin – to strengthen greatly
Concetta	Italian – ingenious idea
Concha	Latin – seashell
Concordia	Latin – harmony, concord
Constance	Latin – constant, steadfast, faithful. Short/pet form: Connie
Constancy	Variant of Constance
Constantia	Variant of Constance
Consuela	Latin – one who consoles
Content	Content, satisfied
Coorah	Aborigine – woman
Copper	Latin – Cyprian metal
Cora	Greek – maiden, girl
Coral	Latin – jewel of the sea, or possibly derived from Cora. It is also a colour name
Coralie	Variant of Cora
Cordelia	Unclear origin. Possibly Latin – heart; or Celtic – jewel/daughter of the sea. Short/pet form: Delia

CONSUELA

CYNTHIA

CRISPINA

Coreen	Alternative spelling of Corinne. Also Aborigine – the end of the hills
Coriander	Greek – species of herb
Corin	Alternative spelling of Corinne
Corina	Alternative spelling of Corinna
Corine	Alternative spelling of Corinne
Corinna	Variant of Cora *(Corina)*
Corinne	French form of Corinna *(Coreen, Corin, Corine)*
Cornelia	Feminine form of Cornelius, meaning 'horn-like' (cornucopia)
Corolla	Latin – small crown
Corona	Greek – kind
Cosima	Greek – harmony, order, beauty
Cottina	Greek – crown of wild flowers
Courtenay	Alternative spelling of Courtney, used only for girls
Courtney	Aristocratic surname derived from a French place name, and now used as a first name for both girls and boys *(Courtenay)*
Cressa	Old German – from watercress
Cressida	Greek – gold
Crispina	Feminine form of Crispin, derived from Latin, meaning 'curly-haired'
Cristine	Alternative spelling of Christine
Cristy	Alternative spelling of Christie
Crystal	Greek – ice, clear brilliant glass. It is also sometimes regarded as

	the Scottish feminine form of Christopher *(Chrystal, Christel)*
Custance	Variant of Constance
Cyane	Greek – deep blue
Cybele	Latin – name of an Asiatic goddess
Cybil	Alternative spelling of Sibyl
Cybill	Alternative spelling of Sibyl
Cynara	Greek – thistle
Cyndi	Alternative spelling of Cindy Short/pet form Cyn
Cynthia	Title of the Greek goddess of the moon, Artemis, meaning 'of Mount Cynthus'. Short/pet forms: Cindy, Cyn, Cyndi
Cyrene	A river nymph in Greek mythology
Cyrilla	Latin – lordly, proud
Cytheria	Latin – Venus

CORNELIA

DAKOTA

DARCEY

DAPHNE

D

Dada	Yoruba – child with curls
Dagmar	Old Norse – joy of the Danes
Dahlia	Species of flower named after the 18th-century Swedish botanist Anders Dahl
Daisie	Alternative spelling of Daisy
Daisy	Species of flower known as 'day's eye' *(Daisie, Dasie)*. The word became popular as a first name in the late 19th century
Dakota	Native American – ally. Also a US place name used for girls and boys
Dalia	Hebrew – branch, bough
Dallas	Celtic – skilled. Also a US place name used for both girls and boys *(Dalys)*
Dalys	Alternative spelling of Dallas
Damita	Spanish – baby princess
Dana	Name of an ancient Celtic goddess of fertility
Danica	Slavonic – morning star. Short/pet form: Dani
Daniela	Variant of Danielle *(Daniella)*
Daniele	Alternative spelling of Danielle
Daniella	Alternative spelling of Daniela
Danielle	The French feminine form of Daniel, meaning 'God has judged', 'of lions'. Short/pet form: Dani *(Daniele)*
Daphne	Greek – bay tree, laurel. Name of a nymph in Greek mythology who was turned into a laurel tree. Short/pet forms: Daff, Daffy
Dara	Hebrew – compassion, pearl of wisdom
Darcey	Alternative spelling of Darcy, used only for girls
Darcy	Derived from the surname, D'Arcy, which came from a French place name and was brought to England with the Norman Conquest. Used for both girls and boys *(Darcey)*
Daria	Feminine form of the boy's name Darius, a name given to Persian kings *(Darya)*
Darla	Anglo-Saxon – dear, loved one

DARRYL

DEIDRA

DELILAH

Darlene	Variant of Darla	**Dechen**	Tibetan – health and happiness
Darri	Aborigine – track	**Dee**	Originated as a pet name for
Darryl	Anglo-Saxon – beloved. More		anyone whose name began with
	often used for boys (Daryl)		'D', now also an independent name
Darya	Alternative spelling of Daria	**Deena**	Feminine form of Dean, the Anglo-
Daryl	Alternative spelling of Darryl		Saxon meaning of which is 'valley,
Dasie	Alternative spelling of Daisy		dweller in the valley'. Also Latin –
Davan	Gaelic feminine form of David		presiding official (Dena, Dina)
Davida	Variant of Davina	**Deidra**	Variant of Deirdre
Davina	Feminine form of the boy's name	**Deidre**	Alternative spelling of Deirdre
	David, meaning 'beloved', 'darling'	**Deiondre**	Unknown origin – valley
	(Davinia, Devina)	**Deirdre**	Possibly Old Celtic, 'the raging
Davinia	Alternative spelling of Davina		one', 'tempestuous', or Gaelic,
Davita	Variant of Davina		'the broken hearted' (Deidre)
Dawn	Old German – daybreak. Translation	**Delaney**	Gaelic – descendant of the challenger
	of aurora, the Latin word for 'dawn'	**Delfina**	Feminine form of Delvin, meaning
Deandra	Latin – divine		'dolphin'
Deanna	Variant of Diana	**Delia**	German – another name for the
Deanne	Variant of Diane, the French form		Greek moon goddess, Artemis,
	of Diana. The use of the 'e' in		meaning 'from Delos'. Also
	place of the 'i' in the spelling		short/pet form of Cordelia
	emphasizes the correct French	**Delicia**	Latin – pleasant, delightful one
	pronunciation	**Delila**	Alternative spelling of Delilah
Debora	Alternative spelling of Deborah	**Delilah**	Biblical temptress who betrayed
Deborah	Hebrew – bee. The name of the		Samson to the Philistines by
	Old Testament prophetess.		cutting off his hair (Delila)
	Short/pet forms Debbie, Debby	**Delinda**	Old German – gentle
	(Debora, Debra)	**Delise**	Variant of Delicia (Delys)
Debra	Alternative spelling of Deborah	**Delissa**	Variant of Delicia

DELPHINIA

DIDO

DESTINY

Della	Old German – originally derived from Adele, but it is now also an independent name
Delores	Alternative spelling of Dolores
Delphia	Greek – of the oracle at Delphi
Delphine	Variant of Delphia
Delphinia	Variant of Delphia
Delta	Hebrew – mouth of a river
Delys	Alternative spelling of Delise
Delyth	Welsh – pretty
Dema	Anglo-Saxon – arbiter
Demeter	Goddess of the harvest in Greek mythology, equivalent to the Roman goddess, Ceres
Demi	French – half, small
Dena	Alternative spelling of Deena
Denice	Alternative spelling of Denise
Denise	Feminine form of the boy's name Denis, derived from Dionysius, the god of wine and revelry in Greek mythology *(Denice, Denyse)*
Denyse	Alternative spelling of Denise
Desdemona	Spanish – name of the tragic heroine in Shakespeare's *Othello*
Desideria	Variant of Desirée
Desirée	Latin – desired, so long hoped for
Desta	Ethiopian – happiness
Destiny	Latin – one's fate
Devina	Alternative spelling of Davina

Devona	Derived from English place, Devon
Diadema	Greek – diadem
Diamanta	French – of diamonds/diamond like
Diamond	Diamond gemstone
Diana	Goddess of the moon and hunting in Roman mythology, equivalent to the Greek goddess Artemis *(Dianna)*
Diane	French form of Diana *(Dianne, Dyan, Dyanne)*
Dianna	Alternative spelling of Diana
Dianne	Alternative spelling of Diane
Dianthe	Greek – divine flower
Diaphenia	Greek – transmitting light
Didi	Variant of Diana
Dido	Legendary queen of Carthage in Roman mythology, also known as Elissa

DEVONA

DIANE

DINAH

DORCAS

DOLORES

Diella	Latin – worships God
Digna	Latin – worthy
Dilys	Welsh – sincere, genuine
Dina	Alternative spelling of Deena
Dinah	An ancient biblical name, meaning 'judged'. It is not a variant of the name Diana
Diona	Variant of Diana
Diona	Variant of Dionne
Dione	Alternative spelling of Dionne
Dionne	Consort of the god Zeus and the mother of Aphrodite in Greek mythology *(Dione)*
Dior	French – golden
Disa	Old Norse – active spirit
Dixie	Anglo-Saxon – from the south part of the USA
Docila	Latin – willing to learn *(Docilla)*
Docilla	Alternative spelling of Docila
Doda	Unknown origin – aunt
Dodi	Alternative spelling of Dodie
Dodie	Short/pet form of Dorothy, now also an independent name *(Dodi)*
Dollie	Alternative spelling of Dolly
Dolores	Derived from a Spanish name used as a shortened form for Maria de los Dolores, 'Mary of 'the sorrows', one of the titles of the Virgin Mary *(Delores)*

Dominica	Variant of Dominique. It is also a place name
Dominique	French feminine form of Dominic, meaning 'belonging to the Lord'
Dominy	Variant of Dominique
Donabella	Latin – beautiful lady. Short/pet forms: Bella, Donna
Donalda	Celtic – little mistress
Donata	Italian – gift from God
Donella	Latin – little damsel
Donna	Italian – lady, implying a woman worthy of respect
Donnica	Variant of Donna
Dora	Greek – gift
Dorcas	Greek – gazelle. Translation of the Aramaic name, Tabitha
Dore	Variant of Dora
Dorea	Alternative spelling of Doria

CLASSICAL
MYTHOLOGY

Packed with gods, goddesses, Titans, monsters and heroes, classical mythology includes many stories that are not only amusing and entertaining but also deal with love, war, death and the sins and strengths of mankind – such as pride, tyranny, wisdom, loyalty and courage. Some classical names might be too outdated for your taste, but there are plenty of others that are still in common use today.

At the end of each entry (G) or (R) denotes whether the name comes from Greek or Roman mythology.

HELIOS

IRIS

DIONYSUS

MAIA

JOCASTA

REMUS

Boys

Adonis Handsome young man killed while hunting (G)

Atlas A Titan forced to bear the world on his shoulders (G)

Cecil Son of Vulcan, the Roman god of fire and craftsmanship (R)

Dionysus God of wine and revelry (G)

Dymas Father of Hecate, goddess of the underworld (G)

Eros Greek god of love (G)

Hector Trojan hero who led the fight against the Greeks for ten years (G)

Helios Greek god of the sun, equivalent to Sol, who rode across the sky daily in a horse-drawn chariot (G)

Hercules Mighty hero who had 12 labours to complete (G + R)

Hermes Messenger of the Greek gods (G)

Homer Greek poet who wrote the classic works, *The Iliad* and *The Odyssey*

Janus Roman god of passages, gateways and beginnings, after whom January is named (R)

Jason Leader of the Argonauts, who sought the Golden Fleece (G)

Leander Lover of Hero who drowned in the Hellespont during a storm (G)

Odysseus Greek hero in the Trojan War (G)

Orion Great hunter killed by a scorpion sent by Artemis (G)

Remus Brother of Romulus, with whom he founded Rome (R)

Silvanus God of forests (R)

Zeus Father of the Greek gods (G)

Girls

Acantha Nymph loved by Apollo (G)

Andromeda Beautiful Greek maiden rescued by Perseus (G)

Bellona Goddess of war (R)

Cassandra Prophetess who foresaw the fall of Troy (G)

Diana Roman goddess of the moon and hunting, equivalent to Artemis (R)

Dionne Consort of the Greek god Zeus and the mother of Aphrodite (G)

Feronia Goddess of springs and woods (R)

Fortuna Roman goddess of fortune, equivalent to Tyche (R)

Hebe Greek goddess of youth and spring (G)

Iris Greek goddess of the rainbow and messenger of the gods (G)

Jocasta Mother and unwitting wife of Oedipus (G)

Leda Seduced by Zeus when he took the form of a swan (G)

Maia Goddess of spring (R)

Melissa Nymph who cared for the young Zeus (G)

Minerva Goddess of wisdom, civilization and practical skills (R)

Phoebe Epithet of Artemis the Greek goddess of the moon, animals and hunting, equivalent to Diana (G)

Selene Greek goddess of the moon (G)

Venus Roman goddess of love and beauty (R)

DYANNE

Doreen	French – golden
Dorena	Variant of Doreen
Dori	Variant of Dora
Doria	Variant of Dora *(Dorea)*
Dorie	Variant of Doris
Dorina	Hebrew – perfection
Dorinda	Variant of Dorothy
Doris	Greek – wealth of the sea
Dorit	Variant of Doris
Dorothea	Variant of Dorothy. Also reversed form of Theodora. Short/pet form: Thea
Dorothy	Greek – divine gift. Short/pet forms: Dodi, Dodie, Dollie, Dolly, Dot, Dotty, Totie
Dova	Old German – dove
Dreama	Greek – joyous music
Drena	Variant of Andrea
Drusilla	Derived from the family name of an old Roman clan. And a biblical name
Duana	Gaelic – little dark-haired maiden. Feminine form of the Gaelic boy's name Duane, meaning 'black'
Dulce	Variant of Dulcie
Dulcea	Variant of Dulcie
Dulcibella	Variant of Dulcie. Short/pet form: Bella
Dulcie	Latin – sweet *(Dulcy)*
Dulcinea	Variant of Dulcie

Dulcy	Alternative spelling of Dulcie
Duretta	Spanish – little steadfast one
Durga	Sanskrit – unattainable.
Dusty	From Thor's stone, fighter
Dyan	Alternative spelling of Diane
Dyanne	Alternative spelling of Diane
Dymphna	Gaelic – suitable one, eligible, virgin saint *(Dympna)*
Dympna	Alternative spelling of Dymphna
Dyna	Greek – power
Dysis	Greek – sunset

E

Earlene	Old German – noble woman
Earnestine	Alternative spelling of Ernestine
Eartha	Anglo-Saxon – of the earth
Easter	Name used for girls born at Eastertime, the annual Christian festival, derived from Ostern or Eostre, the name of an Anglo-Saxon goddess of spring and fertility
Ebony	Ebony wood; the name implies strength, value and durability
Echo	Greek – echo. Nymph in love with Narcissus in Greek mythology
Edana	Gaelic – zealous, fiery
Edelin	Variant of Adeline
Edeline	German – high born
Eden	Hebrew – delight. Name of biblical paradise. Used for girls and boys
Edena	Variant of Edith
Edeva	Variant of Edith
Edina	Variant of Edwina
Edita	Spanish form of Edith
Edith	Anglo-Saxon – successful in war. A royal name that survived the Norman Conquest. Short/pet forms: Eda, Ede, Edie *(Edythe)*

Edlyn	Old German – rich, gentlewoman
Edna	Variant of Edith
Edwena	Alternative spelling of Edwina
Edwina	Feminine form of Edwin *(Edwena, Edwyna)*
Edwyna	Alternative spelling of Edwina
Edythe	Alternative spelling of Edith
Eereena	Greek – messenger of peace
Effie	Greek – melodious talk
Eilean	Alternative spelling of Eileen
Eileen	Derived from the Celtic names Eibhlin and Aibhlin, being a form of Eve/Evelyn. Also a variant of Helen *(Aileen, Eilean, Eilene, Eilleen, Ilene)*
Eilene	Alternative spelling of Eileen
Eilleen	Alternative spelling of Eileen
Eirene	Greek – peace
Eirwen	Welsh – white, blessed

EILEAN

ELANORA

ELISABETH

Ela	Alternative spelling of Ella
Elaine	Old French form of Helen. It was popular in the late 20th century
Elan	Variant of Elaine
Elana	Hebrew – tree
Elanora	Aborigine – home by the sea
Elata	Latin – elevated
Elberta	Old German – nobly bright
Elda	Anglo-Saxon – woman of noble family
Eldora	Spanish – golden
Eleanor	Old French form of Helen. First used in Great Britain in the 12th century Short/pet forms: Elie, Elli, Ellie, Elly *(Elena, Elinor)*
Electra	Greek – amber, bright, radiant
Elena	Alternative spelling of Eleanor
Elera	Uncertain origin – possibly Anglo-Saxon, meaning 'elfin wisdom'
Elfrieda	Variant of Freda
Elgiva	Old German – gift of the elves, clever
Eliana	Hebrew – from the sun
Eliane	Variant of Eliana
Elie	Alternative spelling of Ellie
Elina	Greek – pure
Elinor	Alternative spelling of Eleanor
Elisa	Alternative spelling of Eliza
Elisabeth	Alternative spelling of Elizabeth
Elisavet	Variant of Elizabeth
Elise	French form of Elisa

Elissa	Variant of Alice. Also name of Dido, legendary queen of Carthage in Roman mythology
Elita	French – special one
Eliza	Derived from Elizabeth *(Elisa)*
Elizabeth	Derived from the Hebrew Elisheba meaning 'oath of God'. Short/pet forms: Bess, Bessie, Bet, Beth, Bette, Bettie, Betty, Elsie, Libba, Libbi, Libby, Lisbet, Lisbeth, Liz, Lizzie, Lizzy *(Elisabeth)*
Elke	German form of Alice
Elkie	Variant of Elke
Ella	Norman French, originating from the Old German name Aila, meaning 'all' *(Ela)*
Elle	French – woman, girl
Ellen	Anglo-Saxon form of Helen. Short/pet forms: Elie, Elli, Ellie, Elly
Ellenis	Variant of Ellen
Ellerie	Alternative spelling of Ellery
Ellery	A surname meaning 'one who lives near the elder tree', now used as a first name for both girls and boys *(Ellerie)*
Elli	Alternative spelling of Ellie
Ellie	Short/pet form of Eleanor and Ellen, now also an independent name *(Elie, Elli, Elly)*

ELWYN

ELOUERA

ERANTHE

Ellien	Unknown origin – light	**Emelita**	Variant of Amelia
Elly	Alternative spelling of Ellie	**Emerald**	Emerald gemstone
Elma	Short/pet form of Guilielma, the	**Emilia**	Variant of Emily
	Italian feminine form of William,	**Emilie**	Alternative spelling of Emily
	now also an independent name	**Emily**	Variant of Amelia. Short/pet
Elodie	Greek – marshy, white blossom		forms: Millie, Milly *(Emilie)*
Eloise	Variant of Lois or Louise	**Emma**	Old German – whole, universal,
Elouera	Aborigine – from the pleasant place		all-embracing
Elra	Old German – elfin wisdom	**Emogene**	Alternative spelling of Imogen
Elsa	Old German – noble maiden.	**Endora**	Hebrew – fountain
	Also a variant of Elizabeth *(Ailsa)*	**Enid**	Welsh – life
Else	Variant of Elsie	**Enyonyam**	Ewe – it is good for me
Elsie	Short/pet form of Elizabeth,	**Eranthe**	Variant of Erianthe
	now also an independent name	**Erda**	Old German – earth goddess, worldly
Elspeth	Variant of Elizabeth	**Erianthe**	Greek – sweetness, many flowers
Elu	Native American – full of grace	**Erica**	Feminine form of the boy's name
Elva	Anglo-Saxon – elfin		Eric, meaning 'ever ruler', 'fierce
Elvetta	Old German – wise home ruler		warrior'. Also the Latin name for
Elvia	Old German – of keen mind		heather *(Erika)*
Elvina	Anglo-Saxon – feminine form of	**Erika**	Alternative spelling of Erica
	the boy's name Elvin, meaning	**Erin**	Gaelic – western isle, ie Ireland
	'friend of elves'		*(Errin)*
Elvira	Spanish. Unclear meaning,	**Eris**	Goddess of strife and discord
	possibly means 'wise advice'		in Greek mythology, equivalent to
Elwyn	Welsh – white-browed		the Roman goddess Discordia
Elysia	Latin/Greek – blissful, of paradise	**Erlina**	Anglo-Saxon – little elf
Emalia	Latin – flirt	**Erlinda**	Hebrew – lively
Emaline	Variant of Emma	**Erma**	Alternative spelling of Irma
Emele	Variant of Emily	**Erminia**	Latin – regal

ERNESTINE

EVANGELINE

EUDORA

Ermintrude	Old German – wholly beloved. Short/pet forms: Erma, Irma, Trudi, Trudie, Trudy
Erna	Variant of Ernestine
Ernestine	Feminine form of the boy's name Ernest, meaning 'serious', 'earnest' *(Earnestine)*
Errin	Alternative spelling of Erin
Esme	Latin – esteemed, loved
Esmeralda	Spanish form of Emerald
Esperanza	Spanish – hope
Esta	Italian – from the east
Estel	Alternative spelling of Estelle
Estella	Variant of Estelle
Estelle	Old French – star. Short/pet form: Essie *(Estel)*
Ester	Alternative spelling of Esther
Estera	Variant of Estelle
Esther	Persian – star. Short/pet forms: Ettie, Etty, Hetty *(Ester)*
Etana	Hebrew – determination
Ethel	Anglo-Saxon – noble
Ethelwyn	Old German – noble friend
Etna	Volcano name
Etta	Short/pet form of Henrietta/Harriet, now also an independent name
Eudocia	Greek – esteemed
Eudora	Greek – gift without limits
Eugenia	Variant of Eugenie

Eugenie	Feminine French form of the boy's name Eugene, originally from the Greek and meaning 'born lucky'
Eulalia	Greek – fair of speech. Short/pet forms: Lali, Lalla, Lallie, Lally
Eulalie	Variant of Eulalia
Eunice	Greek – happy/good victory *(Younice)*
Eustacia	Feminine form of the boy's name Eustace, meaning 'bountiful'
Eva	Variant of Eve
Evadne	Greek – a water nymph
Evalina	Variant of Eve
Evana	Variant of Ivana
Evangelina	Variant of Evangeline
Evangeline	Greek – bringer of good news
Evanthe	Greek – flower
Eve	Hebrew – life-giving. Name of the first woman and mother in the Bible. The name was believed to bring longevity. Short/pet form: Evie
Evelien	Alternative spelling of Eveline
Eveline	Variant of Eve
Eveline	Variant of Eve *(Evelien)*
Evelyn	Variant of Eve
Evette	Diminutive of Eve
Evita	Variant of Eve
Evodie	Greek – she who takes the right path
Evonne	Variant of Eve

FAITH

FAWNE

F

Fabienne	Latin – bean grower
Fabrianne	Latin – maid of good works
Fae	Variant of Faith
Fahima	Swahili – learned, understanding
Faith	Latin – trust, faith. One of the 'virtue' names, introduced by the Puritans, at the time of the Reformation
Fallon	Irish – grandchild of the ruler
Fanny	Short/pet form of Frances, now also an independent name
Farah	Arabic – joy
Farrah	Anglo-Saxon – beautiful
Fatima	Arabic – name of the daughter of Muhammad
Faustina	Latin – good luck
Faustine	Variant of Faustina
Fawn	Latin – young deer. Also a colour name (Fawne)
Fawne	Alternative spelling of Fawn
Fay	Possibly from the Anglo-Saxon word fay meaning 'faith', or perhaps derived from the Old French fae, meaning 'fairy' or 'elf' (Faye)
Faye	Alternative spelling of Fay

Faylinn	Variant of Fay
Fayme	French – highly esteemed
Fedora	Variant of Theodora
Felda	Old German – inspired (Velda)
Felice	Variant of Felicity
Felicia	Variant of Felicity (Phylicia)
Felicite	Alternative spelling of Felicity
Felicity	Feminine form of the boy's name Felix, derived from the Latin felicitas, meaning 'happiness'. Short/pet forms: Fee, Flic, Flick (Felicite)
Felipa	Alternative spelling of Philippa
Fenella	Anglicized form of Fionnhuala
Fern	Fern
Feronia	Goddess of springs and woods in Roman mythology
Ffion	Variant of Fiona (Fionn)
Fflur	Alternative spelling of Fleur
Fidelia	Spanish – faithful
Fidella	Variant of Fidelia
Fidonia	Greek – thrifty
Fifi	French – derived from Josephine
Fifine	Variant of Fifi
Filomena	Alternative spelling of Philomena
Finna	Variant of Fiona
Finola	Variant of Fenella
Fiona	Gaelic – fair, white (Fionna)
Fionn	Alternative spelling of Ffion, itself a variant of Fiona

Fionna	Alternative spelling of Fiona	**Florinda**	Variant of Florentina
Fionnhuala	Gaelic – white-shouldered; pronounced 'finn-nu-lah'. Legend has it that the beautiful Fionnhuala was transformed into a swan by her evil stepmother, wandering the lakes and rivers endlessly. She could not be released from the spell until Christianity came to Ireland	**Floris**	Variant of Flora
		Flower	Variant of Florence
		Flur	Alternative spelling of Fleur
		Fortuna	Goddess of fortune in Roman mythology
		Frances	Latin – Frenchman, from France. Old German/Old French – free. Short/pet forms: Fanny, Fran
Fiorenza	Italian – flower	**Francesca**	Italian form of Frances. Short/pet form: Fran
Flanna	Feminine form of Flannan, meaning 'ruddy', 'red-haired'	**Francie**	Variant of Frances
Flavia	Latin – yellow, blonde	**Francine**	Variant of Frances
Flavie	Variant of Flavia	**Franke**	Variant of Frances
Fleta	Anglo-Saxon – swift as an arrow	**Freda**	Derived from Alfreda, Frederica or Winifred *(Frida, Frieda)*
Fleur	French form of Florence *(Flur, Fflur)*		
Flora	Latin – flowers. Short/pet form: Flo	**Frederica**	Feminine form of the boy's name Frederick, meaning 'gentle/peaceful ruler'. Short/pet forms: Freda, Freddy *(Fredrica)*
Floranthe	Variant of Flora		
Flore	Variant of Flora		
Florella	Variant of Flora		
Florence	Latin – blooming. Also Italian place name. Short/pet forms: Flo, Florrie, Flossie	**Fredrica**	Alternative spelling of Frederica
		Freja	Alternative spelling of Freya
		Fresa	Old German – curly-haired
Florentina	Latin – flowering, flowery. Short/pet forms: Flo, Florrie, Flossie	**Freya**	Name of Norse goddess of love and fertility, also 'noble lady' *(Freja)*
Floria	Variant of Florentina	**Frida**	Alternative spelling of Freda
Florian	Variant of Florentina	**Frieda**	Alternative spelling of Freda
Florida	Latin – flourishing. Short/pet forms: Flo, Florrie	**Fronde**	Latin – leafy branch
		Fuscienne	Latin – black

GABRIELLA

GEORGEANNE

GARNET

G

Gabby	Alternative spelling of Gabi
Gabi	Short/pet form of Gabriella, now also an independent name *(Gaby, Gabby)*
Gabriela	Alternative spelling of Gabriella
Gabriella	Italian feminine form of the boy's name Gabriel, meaning 'man of God'. Short/pet forms: Gabi, Gaby, Gabby *(Gabriela)*
Gabrielle	Variant of Gabriella
Gaby	Alternative spelling of Gabi
Gaea	Alternative spelling of Gaia
Gaenor	Welsh form of Gaynor
Gaia	Greek – earth. Goddess of the earth in Greek mythology *(Gaea)*
Gail	Derived from Abigail *(Gale, Gayle)*
Gale	Alternative spelling of Gail
Galina	Greek – calm
Gardenia	Anglo-Saxon – species of flower
Garlanda	Latin – adorned with flowers
Garnet	Garnet gemstone
Gay	French – lively. Also derived from Gaia *(Gaye)*
Gaye	Alternative spelling of Gay
Gayle	Alternative spelling of Gail

Gayner	Alternative spelling of Gaynor
Gaynor	Variant of Guinevere, the name of King Arthur's wife who fell in love with Lancelot, which means 'fair lady' *(Gaenor, Gayner)*
Gemma	Italian – gem *(Jemma)*
Geneva	French – juniper berry. Also Swiss place name
Genevieve	A French name whose origin and meaning are uncertain. The fifth-century St Genevieve is the patron saint of Paris
Genna	Variant of Geneva
Georgeanne	Variant of Georgia
Georgette	French form of Georgia
Georgia	Feminine form of the boy's name George, meaning 'labourer', 'farmer'. Also a place name. Short/pet form: Georgie.

NAME YOUR
LITTLE TREASURE

Your child is precious, so why not name him or her after a precious gem or mineral? You could choose a name simply because you like it, or you might like to choose a gem name that suits your new arrival's date of birth – your child's birthstone. Alternatively you could choose a gemstone for its specific quality – for example, topaz symbolizes good fortune and longevity. However the attributes associated with each stone appear to vary widely, depending on the source consulted!

Thanks to the female penchant for beautiful things, there are inevitably more girls' than boys' names when it comes to treasure. This is evident in the lists opposite.

Birthstones

Birthstones, as we know them in general terms in the West, are gemstones matched to months of birth, standardized at a meeting of the National Association of Jewelers in Kansas in 1912. The birthstones associated with the signs of the zodiac and other disciplines may differ. It is thought that the association of a specific gem with each month has a biblical origin, thanks to a description of Aaron's breastplate being decorated with 12 precious stones.

Of course, not all birthstones provide suitable names for your child but they may provide you with other ideas that you can explore – think of the colours of the stones, for example...

CASPER

JADE

HAVILAH CORAL

AMBER

TOPAZ

SAPPHIRE

Birthstones

January	garnet
February	amethyst
March	blood stone
	(or aquamarine)
April	diamond
May	emerald
June	pearl (or moonstone)
July	ruby
August	sardonyx (or peridot)
September	sapphire (deep blue)
October	opal (or tourmaline)
November	topaz
December	turquoise (or lapis lazuli)

Boys

Aneurin (gold)	**Haima** (made
Casper (treasure)	of gold)
Cornelian	**Havilah** (treasure)
(carnelian)	**Jasper** (treasure)
Ezar (treasure)	**Peridot**
Flint	**Shale**
Gasper	**Slate**
(treasure)	**Zircon**

Girls

Agate	**Crystal**	**Greta** (pearl)	**Ophira** (gold)
Amber	**Diamond**	**Iona** (violet-coloured	**Pearl**
Amethyst	**Doreen** (golden)	stone)	**Pearla**
Beryl (precious stone)	**Emerald**	**Jade**	**Precious**
Cameo	**Esmeralda**	**Jemma** (gem)	**Ruby**
Carnelian	**Garnet**	**Jet**	**Sapphira**
Christel	**Gemma** (gem)	**Jewel**	**Sapphire**
Copper	**Gina** (silvery)	**Margaret** (pearl)	**Silver**
Coral	**Golda**	**Mica**	**Topaz**
Coralie	**Goldie**	**Opal**	**Ula** (jewel of the sea)

Georgiana	Variant of Georgia
Georgina	Variant of Georgia. Short/pet forms: Georgia, Gina
Geralda	Old German – courageous
Geraldene	Alternative spelling of Geraldine
Geraldine	Feminine form of the boy's name Gerald, meaning 'ruler by spear'. Short/pet forms: Geri, Jeri (Geraldene)
Germaine	Feminine form of the French boy's name Germain, meaning 'akin', 'belonging', 'brother'
Gertrude	Old German – spear maiden. The seventh-century St Gertrude of Belgium was the patron saint of travellers. Short/pet forms: Gerda, Gertie, Trudi, Trudie, Trudy
Giacinta	Italian – hyacinth
Gianina	Variant of Gianna
Gianna	Italian form of Jane (Jianna)
Gilberta	Feminine form of the boy's name Gilbert, meaning 'bright pledge'
Gilda	Italian – servant of God, gilded
Gill	Alternative spelling of Jill
Gillian	Variant of Julie/Juliana, the feminine form of the boy's name Julian, meaning 'soft-haired', 'downy-bearded'. Short/pet forms: Gill, Gilly, Jill, Jilly (Gillianne, Jillian)

Gillianne	Alternative spelling of Gillian
Gimbya	Swahili – princess
Gina	Short/pet form of Georgina and Regina, now also an independent name. Also Japanese – silvery
Ginevra	Variant of Guinevere
Ginger	Derived from Virginia. Also used descriptively to mean 'red-haired'
Ginnie	Alternative spelling of Ginny
Ginny	Short/pet form of Virginia, now also an independent name (Ginnie)
Giralda	Old German – powerful contender
Gisela	Variant of Giselle
Giselle	German – a pledge
Gita	Sanksrit – song
Gitana	Spanish – gypsy
Gladys	Welsh – ruler over territory. Short/pet form: Glad
Gleda	Anglo-Saxon – to make happy
Glenda	Gaelic – holy, goodness
Glendora	Old German – gift of the glen
Glenna	Gaelic – valley
Glennis	Alternative spelling of Glenys
Glenys	Variant of Glynis (Glennis)
Glora	Variant of Gloria
Gloria	Latin – glory
Gloriana	Variant of Gloria
Gloriosa	Variant of Gloria
Glory	Variant of Gloria

GRIZELDA

GOEWYN

GWYNNETH

Glynis	Feminine form of the Welsh boy's name Glyn, meaning 'little valley', 'from the valley'
Goewin	Welsh – sprightly *(Goewyn)*
Goewyn	Alternative spelling of Goewin
Golda	Variant of Goldie
Goldie	Anglo-Saxon – made of gold *(Goldy)*
Goldy	Alternative spelling of Goldie
Grace	One of the 'virtue' names favoured by the Puritans, derived from the Latin *gratia*, meaning 'grace'
Gracia	Variant of Grace *(Gratia)*
Gracie	Variant of Grace
Graine	Variant of Grania *(Grainne)*
Grainne	Alternative spelling of Graine
Grania	Gaelic – affectionate, love
Gratia	Alternative spelling of Gracia
Grazia	Variant of Grace
Greta	Derived from Margaret
Gretchen	Derived from Margaret
Gretel	Derived from Margaret
Grette	Derived from Margaret
Griselda	Old German – grey warrior, battle maid *(Grizelda)*
Grizelda	Alternative spelling of Griselda
Guadalupe	Spanish – mother of God
Gudrid	Old German – divine impulse
Gudrun	Old German – God's secret
Guenevere	Alternative spelling of Guinevere
Guinevere	Celtic – fair and yielding, fair wife, fair one. Short/pet form: Gwinny *(Guenevere)*
Gusta	Derived from Augusta
Gwen	Variant of Gwyn. Also a short/pet form of Gwendolen
Gwenda	Variant of Gwendolen
Gwendolen	Celtic – white-browed. Short/pet forms: Gwen, Gwenny, Wendy, Wendi, Wendie *(Gwendolyn)*
Gwendoline	Variant of Gwendolen. Also the name of the Celtic moon goddess
Gwendolyn	Alternative spelling of Gwendolen
Gwendydd	Welsh – morning star. Short/pet forms: Gwen, Gwenny
Gwenhwyvar	Variant of Guinevere
Gwyn	Welsh – fair, white, blessed, holy. Also short/pet form of Gwyneth *(Gwynne)*
Gwyneth	Anglicized form of Gwynedd, the Welsh name for North Wales. Short/pet forms: Gwinny, Gwyn, Gwynne *(Gwynneth, Gwynyth)*
Gwynne	Alternative spelling of Gwyn
Gwynneth	Alternative spelling of Gwyneth
Gwynyth	Alternative spelling of Gwyneth
Gypsy	Uncertain origin, possibly Indian – wanderer, traveller

HALCYON

HARRIET

H

Hafwen	Welsh – fair summer
Haidee	Greek – modest
Haile	Alternative spelling of Hayley
Hala	Arabic – halo
Halcyon	Greek – calm, of the sea. Short/pet forms: Hali, Hallie
Haleigh	Alternative spelling of Hayley
Haley	Alternative spelling of Hayley
Hameline	Old German – home lover
Hana	Japanese – flower, blossom
Hanna	Alternative spelling of Hannah

Hannah	Hebrew – God has favoured me. An old name from which Ann and all its variants derive *(Hanna)*
Hanne	Variant of Hannah
Hanya	Aborigine – stone
Harmonia	Greek – harmony, unity, agreement
Harmony	Variant of Harmonia
Harriet	Feminine form of Harry, itself a nickname for Henry, meaning 'ruler at home'. Short/pet forms: Ettie, Etty, Harrie, Hattie, Hatty, Hetty *(Harriot)*
Harriot	Alternative spelling of Harriet
Haru	Japanese – spring
Harva	Feminine form of the boy's name Harvey, meaning 'warrior'
Hattie	Short/pet form of Harriet and Henrietta, now also an independent name *(Hatty)*
Hatty	Alternative spelling of Hattie
Haylee	Alternative spelling of Hayley
Hayley	Anglo-Saxon – hay meadow *(Haile, Haleigh, Haley, Haylee)*
Hazel	Hebrew. Species of plant – one of the tree and flower names first taken up as personal names at the end of the 19th century. The ancient hazel wand symbolized wisdom and protection. Also an old German colour name *(Hazell, Hazelle)*

HERMIONE

HEBE

HESTIA

Hazell	Alternative spelling of Hazel
Hazelle	Alternative spelling of Hazel
Heather	Old German – species of flower. A name adopted at the end of the 19th century. Short/pet form: Hetty
Heavenly	Vocabulary name meaning 'of the sky', 'of eternal happiness'
Hebe	Goddess of youth and spring in Greek mythology, equivalent to the Roman goddess Juventas
Hedwig	Old German – contention, battling. Short/pet forms: Hedda, Hedy
Heidi	Derived from the German name Adelheid, meaning 'nobility'
Helaine	Alternative spelling of Helene
Helen	Greek – the bright one. A well-known name thanks to Helen of Troy, and the origin of many different variations
Helena	Variant of Helen
Helene	Variant of Helen (*Helaine*)
Helga	Old German – happy, holy, healing
Helianthe	Greek – sunflower
Heloise	Helen + Lois or Louise
Hendrika	Variant of Henrietta
Henrietta	Feminine form of the boy's name Henry meaning 'ruler of the home', 'mistress of the home', which came to Britain via Henrietta Maria, the

	French wife of Charles I. Short/pet forms: Ettie, Etty, Harrie, Hattie, Hatty, Hetty
Henriette	Variant of Henrietta
Hermia	Variant of Hermione
Hermione	Derived from Hermes, the messenger of the gods in Greek mythology
Hero	Greek – hero
Hesper	Greek – night star
Hessa	Arabic – destiny
Hester	A variant of Esther. Short/pet form: Hetty
Hestia	Goddess of the hearth in Greek mythology
Heulwen	Welsh – sunshine
Hibernia	Latin – a woman from Ireland

HENDRIKA

HILDA   HORTENSIA

HILLARY

Hilaire	French form of Hilary
Hilary	Greek – cheerful, merry. The name was known in England from the 13th century, when it was applied to both sexes. Today the name is largely given to girls *(Hillary)*
Hilda	Old German – battle maid, protector *(Hilde)*
Hilde	Alternative spelling of Hilda
Hildegard	Variant of Hilda
Hillary	Alternative spelling of Hilary
Holli	Alternative spelling of Holly
Hollie	Alternative spelling of Holly
Holly	Taken from the name of the holly tree and often used for girls born around Christmas time. The bright red berries of the tree symbolize life *(Holli, Hollie, Hollye)*
Hollye	Alternative spelling of Holly
Honesta	Variant of Honesty
Honesty	Latin – honourable, honest. Also species of plant
Honey	Sweet one. Also variant of Honor
Honey-blossom	Sweetness, flower
Honor	Latin – honour, reputation. Originally used as Honoria, but later favoured by the Puritans as one of the 'virtue' names *(Honour)*

Honora	Variant of Honor
Honoria	Variant of Honor
Honour	Alternative spelling of Honor
Hope	Anglo-Saxon – optimism, trust, faith. Another of the 'virtue' names favoured by 17th-century Puritans
Hortense	French form of an old Roman family name, Hortensius, meaning 'of the garden'
Hortensia	Variant of Hortense
Hue	Vietnamese – lily
Hyacinth	Greek – species of flower. Also a colour name

INDYGO

IMOGEN

I

		Imogen	The name of the heroine in Shakespeare's *Cymbeline*, believed to be originally a misprint of Innogen, perhaps from
Ianna	Feminine form of the boy's name Ian, itself derived from John, meaning 'God is gracious'		the Celtic word *ingen*, meaning 'daughter' or 'girl'. Alternatively, it could be derived from the Latin
Ianthe	Greek – a violet-coloured flower		for image. Short/pet form: Immy
Ida	Old German – happy, industrious		*(Emogene, Imogene)*
Idalee	From Ida + Lee	**Imogena**	Variant of Imogene
Idalia	Variant of Idalee	**Imogene**	Alternative spelling of Imogen
Idana	From Ida + Anna	**Ina**	Latin – mother
Idelle	Greek/Old German – clever, happy	**Inaya**	Swahili – providence
Idola	Greek – idolized	**India**	The country. Originally from the
Idonia	German – industrious		Greek *indos*, meaning the river
Idun	Name of Norse goddess of spring		Indus. Indira is the Hindi form
Ila	French – from the island. Anglo-Saxon – island dweller *(Isla)*		of India
		Indigo	Greek – of India. Also a colour
Ilana	Hebrew – tree		name *(Indygo)*
Ilene	Alternative spelling of Eileen	**Indygo**	Alternative spelling of Indigo
Illeana	Variant of Ilona	**Ines**	Spanish form of Agnes *(Inez)*
Illeane	Variant of Ilona	**Inez**	Alternative spelling of Ines
Ilona	Modern variant of Eleanor, and so another variant of Helen. Ilona also means 'beautiful' in Hungarian	**Inga**	Alternative spelling of Inge
		Inge	Variant of Ingrid *(Inga)*
		Ingrid	Derived from the Old Norse
Ilsa	Variant of Ailsa		name Ing, the god of fertility.
Ima	Japanese – now, the present		Short/pet form: Inky
Imelda	Uncertain origin – possibly Latin or Old German	**Iola**	Alternative spelling of the name Iole
		Iolanthe	French – violet

Iole	Greek – violet. A name from Greek mythology revived by the Victorians in the late 19th century *(Iola)*	**Isabella**	Variant of Isabel. Short/pet forms: Bella, Ibby, Isa, Isi
Iona	Greek – violet-coloured stone; also the name of a Hebridean island	**Isabelle**	Alternative spelling of Isabel
Ira	Hebrew – watcher. Also short/pet form of Irina	**Isadora**	Variant of Isidore – a Greek name referring to Isis, who is the Egyptian goddess of the moon and fertility *(Isidora)*
Ireland	Place name		
Irena	Variant of Irene	**Isha**	Hebrew – woman
Irene	Greek – peace. Name of goddess of peace in Greek mythology. Short/pet forms: Rene, Renie	**Isidora**	Alternative spelling of Isadora
		Isis	Variant of Isadora
Irenna	Variant of Irene	**Isla**	Alternative spelling of Ila
Irette	Old German – little wrathful one	**Isleta**	Spanish – little island
Iria	Variant of Iris	**Ismena**	Greek – learned one
Irina	Russian form of Irene. Short/pet form: Ira	**Isobel**	Alternative spelling of Isabel
		Isolde	Celtic – fair one
Iris	Greek – goddess of the rainbow and messenger of the gods in Greek mythology. Also a species of flower and a colour name	**Isra**	Arabic – nocturnal journey
		Italy	Place name
		Ivana	Feminine form of the boy's name Ivan, itself derived from John, meaning 'God is gracious' *(Ivanna)*
Irisa	Variant of Iris		
Irma	German origin. A short/pet form of Ermintrude and the name of a god of war *(Erma)*	**Ivanna**	Alternative spelling of Ivana
		Ivi	Alternative spelling of Ivy
		Ivie	Alternative spelling of Ivy
Isa	Old German – iron spirit. Also short/pet form of Isabel/Isabella	**Ivory**	Anglo-Saxon – a colour name
		Ivy	Greek – clinging vine, constancy *(Ivi, Ivie)*
Isabel	Variant of Elizabeth. Short/pet forms: Ibby, Isa, Isi *(Isabelle, Isobel)*	**Izellah**	Unknown origin – little princess
		Izora	Arabic – dawn

JACARTA

JANELLE

JAIMIE

J

Jacalyn	Alternative spelling of Jacqueline
Jacarta	Alternative spelling of Jakarta
Jacinda	Greek – beautiful
Jacinta	Greek – derived from Hyacinth
Jacinth	Variant of Jacinta
Jacintha	Variant of Jacinta
Jackie	Short/pet form of Jacqueline, now also an independent name (*Jacky, Jacqui*)
Jacky	Alternative spelling of Jackie
Jaclyn	Alternative spelling of Jacqueline
Jacoba	Variant of Jacqueline
Jacolyn	Alternative spelling of Jacqueline
Jacqueline	Feminine form of the French boy's name Jacques (James), meaning 'supplanter'. Short/pet forms: Jackie, Jacky, Jacqui (*Jacalyn, Jaclyn, Jacolyn, Jacquelyn*)
Jacquelyn	Alternative spelling of Jacqueline
Jacquetta	Variant of Jacqueline
Jacquette	Variant of Jacqueline
Jacqui	Alternative spelling of Jackie
Jade	A green, semi-precious gemstone
Jaime	French – I love
Jaimie	Variant of Jaime

Jakarta	Indonesian place name (*Jacarta*)
Jalene	From James + Lenore
Jamie	Short/pet form of the boy's name James, now also an independent name for both girls and boys
Jamila	Egyptian – beautiful
Jana	Slavonic form of Jane
Janae	Variant of Jane
Janda	Slavonic form of Jane
Jane	One of the feminine forms of the Hebrew boy's name John. Short/pet forms: Janey, Janie, Jinny (*Jayne*)
Janelle	Variant of Jane
Janet	Little Jane. The name evolved in Scotland from the French Jeanette. Short/pet form: Jan (*Jannet*)
Janice	Variant of Jane (*Janis*)
Janina	Variant of Janine

CALENDAR
CONNECTIONS

You may be stuck for names for your baby but something you will know for sure is the time of year he or she is due to be born. This can be an invaluable source of inspiration when it comes to ideas for names, whether they have true calendar connections or simply have a loose association with the time of year, such as typical weather or seasonal customs and plants.

(For birthstones and astrological star signs, which are also dictated by the date of birth, see pages 164 and 144 respectively.)

Birth days

You could even go by the actual day, or time of day, on which your child is born. For example, Monday and Friday are names to suit either a boy or a girl, while Tuesday is a girl's name. Thora suits a girl born on a Thursday (derived from Thor's day), while Abina means 'a girl born on a Tuesday' and Neda is a girl's name meaning 'Sunday's child'. In early times Lucius (or Lucy), meaning 'light' in Latin, was the name given to children born at daybreak. Dawn is also an apt name for a girl born at this time of day. The girl's name Leila derives from a Persian word meaning 'born at night', as does the boy's name Daren, which is of Nigerian origin.

Spring (March–May)

Boys

Beltane (May Day)
Marcus/Mark/Martin (after March)
Pascal (Easter)
Quentin (fifth)

Girls

Anthea (lady of flowers)
April
Aviva (joyful spring)
Avril (after April)
Cerelia (of the spring)
Chloe (tender budding plant, green shoots)
Easter
Eranthe (spring flower)

Fleur (flowers)
Flora (Roman goddess of flowers and spring)
Haru (spring)
Idonea (goddess of spring)
Laverne (spring-like)
Mae/Maya (after the month name)
Magda (after Mary Magdalene)
May
Persephone (after the Roman goddess responsible for changing the seasons)
Rain
Spring

Summer (June–August)

Boys

Auguste/Gus (after the month name)
Juan (after the month name)
Jules/Julian (after the month name)
Leo/Leon (after the zodiac sign)
Octavio (eighth)

Girls

Augustine (after the month name)
Hafwen (fair summer)
Julia/Juliette (after the month name)
June
Summer
Octavia (eighth)

Autumn (September–November)

Boys

Aki (autumn)
Demetrius (from Demeter, the Greek goddess of the harvest)
Sivan (ninth month)
Virgil (after the zodiac sign)

Girls

Autumn
Leaf
Misty
Nona (ninth)
September
Virginia (after the zodiac sign)

Winter (December–February)

Boys

Angelo (after the Nativity story)
Christmas
Gabriel
Janus (after the month name)
Joseph (after the Nativity story)
Nicholas/Nick (after St Nicholas)
Nimbus
Noel (Christmas)
Robin
Rudolf/Rudolph
Santa
Valentine (after the Roman saint martyred on 13 February)
Yule

Girls

Angel
Brandy
Carol
Christmas
Gabriella
Holly
Ivy
Mary
Natalie (meaning 'born at Christmas')
Noelle
Robin
Sherry
Star
Storm
Tiffany (for girls born at Epiphany – 6 January)
Valentina/Valtina
Winter

Janine	Variant of Jane/Janet
Janis	Alternative spelling of Janice
Janna	Hebrew – flourishing
Jannali	Aborigine – moon
Jannet	Alternative spelling of Janet
Jannette	Variant of Janet
Jannike	Scandinavian form of Jane
Jara	Slavonic form of Gertrude
Jarita	Hindi – motherly devotion
Jasmine	Persian – species of flower
Javan	Latin – angel of Greece
Jayne	Alternative spelling of Jane
Jean	Variant of Joanna, having evolved from the Old French Jehane. Formerly regarded as a Scottish form of Jane (*Jeanne*)
Jeanette	Diminutive of Jean
Jeanine	Variant of Jean
Jeanne	Alternative spelling of Jean
Jelena	Russian – shining light
Jemima	Feminine form of the boy's name Benjamin, meaning 'son of the right hand'. Short/pet forms: Jem, Jemmy, Mima
Jemma	Alternative spelling of Gemma
Jenna	Celtic form of Jennifer
Jennelle	From Jenny + Nell
Jennet	Variant of Janet
Jennie	Alternative spelling of Jenny

Jennifer	Variant of Jenifer, the old Cornish form of Guinevere. Short/pet forms: Jen, Jennie, Jenny
Jenny	Variant of Jane/Janet. Also short/pet form of Jennifer (*Jennie*)
Jeri	Alternative spelling of Geri
Jerusha	Hebrew – inheritance
Jessamine	French – jasmine
Jessica	Feminine form of the boy's name Jesse, meaning 'the Lord exists' in Hebrew. Short/pet forms: Jess, Jessie, Jessye
Jet	Greek – name of a black mineral
Jetta	Variant of Jet
Jewel	Latin – joy (*Jewell*)
Jewell	Alternative spelling of Jewel
Jezebel	Hebrew – follower of idols
Jianna	Alternative spelling of Gianna

Jill	Short/pet form of Gillian, now also an independent name *(Gill)*
Jillian	Alternative spelling of Gillian
Jinx	Latin – a charm
Jo-Ann	Variant of Joanne
Joan	Variant of Joanna. The name first came from France as Jhone or Johan in the 12th century, took its present form by the 13th century, and it predates both Jane and Jean
Joann	Alternative spelling of Joanne
Joanna	Feminine form of the boy's name John, meaning 'God is gracious'. Short/pet forms: Jo, Joey, Josie
Joanne	Variant of Joanna *(Joann)*
Jobina	Hebrew – persecuted
Jocasta	In Greek mythology, the mother and unwitting wife of Oedipus
Jocelin	Alternative spelling of Jocelyn
Joceline	Alternative spelling of Jocelyn
Jocelyn	Old French – of the Goths. Referring to the German people, the name was introduced by the Normans and given only to boys until the 20th century. It is now more commonly used for girls. Short/pet form: Joss *(Jocelin, Joceline, Joscelyn)*
Jocosa	Latin – gleeful
Jocunda	Latin – mirthful
Jodette	Latin – sporting
Jodi	Alternative spelling of Jodie
Jodie	Short/pet form of Judith, now also an independent name *(Jodi, Jody)*
Jodis	Old German – horse sprite
Jody	Alternative spelling of Jodie
Joelle	French feminine form of the boy's name Joel, meaning 'Jehovah is the Lord'
Joelliane	Variant of Joelle
Jofrid	Old German – lover of horses
Johanna	Variant of Joanna
Johari	Swahili – something valuable
Joia	Variant of Joy *(Joya)*
Joie	Alternative spelling of Joy
Jolene	From Jo + 'lene' *(Joline)*
Joletta	Latin – violet flower
Jolie	French – pretty, merry
Joline	Alternative spelling of Jolene
Jonina	Hebrew – dove
Jordana	Feminine form of the boy's name Jordan, after a river
Jorna	Spanish – traveller
Joscelind	Latin – gentle playmate
Joscelyn	Alternative spelling of Jocelyn
Josephine	French feminine diminutive of the boy's name Joseph, meaning 'may the Lord add'. Short/pet forms: Jo, Joey, Josie, Pheeny

JULIANNE

J

Jovita	Variant of Joy
Joy	Latin – joyful, happy, rejoicing (*Joie*). Favoured by the Puritans in the 17th century, popular in the 19th century and still widely used
Joya	Alternative spelling of Joia
Joyan	Variant of Joy
Joyce	Derived from the Celtic Jodoc, a seventh-century Breton saint. A medieval name for both sexes, it appeared in many forms. The most common Anglo-Saxon version was Josse, and the name was often registered as Jocea or Jocosa
Joyleen	Variant of Joy
Joyvita	Variant of Joy
Juana	Spanish form of Jane
Juanee	Native American – warrior princess
Juanita	Spanish form of Joanne. Short/pet form: Nita
Judi	Alternative spelling of Judy
Judith	Hebrew – a Jewess, woman of Judea. Short/pet forms: Jodi, Jodie, Jody, Jude, Judi, Judy
Judy	Short/pet form of Judith, now also an independent name (*Judi*)
Julia	Variant of Julie
Juliana	Alternative spelling of Julianna
Julianna	Variant of Julianne (*Juliana*)

Julianne	From Julia + Anne. Short/pet form: Jules
Julie	Feminine form of the old Roman name Julius, meaning 'soft-haired', 'youthful'. Short/pet form: Jules
Julie-Ann	Variant of Julianne
Juliet	Derived from the Italian name *Guilietta*, a diminutive of *Guilia*, from which comes Julia. Its popularity is due to its use in Shakespeare's *Romeo and Juliet* (*Juliette*)
Julietta	Variant of Juliet
Juliette	Alternative spelling of Juliet
June	The name of a month; it originates from the important Roman family, Junius, and from Juno, queen of the gods in Roman mythology
Juniata	Latin – ever-youthful maid
Junilla	Variant of Juniata
Juno	Wife of Jupiter and queen of the gods in Roman mythology, she is equivalent to Greek goddess Hera
Justina	Variant of Justine
Justine	Feminine form of the boy's name Justin, meaning 'just', 'fair'
Justise	Variant of Justine
Juventia	Derived from Juventas, the Roman goddess of youth, equivalent to the Greek goddess, Hebe

KATINA

KASSIA

K

Kaatje	Dutch – pure
Kabibe	French – little lady
Kachine	Variant of Kachina
Kacy	Name derived from the initials KC
Kailey	Alternative spelling of Kayley
Kaitlin	Alternative spelling of Caitlin
Kaitlyn	Alternative spelling of Caitlin
Kaley	Alternative spelling of Kayley
Kalma	Old German – calm
Kalonice	Greek – beauty's victory
Kalya	Sanskrit – healthy
Kalyana	Sanskrit – one who is virtuous
Kamilah	Arabic – perfect one
Kamilia	Slavonic – sweet flower
Kara	Variant of Cara
Karan	Alternative spelling of Karen
Karen	Danish form of Catherine *(Karan, Karin, Karon)*
Karena	Variant of Karen *(Karina)*
Karin	Alternative spelling of Karen
Karina	Alternative spelling of Karena
Karla	Alternative spelling of Carla
Karli	Turkish – covered with snow
Karly	Alternative spelling of Carly
Karolyn	Alternative spelling of Carolyn

Karon	Alternative spelling of Karen
Kasi	Hindi – from the Holy City
Kasia	Alternative spelling of Kassia
Kassia	Variant of Catherine/Katherine *(Kasia)*
Kate	Short/pet form of Katherine, now also an independent name
Katelin	Alternative spelling of Caitlin. Short/pet form: Kate
Katelyn	Alternative spelling of Caitlin. Also from Katherine + Lynn
Katharine	Alternative spelling of Katherine
Katherine	*See* Catherine. Short/pet forms: Kat, Kate, Kath, Kathie, Kathy, Katie, Katy, Kitty *(Katharine, Kathryn)*
Kathini	Kikuyu – little bird
Kathleen	Derived from the phonetic spelling of Caitlin *(Cathleen)*
Kathryn	Alternative spelling of Katherine
Katie	Short/pet form of Katherine, now also an independent name *(Katy)*
Katina	Variant of Catherine/Katherine
Katinka	The Russian form of Catherine/Katherine
Katja	Variant of Catherine/Katherine
Katrien	Dutch form of Katrine
Katrina	Phonetic spelling of Caitriona. Short/pet form: Trina
Katrine	Variant of Katrina

KELLY

KAYLANA

K

KIANDRA

Katy	Alternative spelling of Katie
Katya	Short/pet form of Yekaterina, now also an independent name
Katyin	Aborigine – water
Kay	Greek – rejoice. Short/pet form of any name beginning with 'K' *(Kaye)*
Kaye	Alternative spelling of Kay
Kayla	Variant of Catherine/Katherine
Kaylana	From Kay + Lana
Kayleah	Alternative spelling of Kayley
Kaylee	Alternative spelling of Kayley. Also from Kay + Lee
Kayleen	Variant of Kayley
Kayleigh	Alternative spelling of Kayley
Kayley	Variant of Kelly *(Caileigh, Caleigh, Kailey, Kaley, Kayleah, Kaylee, Kayleigh)*
Kaysa	Scandinavian variant of Catherine/Katherine
Kealy	Alternative spelling of Keeley
Keeley	Variant of Kelly or Keelin *(Kealy, Keely)*
Keelia	Variant of Keeley, itself a variant of Kelly
Keelin	Celtic – slender, fair *(Caoilinn)*
Keely	Alternative spelling of Keeley
Keera	Alternative spelling of Kiera
Kefira	Hebrew – young lioness
Kelda	Old Norse – spring or fountain

Kellee	Alternative spelling of Kelly
Kelli	Alternative spelling of Kelly
Kellie	Alternative spelling of Kelly
Kelly	Modern anglicized form derived from a Gaelic name Caelach, meaning 'warrior' or 'strife' *(Kellee, Kelli, Kellie)*
Kendra	Anglo-Saxon – knowledgeable woman, understanding
Kenisha	Unknown origin – gorgeous woman
Kenya	Name of a country
Keona	Hawaiian – God's gracious gift
Kerley	Variant of Kelly
Kerri	Alternative spelling of Kerry
Kerrie	Alternative spelling of Kerry
Kerry	Gaelic – dark one. Also an Irish place name *(Kerri, Kerrie)*
Kersteen	Alternative spelling of Kirsteen
Kevina	Feminine form of the boy's name Kevin, which means 'comely at birth', 'handsome'
Kiandra	Variant of Kendra
Kiara	Alternative spelling of Ciara
Kiera	Feminine form of the Gaelic name Kieran, meaning 'black', 'dark-skinned', 'dark-haired' *(Keera)*
Kiki	Short/pet form of any name beginning with 'K'
Kiku	Japanese – chrysanthemum

KIMBERLEY

KYLIE

KOLORA

Kiley	Alternative spelling of Kylie	**Kita**	Japanese – north
Kim	Short/pet form of Kimberley, now also an independent name	**Klara**	Alternative spelling of Clara
		Kohana	Japanese – little flower
Kimber	Variant of Kimberley	**Kolina**	Greek – pure
Kimberlee	Alternative spelling of Kimberley	**Kolora**	Aborigine – freshwater lagoon
Kimberley	Derived from the Anglo-Saxon name Kimball, meaning 'bold'. Although once a boy's name, it is now regarded largely as a girl's name. Short/pet forms: Kim, Kimmy (*Kimberlee, Kimberly*)	**Kore**	Variant of Cora
		Krista	Variant of Kristen
		Kristen	Variant of Christine (*Kristin*)
		Kristin	Alternative spelling of Kristen
		Kristina	Alternative spelling of Christina
		Kristine	Alternative spelling of Christine
Kimberly	Alternative spelling of Kimberley	**Krystyna**	Alternative spelling of Christina
Kina	Variant of Kineta	**Kumari**	Sanskrit – a girl or daughter
Kineta	Greek – active one, messenger	**Kuni**	Japanese – country born
Kinta	Native American – beaver	**Kyara**	Alternative spelling of Ciara
Kiona	Native American – brown hills	**Kyla**	Variant of Kyle
Kiran	Hindi – ray	**Kyle**	Gaelic – comely, handsome. This name is much more often used for boys than it is for girls
Kirsteen	Variant of Kirsten (*Kersteen*)		
Kirsten	Originally a Scandinavian form of Christiana or Christine, it is now regarded chiefly as a Scottish variant and means 'anointed'. Short/pet forms: Kirstie, Kirsty (*Kirstin, Kirstyn*)		
		Kylee	Alternative spelling of Kylie
		Kyleigh	Alternative spelling of Kylie
		Kyli	Alternative spelling of Kylie
		Kylie	Possibly derived from Kyle. Also used by Australian Aborigines to describe a boomerang (*Kiley, Kylee, Kyleigh, Kyli, Kyly*)
Kirstie	Alternative spelling of Kirsty		
Kirstin	Alternative spelling of Kirsten		
Kirsty	Short/pet form of Kirsten, now also an independent name (*Kirstie*)	**Kyly**	Alternative spelling of Kylie
		Kyna	Gaelic – wise
Kirstyn	Alternative spelling of Kirsten	**Kyrene**	Greek – Lord, God

LAUREEN
LALEH
LAVINIA

L

Lacey	Variant of Larissa *(Lacie, Lacy)*
Lacie	Alternative spelling of Lacey
Lacy	Alternative spelling of Lacey
Laila	Old Norse – night
Laina	Swahili – soft and gentle
Lala	Slavonic – tulip
Laleh	Variant of Leila
Lan	Vietnamese – flower name
Lana	Variant of Alana. Also means 'to float' in Polynesian
Lani	Hawaiian – sky, heaven
Lara	Variant of Laura and Larissa *(Larah)*
Larah	Alternative spelling of Lara
Laraine	Latin – sea bird
Lareina	Spanish – queen
Larisa	Alternative spelling of Larissa
Larissa	Latin – playful, cheerful one *(Larisa, Laryssa)*
Lark	Anglo-Saxon – name of a songbird
Laryssa	Russian form of Larissa
Lassie	Anglo-Saxon – young girl, maiden
Latanya	Daughter of Tanya. Short/pet forms: Tania, Tanya, Toni, Tonia, Tonya
Latisha	Alternative spelling of Letitia
Latonia	Latin – mother of Apollo and Diana. Short/pet forms: Tania, Tanya, Toni, Tonia, Tonya
Laura	Derived from the Latin *laurus*, meaning 'laurel'.
Laureen	Variant of Laura
Laurel	Variant of Laura
Lauren	Variant of Laura *(Lauryn, Loren)*
Lauretta	Alternative spelling of Loretta
Laurette	Variant of Laura
Lauri	Variant of Laura
Laurie	Variant of Laura
Laurinda	Variant of Laura
Laurissa	Variant of Laura
Lauryn	Alternative spelling of Lauren
Laveda	Latin – innocent one
Lavender	Anglo-Saxon. A species of flower. It is also a colour name
Laverne	French – spring-like
Lavina	Variant of Lavinia
Lavinia	Latin – a classical name, that of the second wife of Aeneas in Roman mythology. Short/pet form: Vina
Lawana	Native American – laughing water
Layla	Variant of Leila *(Lela)*
Lea	Alternative spelling of Leah
Leaf	Leaf
Leah	Hebrew – fatigued, weary. A biblical name *(Lea)*

LEANNE

LEXINE

LEONORA

Leala	French – loyal one	**Lentula**	Celtic – mild
Leana	Alternative spelling of Leanne	**Leola**	Variant of Leonie
Leandra	Latin – like a lioness	**Leoma**	Variant of Leonie
Leann	Alternative spelling of Leanne	**Leona**	Variant of Leonie (Liona)
Leanna	Variant of Leanne (Leana, Liana)	**Leonarda**	Variant of Leonie
Leanne	Possibly derived from the French	**Leonie**	Latin/Greek – brave as lion, lioness
	Liane, meaning 'climbing vine',	**Leonora**	Possibly derived from Eleanor or
	or from Lee + Anne/Anna		from the same root as Leonie
	(Leann, Lian, Liane)	**Lesley**	A Scottish surname originally derived
Lecea	Variant of Alice		from an Aberdeenshire place name,
Leda	Greek – beautiful temptress. Name		probably meaning 'little meadow', it
	of the woman seduced by Zeus in the		is now used as a first name for both
	form of a swan in Greek mythology		girls and boys. The usual feminine
Ledell	Variant of Leda		form is Lesley and the masculine
Lee	Anglo-Saxon – meadow. More		Leslie, but the spellings are
	often used for boys (Leigh)		interchangeable. Short/pet form: Les
Leewana	Aborigine – wind	**Leta**	Variant of Letitia
Leigh	Alternative spelling of Lee	**Letha**	Greek – oblivion
Leila	Persian – dark-haired, dark beauty,	**Leticia**	Alternative spelling of Letitia
	born at night (Leilah, Lila, Lilah)	**Letitia**	Latin – full of joy, happiness. Lettice
Leilah	Alternative spelling of Leila		is a variant and used to be common
Leilani	Hawaiian – heavenly child		in Tudor England (Latisha, Leticia)
Lela	Alternative spelling of Layla	**Levana**	Latin – rising sun
Lena	Variant of Helen	**Lexia**	Derived from Alexandra
Lene	Old Norse – illustrious	**Lexine**	Derived from Alexandra
Lenice	Greek – brave as a lion	**Leya**	Variant of Leonie
Lenka	Slavonic – light	**Leyla**	Arabic – night
Lenora	Variant of Leonora	**Lian**	Alternative spelling of Leann
Lenore	Variant of Leonora	**Liana**	Alternative spelling of Leanna

POPULAR NAMES THROUGH
THE DECADES

You have only to look at the names of your grandparents and others of their generation to see how their names are generally quite different from those of you and your friends. Parents' choice of first names for their children invariably follows a cyclical fashion over the decades. While Jack and Chloe are today's favourites (see page 30 for the current Top 10 UK baby names), for example, neither of these were among even the Top 100 most popular names in 1974. Similarly, although John and Mary were extremely popular names in the first half of the 20th century, they are both currently outside the Top 50.

The following lists show the top five most popular first names for boys and for girls in England and Wales within specific years during the last century, up to the millennium.

WILLIAM   JAMES
       CLAIRE
  GEORGE   PATRICIA
          THOMAS

1900

Boys	Girls
1. John	Mary
2. William	Helen
3. James	Anna
4. George	Margaret
5. Charles	Ruth

1934

Boys	Girls
1. John	Margaret
2. Peter	Jean
3. William	Mary
4. Brian	Joan
5. David	Patricia

1994

Boys	Girls
1. Thomas	Rebecca
2. James	Lauren
3. Jack	Jessica
4. Daniel	Charlotte
5. Matthew	Hannah

1904

Boys	Girls
1. William	Mary
2. John	Florence
3. George	Doris
4. Thomas	Edith
5. Arthur	Dorothy

1964

Boys	Girls
1. David	Susan
2. Paul	Julie
3. Andrew	Karen
4. Mark	Jacqueline
5. John	Deborah

2000

Boys	Girls
1. Jack	Chloe
2. Thomas	Emily
3. James	Megan
4. Joshua	Lauren
5. Daniel	Charlotte

1924

Boys	Girls
1. John	Margaret
2. William	Mary
3. George	Joan
4. James	Joyce
5. Thomas	Dorothy

1974

Boys	Girls
1. Paul	Sarah
2. Mark	Claire
3. David	Nicola
4. Andrew	Emma
5. Richard	Lisa

Source for all: Office for National Statistics, England and Wales

Liana	Latin – youth
Liane	Alternative spelling of Leanne. Also a species of plant
Lida	Greek – beloved by all, people's love
Liese	Variant of Liesel
Liesel	Variant of Elizabeth
Lila	Alternative spelling of Leila
Lilac	Persian – blueish
Lilah	Alternative spelling of Leila
Lilia	Variant of Lilian and Lilac
Lilian	Possibly derived from a pet form of Elizabeth, or a variant of Lily. Short/pet forms: Lil, Lilli, Lillie, Lilly, Lily *(Lillian)*
Liliana	Variant of Lilian
Lilias	Scottish form of Lilian
Lilith	Hebrew – spirit/woman of the night
Lilli	Alternative spelling of Lily
Lillian	Alternative spelling of Lilian
Lillie	Alternative spelling of Lily
Lilly	Alternative spelling of Lily
Lilo	Hawaiian – generous one
Lily	Latin/Greek – species of flower symbolizing purity. Also a short/pet form of Lilian. Short/pet forms: Lil *(Lilli, Lillie, Lilly)*
Lilybelle	From Lily + Belle; beautiful lily
Lina	Derived from the name Adeline. Also Arabic – tender
Linda	Variant of Belinda. Short/pet forms: Lin, Lindy, Lyn, Lynn, Lynne *(Lynda)*
Lindsay	Ancient Scottish surname taken from a place name, Lindon's Isle. Used initially for boys, now more commonly for girls. Short/pet forms: Lin, Lindy, Lyn, Lynn, Lynne *(Lindsey, Linzi, Lyndsey, Lynsey)*
Lindsey	Preferred English spelling of the Scottish name Lindsay
Lindy	Short/pet form of Linda, now also an independent name
Linette	Alternative spelling of Lynette
Linnea	Old Norse – lime tree, national flower of Sweden
Linnet	Alternative spelling of Lynette. Also variant of an old Welsh name Eluned, and the name of a songbird
Linzi	Alternative spelling of Lindsay
Liona	Alternative spelling of Leona
Lisa	Derived from Elisa, itself derived from Elizabeth *(Lysa)*
Lise	Derived from Elise, a French form of Elizabeth
Lisette	Diminutive of Lise
Lisha	Hausa – full of secrets
Liza	Derived from Eliza
Lizbeth	Variant of Elizabeth
Lizette	Diminutive of Liz

LORAINE
LOURDES
LORNA

Lois	Greek – good, worthy of desire	**Lorrie**	Alternative spelling of Lori
Lola	Derived from Dolores	**Lotus**	Greek – dream-like, lotus flower
Lolita	Derived from Dolores or Charlotte	**Louella**	From Louise + Ella. Short/pet forms: Lou, Louie (*Luella*)
Lona	Derived from Maelona		
Lora	Alternative (older) spelling of Laura	**Louisa**	Variant of Louise
Loraine	Alternative spelling of Lorraine	**Louise**	French feminine form of the boy's name Louis, meaning 'famous warrior', 'glorious in battle'. Short/pet forms: Lou, Louie
Lorayne	Alternative spelling of Lorraine		
Lorelei	German – siren of the river, lure to the rocks		
Lorella	Variant of Laura	**Loura**	Like Lora, an older spelling of Laura
Loren	Alternative spelling of Lauren	**Lourana**	From Laura + Ana
Lorena	Variant of Lorna	**Lourdes**	Spanish, derived from the French place name
Loretta	A well-used Roman Catholic name, possibly deriving from Our Lady of Loreto in Italy, or even from the name Laura (*Lauretta, Lorretta*)		
		Lourine	Variant of Laura
		Love	Anglo-Saxon – love, loved one. Short/pet forms: Lovie, Lovey
Lori	Short/pet form of Lorraine, now an independent name. In Australia a lory is a brightly coloured Australian parrot, which dines on the nectar and pollen of flowers (*Lorrie*)		
		Lowanna	Aborigine – girl
		Luana	Old German – female warrior
Lorna	Derived from the Scottish place name, Lorn. The name was popularized in RD Blackmore's 1869 novel *Lorna Doone*		
Lorraine	Variant of Laura. Also a French place name. Short/pet forms: Lori, Lorrie (*Loraine, Lorayne*)		
Lorretta	Alternative spelling of Loretta		

LUCILLA

LUPITA

Lubaya	Swahili – young lioness	**Lula**	Native American – jumping water
Lucia	Italian form of Lucy	**Lulu**	Derived from Louise. Also Native
Lucie	Alternative spelling of Lucy		American – rabbit
Lucile	Alternative spelling of Lucille	**Luna**	Latin – moon
Lucilla	Variant of Lucille. Short/pet form: Cilla	**Lunetta**	Little moon
		Lunette	Variant of Lunetta
Lucille	Variant of Lucy *(Lucile)*	**Lupe**	Variant of Lupita
Lucinda	Latin – bright, shining. Short/pet form: Cindy	**Lupita**	Feminine form of the boy's name Guadalupe, which means 'mother of God'
Lucretia	Latin – associated with virgin purity, being the name of the Roman woman who committed suicide in shame after being raped by Tarquinius. Short/pet form: Crete	**Lycia**	Variant of Alice
		Lydia	Greek – woman of Lydia. Short/pet form: Liddy
		Lyn	Alternative spelling of Lynn
Lucy	Feminine form of the boy's name Lucius, meaning 'bringer of light'. In early times the name was given to children born at daybreak *(Lucie)*	**Lynda**	Alternative spelling of Linda
		Lyndsey	Alternative spelling of Lindsay
		Lynette	Diminutive of Lynn *(Linette, Linnet, Lynnette)*
Luella	Alternative spelling of Louella	**Lynn**	Short/pet form of Linda and Lindsay, now also an independent name *(Lyn, Lynne)*
		Lynne	Alternative spelling of Lynn
		Lynnette	Alternative spelling of Lynette
		Lynora	From Lynda + Nora
		Lynsey	Alternative spelling of Lindsay
		Lyris	Greek – musical, player of the lyre
		Lysa	Alternative spelling of Lisa
		Lysandra	Greek – liberator, emancipator
		Lyudmila	Slavonic – grace of the people

MABEL

MAGNOLIA

MADLYN

M

Mabel   Possibly derived from the Anglo-Saxon name Amabel, but may come from the French *ma belle*, meaning 'my beautiful girl' *(Mabelle, Mable)*

Mabella   Variant of Mabel. Short/pet form: Bella

Mabelle   Alternative spelling of Mabel

Mable   Alternative spelling of Mabel

Maddie   Short/pet form of Maddison and Madeline, now also an independent name *(Maddy)*

Maddison   Son of Maude. Short/pet forms: Maddie, Maddy *(Madison)*

Maddy   Alternative spelling of Maddie

Madeleine   French form and preferred spelling of Madeline

Madelia   Variant of Madeline

Madeline   Hebrew – woman of Magdala. St Mary Magdalene was the patroness of penitents. Short/pet forms: Maddie, Maddy *(Madilyn, Madlin, Madlyn, Madoline)*

Madilyn   Alternative spelling of Madeline

Madison   Alternative spelling of Maddison

Madlin   Alternative spelling of Madeline

Madlyn   Alternative spelling of Madeline

Madoline   Alternative spelling of Madeline

Madonna   Variant of Donna, meaning 'my lady', 'mother'

Madra   Latin – mother

Madrona   Variant of Madra

Mae   Alternative spelling of May

Maelona   Welsh – princess

Maeve   Phonetic spelling of the Gaelic name Meadhbh, which means 'intoxicating'

Mafuane   Egyptian – soil

Magda   Short/pet form of Magdalene, now also an independent name

Magdalen   Alternative spelling of Magdalene

Magdalena   Variant of Magdalene

Magdalene   *See* Madeline. Short/pet forms: Madge, Magda *(Magdalen)*

Magenta   Italian place name. Also a colour

Magnolia   French – a species of flower

Magot   Alternative spelling of Margot

Mai   Alternative spelling of May

Maia   Goddess of spring in Roman mythology, after whom the month of May is named – *see* May *(Maya)*

Maida   Old German – unmarried girl, maiden

Maidie   Variant of Maida

Maille   Gaelic form of Molly

MAIREAD

MARCELLA

Mair	Alternative spelling of Maire
Maire	Gaelic form of Mary *(Mair)*
Mairead	Gaelic form of Margaret
Mairin	Another Gaelic form of Mary; pronounced 'more-een'
Maisie	Scottish pet form of Margaret. Also derives from a Greek word meaning 'pearl' *(Maisy)*
Maisy	Alternative spelling of Maisie
Maj	Old Norse – pearl
Makayla	Alternative spelling of Michaela
Malaya	Spanish – free. Also a place name
Malina	Variant of Malinda
Malinda	Greek – gentle
Mame	Alternative spelling of Mamie
Mamie	American pet form of Mary *(Mame, Mamy)*
Mamy	Alternative spelling of Mamie
Manilla	Aborigine – winding river
Manon	French short/pet form of Mary
Manuela	Hebrew – God is with us
Maralyn	Alternative spelling of Marilyn
Marcella	Feminine form of Marcellus, the boy's name derived, like Mark and Marcus, from Mars, the god of war in Roman mythology
Marcelle	Variant of Marcella

Marcia	Feminine form of the name Marcius, a Roman clan name, possibly originating from Mars, the god of war from which the boys' names Mark and Marcus derive
Marcie	Alternative spelling of Marcy
Marcy	Variant of Marcia *(Marcie)*
Mardi	Variant of Martha. It is also French for Tuesday
Maree	Variant of Mary
Marella	From Mary + Ella
Maren	Variant of Marina
Marenda	Variant of Miranda
Margaret	Greek – pearl. Possibly originally derived from a Persian word, meaning 'child of light'. Short/pet forms: Madge, Maggie, Maggy, Marge, Margi, Margie, Meg, Peg, Peggie, Peggy
Margareta	Alternative spelling of Margarita

MARGOT

MARISSA

Margarete	Alternative spelling of Marguerite
Margaretta	Alternative spelling of Margarita
Margarita	Spanish form of Margaret. Short/pet form: Rita *(Margareta, Margaretta)*
Margery	Variant of Margaret, derived from the French form Marguerite. Short/pet forms: Marge, Margi, Margie *(Marjorie)*
Margherita	Italian form of Margaret. Short/pet form: Rita
Margo	Alternative spelling of Margot
Margot	Variant of Margaret *(Magot, Margo)*
Marguerite	French form of Margaret, and translated as 'daisy' *(Margarete)*
Maria	Latin form of Mary, widely used in Italy and Spain
Mariam	Alternative spelling of Maryam
Marian	Alternative spelling of Marianne
Marianne	Derived from the French name Marie. In Anglophile countries it sometimes replaces Marion, and can also be interpreted as a 'double' name from Mary + Anne *(Marian)*
Maribel	From Mary + Belle
Marie	French form of Mary. Short/pet form: Mimi
Mariel	Variant of Mary
Mariella	Variant of Mariel

Marielle	Variant of Mariel
Marietta	Variant of Mary
Marigold	A species of flower, meaning 'Mary's gold'
Marilu	From Mary + Lucille
Marilyn	Anglo-Saxon. Thought to mean 'of Mary's line', referring to descendants of the Virgin Mary. Short/pet forms: Marli, Marlie, Marlo, Marly *(Maralyn, Marrilynne, Marylyn)*
Marin	Contraction of Marilyn
Marina	Latin – of the sea. Short/pet form: Marnie
Marion	*See* Marianne
Mariposa	Spanish – species of lily
Maris	Hebrew – of the sea
Marisa	Variant of Maris *(Marissa)*
Marise	Japanese – infinite
Marisela	Variant of Maris
Marisol	Variant of Maris
Marissa	Alternative spelling of Marisa
Marjeta	Slavonic form of Margaret
Marjorie	Alternative spelling of Margery
Marlee	Aborigine – elder tree
Marleen	Alternative spelling of Marlene
Marlena	Variant of Marlene
Marlene	Variant of Magdalene, being a contraction of Mary Magdalene. Short/pet form: Marla *(Marleen)*

MARVEL

Marmara	Greek – radiant
Marnie	Short/pet form of Marina, now also an independent name
Marrilynne	Alternative spelling of Marilyn
Marsha	Variant of Marcia
Marta	Variant of Martha and Martina
Martha	Aramaic – lady
Marti	Variant of Martha (*Marty*)
Martina	Feminine form of the boy's name Martin, meaning 'warlike'
Martinique	French feminine form of the boy's name Martin. Also a country name
Marty	Alternative spelling of Marti
Marvel	Latin – to wonder, admire
Marvela	Latin – marvellous
Mary	There is some doubt about the origins of Mary, one of the oldest names and the most significant in the Christian Church. The Virgin Mary, mother of Jesus Christ, inspired a cult so fervent that the name was sometimes considered too holy to use. After the 12th century it became the most consistently popular name in Europe – as the Mediterranean Maria, the French Marie, the Welsh Mair or the Gaelic Maire, Moira and Maureen.
Maryam	Arabic form of Mary (*Mariam*)
Marylyn	Alternative spelling of Marilyn
Masika	Egyptian – born during rain
Mathilde	Variant of Matilda
Matilda	Old German – strength, battle, battle maid. Short/pet forms: Mattie, Matty, Tilda, Tillie, Tilly
Maud	A variant of the names Madeline and Matilda (*Maude*)
Maude	Alternative spelling of Maud
Maudie	Pet form of Maud
Maura	Latin – dark. Possible variant of Mary
Maureen	Variant of Maire, a Gaelic form of Mary. Short/pet form: Mo (*Maurine*)
Maurilla	Old German – wise, dark-eyed girl
Maurine	Alternative spelling of Maureen
Maurita	Latin – little dark girl
Mauve	French – purplish
Mavis	Celtic – Song thrush
Maxeen	Alternative spelling of Maxine
Maxima	Variant of Maxime
Maxime	Variant of Maxine
Maxine	French feminine form of the boy's name Maximilian, meaning 'greatest'. Short/pet forms: Max, Maxie, Maxy (*Maxeen*)
May	Derived from the Romans naming their spring month after Maia, their goddess of spring, whom they honoured with festivities on May Day. The name is also a pet form of

MELODY

MELANTHA

	Mary, and sometimes of Margaret *(Mae, Mai)*
Maya	Alternative spelling of Maia
Mayda	Anglo-Saxon – maiden
Mayna	Old German – home woman
Mckayla	Alternative spelling of Michaela
Mea	Latin – mine *(Mia)*
Meagan	Alternative spelling of Megan
Meaghan	Alternative spelling of Megan
Meda	Native American – priestess
Medita	Latin – reflective
Meena	Alternative spelling of Mina
Meg	Short/pet form of Margaret
Megan	Welsh name developed from Meg, which is one of the pet names of Margaret meaning 'pearl' *(Meagan, Meaghan, Meghan)*
Meghan	Alternative spelling of Megan
Mehri	Persian – kind
Meingolda	Old German – my golden flower
Melanie	Greek – dark-complexioned, black. Short/pet forms: Mel, Mellie, Melly *(Melany)*
Melantha	Greek – dark flower. Short/pet forms: Mel, Mellie, Melly
Melany	Alternative spelling of Melanie
Mele	Hawaiian form of Mary
Melia	Greek – ash tree. Short/pet forms: Mel, Mellie, Melly

Melika	Greek – lyrical. Short/pet forms: Mel, Mellie, Melly
Melina	Uncertain origin. Possibly Latin – canary yellow, or Greek – honey. Short/pet forms: Mel, Mellie, Melly
Melinda	From Melina + Linda. Short/pet forms: Mel, Mellie, Melly, Mindy
Melisa	Alternative spelling of Melissa
Melisande	Variant of Mélissande, a French form of Millicent
Melisenda	Spanish – honest, diligent. Short/pet forms: Mel, Mellie, Melly
Melissa	Greek – bee. Short/pet forms: Mel, Mellie, Melly, Misha *(Melisa)*
Melita	Italian form of Melissa. Short/pet forms: Mel, Mellie, Melly
Melodie	Alternative spelling of Melody
Melody	Greek – tune, singer of songs. Short/pet forms: Mel, Mellie, Melly *(Melodie)*
Melonia	Greek – dark. Short/pet forms: Mel, Mellie, Melly
Melosa	Spanish – sweet, gentle. Short/pet forms: Mel, Mellie, Melly
Melva	Variant of Melvina
Melvina	Feminine form of the boy's name Melvin, the origin of which is uncertain. Short/pet forms: Mel, Mellie, Melly

NAMES FROM
MOTHER NATURE

There are inevitably more names for girls to be found among the world of plants than there are for boys. Girls' names based on nature tend to come from the words for flowers and fruit, the more feminine and colourful aspects, whereas boys' names tend to come from trees. The Victorians are the ones responsible for the enthusiastic take up of tree and flower names as first names towards the end of the 19th century. The use of fruit as names such as Peaches and Strawberry is generally a more modern trend.

Aside from specific species of plant, the Latin and French origins of the word 'flower' has given rise to many girls' names, such as Flora, Fleur, Floranthe, Flore, Florella, Florence and Floris, as well as Flower itself, plus Florian for boys.

The following lists include 'vocabulary words' that have come to be used as names, as well as names that have a meaning related to the natural world. For example, Erica is Latin for heather and Daphne is Greek for laurel tree, while many boys' names beginning with 'Ash' are of Anglo-Saxon origin and relate to the ash tree, just as names beginning with 'Wil' relate to willow trees and 'Ald' to the alder tree.

CELANDINE
TUART
LAUREL

Boys

Aldridge	Basil	Heath	Linden	Rowan
Ash	Berrigan	Jarrah	Myall	Taree
Ashley	Birch	Laurel	Natan	Tuart
Ashford	Burnet	Laurence	Oakes	Wilford
Ashton	Fabian	Lian	Perry	Willoughby

Girls

Acacia	Camellia	Helianthe	Myrtle	Rue
Amaryllis	Cassia	Holly	Oleander	Saffron
Anemone	Celandine	Honesty	Olive	Sage
Angelica	Cherry	Hyacinth	Pansy	Savanna
Anise	Cicely	Iris	Peaches	Snowdrop
Aspen	Columbine	Ivy	Peony	Strawberry
Aster	Coriander	Jasmine	Petunia	Tansy
Azalea	Dahlia	Lavender	Plum	Tiger Lily
Blackberry	Daisy	Liane	Poppy	Verbena
Blossom	Daphne	Lily	Primrose	Veronica
Bramble	Erica	Lotus	Primula	Viola
Brier	Fern	Magnolia	Prunella	Violet
Briony	Gardenia	Marigold	Rose	Willow
Buttercup	Hazel	Mariposa	Rosemary	Yasmine
Calla	Heather	Melia	Rowan	Zinnia

M

Memphis	US place name, used for both girls and boys	**Michelle**	French feminine form of the boy's name Michael, meaning 'God-like'. Short/pet forms: Chelle, Chellie, Mica, Misha, Shelley, Shelly *(Michele)*
Mena	Latin – mercy, strength		
Meras	Hebrew – worthy		
Mercedes	Latin – merciful		
Mercia	Variant of Mercy	**Miette**	French – small sweet thing
Mercy	Latin – compassion, mercy	**Mignon**	French – dainty, petite
Meredith	Celtic – great chief. Short/pet form: Merry	**Mikaela**	Alternative spelling of Michaela
		Mikayla	Alternative spelling of Michaela
Merel	Alternative spelling of Meryl	**Miki**	Japanese – flower stalk
Meriel	Celtic – bright as the sea	**Mildred**	Derived from the Anglo-Saxon name Milthryth, meaning 'gentle power'. Short/pet forms: Millie, Milly
Merle	French – blackbird		
Merrill	Alternative spelling of Meryl		
Merry	Anglo-Saxon – happy. Also short/pet form of Meredith	**Mili**	Unknown origin – 'Who is for me?'
		Millicent	Old German – work, strong. Short/pet forms: Millie, Milly
Merryl	Alternative spelling of Meryl		
Merula	Variant of Merle	**Millie**	Short/pet form of Camilla, Amelia/ Emily, Mildred and Millicent, now also an independent name *(Milly)*
Meryl	Variant of Merle *(Merel, Merrill, Merryl)*		
Meta	Latin – ambitious	**Milly**	Alternative spelling of Millie
Mia	Alternative spelling of Mea. Also Danish pet form of Mary	**Mina**	Short/pet form of Wilhelmina. Also Japanese – south *(Meena, Minna)*
Mica	Short/pet form of Michelle. Also a type of lustrous mineral	**Minda**	Native American – knowledge
		Minerva	Goddess of wisdom, civilization and practical skills in Roman mythology, who is equivalent to the Greek goddess Athena
Michaela	Feminine form of the boy's name Michael, meaning 'God-like' *(Makayla, Mckayla, Mikaela, Mikayla)*		
Michaelina	Variant of Michaela	**Minna**	Old German – resolute, strong, love. Also alternative spelling of Mina
Michele	Alternative spelling of Michelle		

MIRABEL   MYFANWY

MONIQUE

Minnie	Scottish pet form of Mary, also a short form of Wilhelmina	**Mona**	Anglicized form of the Gaelic name Maudhnait, meaning 'noble'. Also the Latin for the Isle of Man
Mira	Latin – wonderful. A variant of Mary		
Mirabel	Latin – of great beauty (*Mirabelle*)	**Monica**	Latin – adviser
Mirabella	A variant of Mirabel. Short/pet form: Bella	**Monique**	French form of Monica
Mirabelle	Alternative spelling of Mirabel	**Monita**	A variant of Mona. Short/pet form: Nita
Miranda	Latin – worthy of admiration. Short/pet forms: Manda, Mandi, Mandy	**Mora**	Variant of Morag
		Morag	Gaelic – great, large
Mireille	Alternative spelling of Mirella	**Morgan**	Welsh name of uncertain meaning. Name of King Arthur's jealous step-sister, Morgan La Fey. Used for both girls and boys (*Morgen*)
Mirella	French – Jehovah spoke		
Miriam	Hebrew – earliest form of Mary. Short/pet form: Mimi		
		Morgana	Variant of Morgan
Mirielle	French – miraculous	**Morgen**	Alternative spelling of Morgan
Mirra	Variant of Miranda	**Morna**	Gaelic – beloved (*Myrna*)
Missouri	Native American – canoe. Also US place name	**Morwenna**	Welsh – maiden
		Moya	Celtic – great. Also a variant of Mary
Missy	Anglo-Saxon – young girl		
Misty	Anglo-Saxon – Misty	**Moyra**	Alternative spelling of Moira
Mitra	Persian – angel	**Muriel**	Variant of Meriel
Mitzi	Variant of Mary	**Mya**	Burmese – emerald
Modesty	Latin – without conceit	**Myfanwy**	Welsh – my treasure
Mohana	Sanskrit – bewitching, enchantress	**Myra**	A name invented by the 16th-century poet Fulke Greville, now popular with Scottish parents
Moira	Anglicized form of Maire, the Gaelic form of Mary (*Moyra*)		
Mollie	Alternative spelling of Molly	**Myrna**	Alternative spelling of Morna
Molly	Pet form of Mary (*Mollie*)	**Myrtle**	Greek – species of plant

NADYA

NESTA

NATASHA

N

Nada	Variant of Nadia
Nadeem	Variant of Nadia
Nadia	Short/pet form of the Russian name
	Nadezhda, meaning 'hope' *(Nadya)*
Nadie	Variant of Nadia
Nadine	French form of Nadia
Nadya	Alternative spelling of Nadia
Naida	Latin – water nymph
Nalani	Hawaiian – calmness of the skies
Nalin	Native American – maiden
Nan	Pet form of Ann
Nana	Variant of Ann/Hannah *(Nanna)*
Nancy	Variant of Nan, also possibly
	from Agnes
Nanette	Diminutive of Nan
Nanine	French variant of Ann
Nanna	Alternative spelling of Nana
Naomi	Hebrew – pleasant, sweet
Narelle	Popular girl's name in Australia of
	uncertain origin, probably Aborigine
Nasia	Variant of Natalie
Nastasia	Variant of Anastasia *(Nastasya)*
Nastasya	Alternative spelling of Nastasia
Nastaya	Variant of Nastasia
Nata	Acrobatic, dancer

Natala	Variant of Natalia
Natalia	Less common variant
	of Natalie *(Natalya)*
Natalie	Latin – the Lord's birthday, ie child
	born at Christmas *(Nathalie)*
Natalya	Russian form of Natalia
Natane	Native American – daughter
Natasha	Russian pet form of Natalya.
	Short/pet form: Tasha
Nathalie	Alternative spelling of Natalie
Neala	Celtic – having chieftains
Neena	Spanish form of Nina
Nelia	Feminine form of Neil – 'champion'
Nell	Old pet form of the names
	Eleanor and Helen *(Nelle)*
Nelle	Alternative spelling of Nell
Nellie	Old pet form of of the names
	Eleanor and Helen *(Nelly)*
Nelly	Alternative spelling of Nellie
Neoma	Greek – new moon
Neona	Variant of Neoma
Nerine	Greek – one from the sea, sea born
Nerissa	Greek – sea nymph
Nerys	Welsh – lady
Nesta	A Welsh name and a pet form
	of Agnes. Short/pet forms:
	Ness, Nessa, Nessie
Netanya	Hebrew – God's gift. Short/pet
	forms: Tania, Tanya, Toni, Tonia, Tonya

NICOLA

NORAH

NIXIE

Neva	Spanish – snow	**Noelani**	Hawaiian – beautiful girl from heaven
Neysa	Greek – chaste, pure	**Noeleen**	Variant of Noelle
Nia	Swahili – purpose	**Noella**	Variant of Noelle
Niamh	Gaelic – bright, beautiful; pronounced 'neev'	**Noelle**	Feminine form of the boy's name Noel, meaning 'Christmas'
Nichola	Alternative spelling of Nicola	**Nokomis**	Native American – daughter of the moon
Nichole	Alternative spelling of Nicole		
Nicola	Feminine form of the boy's name Nicholas, meaning 'the people's victory'. Short/pet forms: Nick, Nicki, Nickie, Nicky, Nikky *(Nichola)*	**Nola**	Latin – of high birth
		Nona	Latin – ninth
		Nora	Gaelic short/pet form of the name Honora, meaning 'honour'. Also derived from Leonora *(Norah)*
Nicole	French form of Nicola. Short/pet forms: Nick, Nicki, Nickie, Nicky, Nikky *(Nichole)*	**Norah**	Alternative spelling of Nora
		Noreen	Diminutive of Nora *(Norine)*
Nicolette	Diminutive of Nicole	**Norine**	Alternative spelling of Noreen
Nicolina	Variant of Nicola	**Norma**	Possibly derived from the Latin, meaning 'rule', or simply the feminine form of the boy's name Norman, meaning 'man from the north'
Nigella	Latin – black		
Nijole	Slavonic form of Nicole		
Nina	Short/pet form of the Russian name Antonina or the French name Nanine, both variants of Ann		
		Nova	Variant of Novia
Ninette	Diminutive of Nina	**Novia**	Latin – fresh, new
Ninon	Variant of Nanine	**Noya**	Hebrew – beautiful, ornamented
Nissa	Old Norse – friendly elf	**Nu**	Burmese – tender
Nita	Short/pet form of Anita, Bonita and Juanita. Also derived from a Native American word for bear	**Nuala**	Short/pet form of Fionnhuala, now also an independent name
		Nydia	Latin – homemaker
Nitzana	Hebrew – blossom	**Nyx**	Greek – night. Name of the goddess of the night in Greek mythology
Nixie	German – water sprite		

OCEANA

ORENDA

OLYMPIA

O

Obelia	Greek – pillar of strength
Oceana	Greek – ocean
Octavia	Latin – eighth
Odele	Greek – wealthy
Odelia	Hebrew – heiress, prosperous
Odera	Hebrew – plough
Odessa	Greek – a long journey.
Odette	French form of an Old German boy's name, Oda, meaning 'rich'
Oenone	A nymph in Greek mythology with the gifts of prophecy and healing
Ola	Greek – virgin, Hebrew – eternal and Old Norse – daughter
Oleander	Greek – species of plant
Olga	Russian name derived from Helga, which means 'holy', 'prosperous'
Oliana	Hawaiian – oleander
Olive	Latin – olive tree, the ancient symbol of peace. Also a colour name. Short/pet forms: Liv, Livi, Livvy, Nollie, Ollie
Olivia	Italian form of Olive. Short/pet forms: Liv, Livi, Livia, Livvy, Nollie, Ollie
Olubayo	Yoruba – highest joy
Olwen	Welsh – white footprint. Short/pet form: Ollie

Olympia	Greek – heavenly one, of Olympus, mountain of the gods
Ona	Gaelic – graceful one
Ondine	Alternative spelling of Undine
Onida	Native American – the expected one
Oona	Modern spelling of Oonagh
Oonagh	Ancient Gaelic name – meaning uncertain, but linked with the Latin for 'one' and Gaelic for 'lamb'
Opa	Native American – owl
Opal	Sanskrit – opal gemstone
Ophelia	Greek – helper
Ophrah	Hebrew – fawn
Ora	Derived from Aurora
Orana	Aborigine – moon
Orella	Latin – she who listens
Orenda	Native American – magic power
Oriana	Latin/Greek – golden (*Orianna*)
Orianna	Alternative spelling of Oriana
Oriel	Alternative spelling of Auriel
Oriole	Alternative spelling of Auriel
Orissa	Indian place name
Orla	Variant of Oriel. Phonetic spelling of the Gaelic name Orfhlaith
Orlena	French – bright maiden
Orpah	Hebrew – female deer
Ottilie	Feminine form of Otto, meaning 'wealthy', 'prosperous'
Ownah	Variant of Una

PALOMA
PEACHES
PARTHENIA

PQ

Pacifica	Latin – peaceful
Page	Alternative spelling of Paige
Paige	Anglo-Saxon – young servant, child *(Page)*
Painton	The name of a country town introduced by the Normans
Pallas	Greek – maiden, wisdom
Palmeda	Greek – inventive
Paloma	Spanish – dove. Like the olive, a symbol of peace
Pamela	Greek – honey-like sweetness. Short/pet forms: Pam, Pammie, Pammy
Pamelia	Variant of Pamela
Pandora	Greek – multi-gifted, talented
Panola	Native American – cotton
Pansy	Greek – species of flower
Panya	Swahili – mouse, little baby
Paola	Alternative spelling of Paula
Paolma	Variant of Paloma
Paris	French and US place name, used for both girls and boys
Parthenia	Greek – virgin, maid
Parveneh	Persian – butterfly
Pascale	French – Passover, Eastertime
Pascha	Hebrew – to pass over
Pat	Short/pet form of Patience and Patricia; now an independent name
Patience	Latin – an abstract 'virtue' name, which came into use in the 17th century. Short/pet form: Pat
Patrice	French form of Patricia. Short/pet form: Pat
Patricia	Feminine form of the boy's name Patrick, meaning 'aristocratic', 'nobleman'. Short/pet forms: Pat, Patsy, Patti, Pattie, Patty, Tricia, Trish, Trisha
Patsy	Short/pet form of Patricia, now also an independent name
Paula	Feminine form of the boy's name Paul, meaning 'small' *(Paola)*
Pauleen	Alternative spelling of Pauline
Paulette	Diminutive of Paula/Pauline
Paulina	Variant of Pauline
Pauline	French feminine form of the boy's name Paul *(Pauleen)*
Pavita	Sanskrit – purified
Peace	Latin/Old French – peace, happiness
Peaches	Derived from the name of the fruit
Pearl	Probably Latin in origin. One of the jewel names in vogue in Victorian times that has survived to today. Short/pet forms: Pearlie, Pearly *Pearle*)
Pearla	Variant of Pearl

PHILLIPPA

PENELOPE

PETRINA

PQ

Pearle	Alternative spelling of Pearl
Peg	Short/pet form of Peggy
Peggie	Alternative spelling of Peggy
Peggy	Pet form of Margaret, this is now also an independent name in its own right *(Peggie)*
Pelagia	Greek – from the sea, mermaid
Penelope	Greek – weaver, or possibly a type of duck. Short/pet forms: Pen, Penney, Penny, Pennie
Penney	Alternative spelling of Penny
Pennie	Alternative spelling of Penny
Penny	Short/pet form of Penelope, now also an independent name *(Pennie, Penney)*
Peony	Greek – species of flower
Pepita	Variant of Josephine
Perdita	Latin – lost. Short/pet forms: Perdy, Purdie
Peri	Feminine form of the boy's name Perry, derived from Peregrine, or possibly meaning 'pear tree'
Perlita	Variant of Pearl
Persephone	Goddess in Greek mythology, equivalent to the Roman goddess Proserpina
Petra	Greek – rock. Also a place name
Petrina	A variant of Petra. Short/pet form: Trina

Petrona	Variant of Petra
Petronella	Latin – the name of an early Christian martyr, used in England since the 12th century
Petula	Latin – one who seeks/asks. Short/pet form: Pet
Petunia	French – species of flower
Phebe	Alternative spelling of Phoebe
Pheby	Alternative spelling of Phoebe
Phenice	Hebrew – of the stately palm tree
Philippa	Feminine form of the boy's name Philip, meaning 'lover of horses'. Short/pet forms: Phil, Pip, Pippa *(Felipa, Phillippa)*
Phillida	Alternative spelling of Phyllida
Phillippa	Alternative spelling of Philippa
Philomena	Greek – nightingale, lover of the moon. Short/pet form: Phil *(Filomena)*
Phoebe	Greek – shining, brilliant. Epithet of Artemis, the Greek goddess of the moon *(Phebe, Pheby)*
Phoenix	Latin – phoenix (mythological bird that rises from the ashes). Also a US place name. Used f or both girls and boys
Phylicia	Alternative spelling of Felicia
Phyliss	Alternative spelling of Phyllis
Phyllida	Variant of Phyllis *(Phillida)*

PIERRETTE

QUINTANA

QUEENA

Phyllis	Greek – leafy, foliage. Short/pet form: Phil (Phyliss)
Pia	Latin – pious, dutiful
Pierrette	Feminine form of Pierre, which is the French version of the boy's name Peter. The latter name means 'a rock'
Pili	Egyptian – born second
Piper	Anglo-Saxon – pipe player
Pippa	Short/pet form of Philippa, now also an independent name. Short/pet form: Pip
Placida	Latin – calm
Pleasance	Old French – to please
Plum	Species of tree/fruit
Pocahontas	Native American – playful one
Polly	Rhyming variant of Molly. Short/pet form: Poll
Pollyanna	From Polly + Anna. Short/pet forms: Anna, Poll, Polly
Poloma	Native American – bow
Poppy	Species of flower
Portia	Latin – an offering to God
Posy	Small flower
Precilla	Alternative spelling of Priscilla
Precious	French – precious, dear
Primrose	Latin – early rose
Primula	Latin – botanical name, used as a first name since the late 19th century

Prisca	Variant of Priscilla
Priscilla	Latin – ancient. Short/pet form: Cilla (Precilla)
Priya	Sanskrit – beloved
Prudence	Latin – prudent, cautious. Short/pet forms: Pru, Prue
Prunella	Latin – little plum. Short/pet forms: Pru, Prue
Queena	Variant of Queenie
Queenie	Anglo-Saxon – the name implies 'a supreme woman', whether she is queen of a man's heart, a house or a realm. Used as an affectionate first name for Queen Victoria, and then by the Edwardians
Quenby	Old Norse – womanly
Querida	Spanish – beloved
Quibilah	Egyptian – peaceful
Quinta	Feminine form of the boy's name Quintin, meaning 'fifth', and much used in Ancient Rome
Quintana	Modern variant of Quinta
Quintina	Variant of Quintana
Quirita	Latin – citizen

AROUND
THE WORLD

With so many more of us travelling further afield these days, either to settle abroad or merely to visit, it is inevitable that there is a common sharing of cultures occurring across the globe. This blending of ideas has introduced subtle changes in our language and customs, such as in our preferences for foods and 'ethnic' art and furnishings and, of course, as well as in the choice of baby names.

There are plenty of reasons for wanting to choose an unusual foreign name for your child. Perhaps an ancestor of yours came from foreign parts. Maybe you have enjoyed living in or visiting a place yourself and, rather than naming your child after the location (see page 50), you wish to borrow a word from the language. Or perhaps you are seeking a foreign name simply because it is different...

BASIM
ARIKA
KHAUL
SEQUOYAH
SAHAR
KACHINA
LATIKA

Boys

Amaroo Aborigine – a beautiful place
Aswad Arabic – black
Bali Hindi – mighty warrior
Basim Arabic – smiling
Burnum Aborigine – a great warrior
Chin Korean – precious
Cobar Aborigine – burnt earth
Givon Arabic – hill, high place
Hemi Maori form of James
Jamal Arabic – beauty
Jian Chinese – healthy
Jiro Japanese – second son

Kale Hawaiian – strong, manly
Kalti Aborigine – spear
Kamal Name of a Hindu god
Kari Aborigine – smoke
Kedar Hindi – mountain lord, powerful
Khalil Arabic – good friend
Kontar Ghanaian – only child
Lei Chinese – thunder
Mandu Aborigine – sun
Marron Aborigine – leaf
Mesha Hindi – ram
Mowan Aborigine – sun
Nuri Arabic – fire

Pita Maori form of Peter
Powhatan Native American – powwow hill
Rafu Japanese – net
Ravi Hindi – benevolent, sun god
Rimon Arabic – pomegranate
Sequoyah Native American – sparrow
Simba Swahili – lion
Taro Japanese – firstborn son
Tomi Japanese – red
Uwan Aborigine – to meet
Zoltan Arabic – sultan, ruler

Girls

Alani Hawaiian – orange tree
An Chinese – peace
Anzu Japanese – apricot
Arika Aborigine – water lily
Aruna Hindi – radiance
Aziza Swahili – precious
Bayo Nigerian – to find joy
Bega Aborigine – beautiful
Cai Vietnamese – female
Carna Arabic – horn
Chieko Japanese – wise child
Corazon Filipino – heart
Ema Polynesian – beloved

Eshe Egyptian – life
Halona Native American – fortunate
Hea Korean – grace
Huan Chinese – happiness
Kachina Native American – sacred dancer
Kalila Arabic – beloved
Kalinda Sanskrit – sun
Kimiko Japanese – dear child
Latika Hindi – elegant
Lokelani Hawaiian – small red rose

Miah Aborigine – the moon
Rani Hindi – queen
Reka Maori – sweet
Rohana Hindi – sandalwood
Sabra Arabic – thorny cactus
Sachiko Japanese – happy child
Sade Nigerian – honour confers a crown
Sahar Arabic – dawn
Shani Swahili – marvellous
Veda Hindi – sacred knowledge
Zada Arabic – lucky one

RHIANNONA
RAMONA
REBECCA

R

Rachael	Alternative spelling of Rachel
Rachel	Hebrew – ewe, innocence. Short/pet forms: Rae, Ray *(Rachael)*
Rachelle	Variant of Rachel
Racquel	Alternative spelling of Raquel
Radcliffe	Anglo-Saxon – from the red cliff
Radinka	Old German – playful
Rain	Rain
Ramona	Feminine form of the boy's name Ramon, Spanish for Raymond
Rana	A name of Asian origin meaning 'a queen of birth'
Rane	Variant of Rana
Raphaela	Feminine form of the boy's name Raphael, meaning 'healed by God'
Raquel	Variant of Rachel *(Racquel)*
Raven	Anglo–Saxon – raven, black
Rea	Alternative spelling of Rhea
Reanna	Obscure origin – possibly Welsh. Moon goddess or nymph
Reba	Variant of Rebecca
Rebecca	Biblical name of uncertain origin. Possibly Hebrew – knotted cord, tied. Short/pet forms: Becca, Becka, Beckie, Becky *(Rebekah)*

Rebekah	Alternative spelling of Rebecca
Regina	Latin – queen. Short/pet form: Gina
Rehani	Swahili – a promise
Reina	Anglicized form of Reine
Reine	French form of Regina
Ren	Japanese – water lily
Rena	Derived from the names Andrea, Irene and Regina
Renata	Latin – born again. Short/pet forms: Rene, Renie *(Renate)*
Renate	Alternative spelling of Renata
Renée	French form of Renata
Renita	Latin – resistance. Short/pet form: Nita
Reva	Old French – dreamer
Rhea	Possibly Greek – stream, river. Goddess of fertility in Greek mythology *(Rea)*
Rhian	Welsh – maiden
Rhiannon	Welsh – nymph, goddess
Rhoda	Greek – rose, or woman of Rhodes
Rhodanthe	Greek – flower of the rose bush
Rhode	Variant of Rhoda
Rhona	Alternative spelling of Rona, or possibly a variant of Rhonda
Rhonda	Welsh place name
Rhonwen	Welsh – possibly means 'white-haired', or 'white lance'
Ria	Spanish – mouth of a river

RIONA

R

ROCHELLE

Richelle	Anglo-Saxon/Old German – brave ruler
Richenda	Feminine form of the boy's name Richard, meaning 'strong ruler'
Rihana	Arabic – sweet basil
Rilla	German – brook
Rimca	Variant of Rebecca
Rimona	Hebrew – pomegranate
Rina	Greek – pure
Riona	Gaelic form of Regina. Phonetic spelling of the Gaelic name Rioghnach
Risa	Japanese form of Lisa
Risa	Latin – laughter
Rita	Short/pet form of Margarita and Margherita; also an independent name
Riva	French – shore
Robbin	Alternative spelling of Robin
Roberta	Feminine form of the boy's name Robert, meaning 'illustrious' or 'fame'. Short/pet forms: Bobbie, Bobby, Robbie, Robby
Robi	Hungarian – shining with fame
Robin	Diminutive of Rob, the short form of Robert, but now an independent name. The first feminine form was Robina but Robin and Robyn are now used for girls as well as for boys. Short/pet forms: Bobbie, Bobby, Robbie, Robby *(Robbin, Robyn)*

Robina	Variant of Roberta and Robin
Robyn	Alternative spelling of Robin, used only for girls
Rochelle	French – little rock. Also French place name
Rohnwen	Variant of Rowan
Roma	Feminine form of the boy's name Roman, meaning 'of Rome'
Romaine	French form of Roma *(Romayne)*
Romana	Variant of Roma
Romayne	Alternative spelling of Romaine
Romilda	Old German – brave little battle maid
Rona	Feminine form of the boy's name Ronald, meaning 'power' + 'force', 'ruler'. Possibly derived from a contraction of Rowena. Also a Scottish place name *(Rhona)*
Ronalda	Feminine form of Ronald *(see Rona)*
Ronalee	From Rona + Lee

R

ROSALEEN

ROSEMARIE

ROSANNA

Rori	Feminine form of the boy's name Rory, meaning 'red'
Ros	Short/pet form of many names beginning with 'Ros', for example Rosalind and Rosamund (Roz)
Rosa	Italian form of Rose
Rosabel	Latin – beautiful rose
Rosalba	Latin – white rose
Rosaleen	Alternative spelling of Rosaline
Rosalia	Variant of Rose
Rosalie	French form of Rosalia
Rosalind	Originally derived from Old German, roslindis, meaning 'horse and serpent', but when the name reached Spain as Rosalinda it took the Spanish meaning of 'rose', and 'pretty' from the Spanish word linda. Short/pet forms: Ros, Rosa, Rosie
Rosalinda	Variant of Rosalind
Rosaline	Variant of Rosalind (Rosaleen)
Rosalyn	Variant of Rosalind
Rosamond	Alternative spelling of Rosamund
Rosamund	Originally derived from Old German meaning 'horse protector'. However, in the Middle Ages scholars decided that it was from Latin, with the more attractive meaning 'rose of the world'. Short/pet forms: Ros, Rosa, Rosie (Rosamond)

Rosanna	Variant of Rosanne
Rosanne	Alternative spelling of Roseanne
Rose	Originally from the German hros, meaning 'horse', an animal revered by the early Germanic people. It is with the flower, however, that the name is usually associated. It is also a short/pet form of Rosemary and a colour name
Roseanne	From Rose + Anne. Short/pet forms: Ros, Rosa, Rosie (Rosanne)
Roselani	Hawaiian – heavenly rose
Roselle	Diminutive of Rose, which means 'little rose'
Rosemarie	An alternative spelling of the name Rosemary

ROSALINDA

ROSINA ROWENA

RYLEE

Rosemary — From Rose + Mary. Also species of herb. Short/pet forms: Ros, Rose, Rosie *(Rosemarie)*

Rosetta — Diminutive of Rosa, meaning 'little rose'

Rosie — Short/pet form of Rose and Rosemary, now also an independent name

Rosina — Italian variant of Rose

Rosita — Spanish variant of Rose

Roslin — Alternative spelling of Roslyn

Roslyn — Variant of Rosalyn and Rosalind. Also a Scottish place name *(Roslin, Roslynn, Rosslyn)*

Roslynn — Alternative spelling of Roslyn

Rossa — Feminine form of the boy's name Ross

Rosslyn — Alternative spelling of Roslyn

Rowan — Gaelic – little red one. Also a species of tree. (The rowan tree is believed to have the power to drive away evil.) Used for both girls and boys. Short/pet form: Ro

Rowena — Variant of Rowan, which is more commonly used than Rowan. Short/pet forms: Ro, Ronnie, Ronny *(Rowina)*

Rowina — Alternative spelling of Rowena

Roxana — Alternative spelling of Roxanna

Roxane — Alternative spelling of Roxanne

Roxanna — Variant of Roxanne *(Roxana)*

Roxanne — Persian – dawn, sunrise. Short/pet form: Roxy *(Roxane)*

Roz — Alternative spelling of Ros

Rozelle — From Rose + Elle

Rozene — Variant of Rose

Ruby — Latin – ruby gemstone; colour name.

Rue — Species of herb

Ruella — Lucky elfin one

Rufina — Feminine form of the boy's name Rufus, derived from the Latin and meaning 'red-haired'

Rukmini — Sanskrit – name of the wife of Lord Krishna. Often used in Indonesia

Ruth — Probably Hebrew – version of beauty, friend, compassion.

Rylee — Variant of Riley

ROXANA

SABRINA

SARENA

SALOME

S

Saba	Greek – woman of Sheba
Sabin	Alternative spelling of Sabine
Sabina	Latin – from the Sabine region (of ancient Italy)
Sabine	Variant of Sabina (Sabin)
Sabreena	Alternative spelling of Sabrina
Sabrina	A poetic Roman name for the river Severn. Also legendary Celtic princess. Short/pet form: Brie (Sabreena, Sabryna, Zabrina)
Sabryna	Alternative spelling of Sabrina
Sacha	Alternative spelling of Sasha
Sadie	Variant of Sarah
Saffron	Species of plant, yellow
Safi	Swahili – pure
Sage	Latin – prophet. Also a herb
Sahar	Arabic – dawn, splendour of the East
Sallie	Alternative spelling of Sally
Sally	Pet form of Sarah. Short/pet form: Sal (Sallie)
Sallyann	From Sally + Ann. Short/pet forms: Ann, Sal, Sallie, Sally,
Salome	Hebrew – peace
Samantha	Of disputed origin – possibly Aramaic, meaning 'heard', a name implying the granting of parents' prayers for a child. Short/pet forms: Sam, Sammie, Sammy
Samara	Hebrew – mountain, outlook, ruled by God
Sancha	Latin – holy (Sancia, Sanchia)
Sanchia	Alternative spelling of Sancha
Sancia	Alternative spelling of Sancha
Sandra	Derived from Alessandra, itself a variant of Alexandra (Zandra)
Sapphira	Variant of Sapphire
Sapphire	Sapphire gemstone. A colour name
Sara	Alternative spelling of Sarah
Sarah	Hebrew – princess (Sara, Sarra)
Sarai	Variant of Sarah
Saree	Arabic – most noble
Sarena	Variant of Sarah
Sarra	Alternative spelling of Sarah
Sasha	Derived from Alessandra (Sacha)
Saskia	A Dutch name, popular in Britain for the last 20 years
Satin	A modern vocabulary name, denoting a smooth, luxurious fabric
Savanna	Spanish – treeless plain, open grassland (Savannah)
Savannah	Alternative spelling of Savanna
Scarlet	Anglo-Saxon – scarlet; probably a cloth trader's surname turned first name (Scarlett, Scarlette)

SELENA   SHEBA

SHARAN

Scarlett	Alternative spelling of Scarlet	**Sharan**	Alternative spelling of Sharon
Scarlette	Alternative spelling of Scarlet	**Sharen**	Alternative spelling of Sharon
Scout	Scout	**Sharene**	Variant of Sharon
Selena	Variant of Selene (Selina)	**Shari**	Variant of Sharon
Selene	Greek – moon. Goddess of	**Sharleen**	Alternative spelling of Charlene
	the moon in Greek mythology,	**Sharlene**	Alternative spelling of Charlene
	who is equivalent to the Roman	**Sharmila**	Sanskrit – the protected one
	goddess Luna	**Sharon**	Hebrew – flat plain. A biblical place
Selia	Gaelic form of Sheila		name (Sharan, Sharen, Sharron)
Selima	Arabic – peace	**Sharron**	Alternative spelling of Sharon
Selina	Alternative spelling of Selena	**Shauna**	Feminine form of the boy's name
September	Latin – name of a month		Shaun, meaning 'God's mercy'
Sera	Derived from Serafina		(Shaunna, Shawna)
Serafima	Hebrew – angel of flame	**Shaunna**	Alternative spelling of Shauna
Serafina	Spanish – seraph, angel (Seraphina)	**Shavon**	Alternative spelling of Shevon
Seraphina	Alternative spelling of Serafina	**Shawna**	Alternative spelling of Shauna
Serena	Latin – calm, serene, clear	**Shawnee**	Native American – southern
Serendipity	A vocabulary name, denoting		people. Used for both girls and boys
	good fortune	**Shayna**	Variant of Sheena
Serenity	Peaceful disposition	**Sheba**	Derived from Bathsheba
Shaina	Variant of Shana	**Sheela**	Alternative spelling of Sheila
Shaine	Variant of Shana	**Sheelagh**	Alternative spelling of Sheila
Shana	Hebrew – beautiful	**Sheelah**	Alternative spelling of Sheila
Shannon	Gaelic – old wise one. Also	**Sheena**	Phonetic spelling of the Gaelic
	the name of an Irish river		name Sine, a form of Jane (Shena,
	(Channon, Shanon)		Sheona, Sheenagh, Sheenah)
Shanon	Alternative spelling of Shannon	**Sheenagh**	Alternative spelling of Sheena
Shantay	French – enchanted	**Sheenah**	Alternative spelling of Sheena
Shara	Variant of Sharon	**Sheera**	Hebrew – song

SHEONA SHEVON

SIAN

Sheila	Phonetic spelling of the Gaelic name Sile, a form of Celia *(Sheela, Sheelagh, Sheelah, Shela, Shelagh)*
Shela	Alternative spelling of Sheila
Shelagh	Alternative spelling of Sheila
Shelley	Anglo-Saxon – clearing on a slope, meadow border. Originally a surname, then a first name for boys. During the 20th century it became known as a girl's name *(Shelly)*
Shelly	Alternative spelling of Shelley
Shena	Alternative spelling of Sheena
Shenandoah	Native American – beautiful star daughter. Also a US place name
Sheona	Alternative spelling of Sheena
Sheral	Alternative spelling of Cheryl
Sheree	Anglicized form of the French word *chérie*, meaning 'darling' *(Sheri, Sherri, Sherrie, Sherry)*

Shereen	Iranian – sweet
Sheri	Alternative spelling of Sheree
Sherill	Alternative spelling of Cheryl
Sherilyn	Alternative spelling of Cheralyn
Sherise	Alternative spelling of Charis
Sherri	Alternative spelling of Sheree
Sherrie	Alternative spelling of Sheree
Sherry	Alternative spelling of Sheree
Sherryl	Alternative spelling of Cheryl
Sheryl	Alternative spelling of Cheryl. Also variant of Shirley
Shevaun	Alternative spelling of Shevon
Shevon	Variant of Siobhan *(Shavon, Shevaun)*
Shirleen	Persian – sweet
Shirley	Anglo-Saxon – bright meadow. Short/pet form: Shirl
Shohan	Hebrew – pearl
Shona	Anglicized form of the Gaelic name Seonaid, the feminine version of Shaun, meaning 'God's mercy'
Shoshana	Hebrew – rose *(Shoshanah)*
Shoshanah	Alternative spelling of Shoshana
Shukura	Egyptian – grateful
Shula	Hebrew – brightness
Sîan	Alternative spelling of Sian
Sian	Welsh form of Jane; pronounced 'sharn' *(Sîan)*
Sibel	Alternative spelling of Sibyl
Sibilla	Alternative spelling of Sibylla

SIBYL SKYE

SIGOURNEY

S

Sibyl	Derived from Ancient Greece and Rome, where it denoted the collective name of the guardians of the Sibylline Oracles. Short/pet form: Sibbie *(Cybil, Cybill, Sibel, Sybil)*	**Sinead**	Gaelic form of Janet; pronounced 'shin-aid'
		Siobhan	Gaelic form of Joan; pronounced 'shah-vawne'
		Sirena	Greek – siren
		Sisley	Alternative spelling of Cicely
Sibylla	Variant of Sibyl *(Sibilla)*	**Sissy**	Gaelic form of Cecilia
Sida	Greek – water lily	**Siti**	Egyptian – lady
Sidney	Alternative spelling of Sydney	**Sky**	Sky
Sidonia	Italian – from Sidonia	**Skye**	Scottish place name
Sidonie	Alternative spelling of Sydney	**Snowdrop**	Species of flower
Siena	Italian place name	**Sofia**	Italian form of Sophia. Place name
Sienna	Italian – colour name	**Sofya**	Alternative spelling of Sophia
Sierra	Spanish – saw-tooth mountain range	**Solana**	Spanish – sun
Signa	Latin – signal, sign	**Solange**	French name derived from the Latin word for 'solemn'
Sigourney	French – daring king		
Sigrid	Old German – beauty, victory	**Soledad**	Spanish – solitary, health
Sile	Gaelic form of Celia; pronounced 'shee-la'	**Solita**	Latin – alone
		Sonia	Alternative spelling of Sonya
Silva	Latin – woodland maid	**Sonja**	Alternative spelling of Sonya
Silvana	Variant of Sylvia *(Sylvana)*	**Sonya**	Russian pet form of Sophia *(Sonia, Sonja)*
Silver	Silver		
Silvia	Alternative spelling of Sylvia	**Sophia**	Greek – wisdom *(Sofya)*
Simona	Variant of Simone	**Sophie**	French form of Sophia *(Sophy)*
Simone	Feminine form of the boy's name Simon, meaning 'snub-nosed'	**Sophy**	Alternative spelling of Sophie
		Sorcha	Celtic variant of Sarah
Sine	Gaelic form of Jane; pronounced 'shee-na'	**Soroya**	Persian – seven stars
		Sorrel	Species of herb
		Souzan	Persian – fire

BE INSPIRED
BY COLOUR!

If you assume colour is only of use within fashion, paint swatches and interior decorating, then be prepared to change your mind! Start thinking laterally and you will soon realize that colours can be yet another valuable source of inspiration for names for your baby.

There are plenty of names, across many languages, that have their origins in the names of colours. Whether you simply have a favourite colour you would like to promote in the form of a name or want a name to describe your baby's skin tone you might find a name here that will suit your requirements.

BRONSON
DONOVAN
HADRIAN

BIANCA
ORIEL PHINEAS
XANTHE

Boys

Adrian (dark one)
Amaro (dark, like a Moor)
Baynard (reddish-brown)
Boyd (yellow)
Brindley (reddish-brown)
Bronson (son of the dark-skinned one)
Burnett (brown)
Clancy (ruddy/red warrior)
Cole (coal black)
Colley (dark, swarthy)
Corcoran (of reddish complexion)
Corvin (raven, black)

Darel (blue sky)
Donovan (dark brown)
Douglas (dark water)
Duff (black, of a dark complexion)
Dunbar (dark branch)
Duncan (dark/brown warrior)
Dunn (brown)
Dyer (colourer of fabrics)
Flannan (ruddy)
Flavian (yellow)
Gannon (fair-complexioned)
Gwyn (white)
Hadrian (dark one)

Kent (white)
Kieran (black, dark-skinned)
Lloyd (grey, dark)
Merrick (dark, swarthy)
Oran (green)
Phineas (black)
Reid (red, ruddy)
Rory (red)
Rudyard (red yard)
Sandy
Slate (grey)
Tomi (red)
Umberto (reddish-brown)
Xanthus (yellow)

Girls

Aurelia (golden one)
Bianca (white)
Bronwen (white-breasted)
Burnetta (little brown one)
Candida (white hot)
Carmine
Cerise (cherry red)
Chenoa (white dove)
Chloris (green)
Cyane (deep blue)
Doreen (golden)
Eirwen (white)
Elwyn (white-browed)

Fenella (white-shouldered)
Fiona (white)
Flanna (ruddy)
Flavia (yellow)
Fuscienne (black)
Gwendolen (white-browed)
Iolanthe (violet)
Joletta (violet flower)
Lilac (blueish)
Magenta
Mauve (purplish)
Melanie (dark-complexioned, black)

Nigella (black)
Nuala (white-shouldered)
Oriel (golden one)
Phoenix (blood red)
Raven (black)
Rosalba (white rose)
Saffron (yellow)
Scarlet
Sienna
Virida (green)
Whitney (white island)
Xanthe (golden yellow)
Yolande (violet flower)

STEPHANIE

SYLVIA

SUSANNAH

Spring	Name of a season
Stacey	Derived from Anastasia and Eustacia *(Stacie, Stacy)*
Stacia	Variant of Stacey
Stacie	Alternative spelling of Stacey
Stacy	Alternative spelling of Stacey
Star	Sanskrit – star
Stefania	Alternative spelling of Stephania
Stefanie	Alternative spelling of Stephanie
Stella	Derived from Estelle
Stephania	Variant of Stephanie *(Stefania)*
Stephanie	French feminine form of Stephen, meaning 'crown', 'garland'. Short/pet forms: Stef, Steffi, Steffie, Steph, Stephie, Stevie *(Stefanie, Stephenie)*
Stephenie	Alternative spelling of Stephanie
Stockard	Anglo-Saxon – from the yard of tree stumps
Storm	A modern 'vocabulary name' used for both girls and boys
Strawberry	Name of a fruit
Sukey	Alternative spelling of Suky
Suki	Alternative spelling of Suky
Sukie	Alternative spelling of Suky
Suky	Variant of Susan *(Sukey, Suki, Sukie)*
Summer	Name of a season
Sunny	Brilliant, of the sun
Susan	Hebrew – lily. Short/pet forms: Sue, Susie, Suzie, Suzy

Susanna	Alternative spelling of Susannah
Susannah	Older biblical variant of Susan. Short/pet forms: Sue, Susie, Suzie, Suzy *(Susanna, Suzanna)*
Susanne	Alternative spelling of Suzanne
Suzanna	Alternative spelling of Susanna
Suzanne	French form of Susan *(Susanne)*
Suzette	Variant of Susan
Svetlana	Russian – star, light. Short/pet form: Sveta
Sybil	Alternative spelling of Sibyl
Sydney	Anglo-Saxon – disciple of St Denis *(Sidney, Sidonie)*
Sylvana	Alternative spelling of Silvana
Sylvia	Latin – wood, woodland *(Silvia)*
Sylvie	French form of Sylvia
Syna	Greek – two together
Syrie	Feminine form of the boy's name Cyril, taken from the Greek meaning 'lordly'

SUMMER

TALLULAH

TARANEH

TAMMY

T

Tabitha	Hebrew – gazelle. Short/pet forms: Tabby, Tabs
Tacita	Latin – to be silent
Tahiya	Swahili – guardian, guarding
Takara	Japanese – treasure
Tala	Native American – wolf
Talia	Alternative spelling of Thalia
Talitha	Young woman
Tallara	Aborigine – rain
Tallulah	Native American – jumping water. Tallulah Falls is a notable beauty spot in the American state of Georgia
Tamara	Hebrew – palm tree. Short/pet form: Tammy
Tamasin	Alternative spelling of Tamsin
Tammy	Short/pet form of Tamara and Tamsin, now also an independent name
Tamsin	Old Cornish form of Thomasina, the feminine form of the boy's name Thomas, meaning 'twin'. Short/pet forms: Tammy (Tamasin, Tamsine, Tamsyn)
Tamsine	Alternative spelling of Tamsin
Tamsyn	Alternative spelling of Tamsin

Tani	Japanese – valley
Tania	Alternative spelling of Tanya
Tansy	Greek – immortality
Tanya	Short/pet form of Antonia, Antoinette and the Russian name Tatiana, now also an independent name (Tania, Tonia, Tonya)
Tara	Irish place name meaning 'hill', 'tower', the ancient coronation site of the Irish kings
Taraneh	Persian – melody
Taree	Japanese – bending branch
Tarra	Aborigine – creek
Taryn	Feminine form of the boy's name Tyrone, meaning 'Owen's country'
Tasia	Derived from Anastasia
Tatiana	A Russian name, used as a first name in Britain since the early 20th century. Short/pet forms: Tania, Tanya (Tatyana)

Tatum	Feminine form of the boy's name Tate, meaning 'spirited', 'cheerful'		form of Althea, Anthea, Dorothea and Theodora
Tatyana	Alternative spelling of Tatiana	**Thelma**	Invented by the novelist Marie Corelli
Tawnie	Romany – little one		for her 1887 novel *Thelma*. Possibly
Tawny	Old French – with yellowish-brown hair		derived from the Greek for wish
		Thema	Egyptian – queen
Taylor	Anglo-Saxon – tailor. An occupational surname turned first name, given usually to girls and less commonly to boys	**Themis**	Goddess of justice and order in Greek mythology
		Theodora	Feminine form of the boy's name Theodore, meaning 'gift of God'. Short/pet form: Thea
Tegan	Welsh – beautiful, blessed		
Tegwen	Variant of Tegan	**Theodosia**	Variant of Theodora
Telma	Variant of Thelma	**Theone**	Greek – godly
Terentia	Greek – guardian	**Thera**	Greek – strength, untamed
Teresa	Possibly Greek – to reap, harvest. Possibly the feminine form of the boy's name Terence. Originally a predominantly Roman Catholic name. Short/pet forms: Tess, Tessa Tesse, Terri, Terry, Tessie *(Theresa)*	**Theresa**	Alternative spelling of Teresa
		Thirza	Hebrew – pleasant
		Thomasa	Variant of Thomasina
		Thomasina	Feminine form of the boy's name Thomas, meaning 'twin'
		Thora	Derived from Thor, the Norse god of thunder and war, after whom Thursday, Thor's day, is named
Terese	Variant of Teresa		
Tertia	Latin – third		
Tesia	Polish – loved by God	**Tiana**	Greek – princess
Tessa	Variant of Esther and short/pet form of Teresa. Short/pet forms: Tess, Tesse, Tessie	**Tierra**	Latin – earth
		Tiffany	Derived from the Greek name Theophinia, 'manifestation of God' and given to girls born at Epiphany, now also an independent name. Short/pet form: Tiff
Thalia	Greek – joyful, blooming *(Talia)*		
Thandine	Variant of Theodora		
Thea	Greek – goddess. Also a short/pet		

TITANIA

TWILA

TRINETTE

Tiger Lily	Species of flower
Tina	Originally a pet form of names ending with 'tina', such as Christina and Martina, now also an independent name
Tisha	Originally derived from shortened forms of Patricia and Letitia, now an independent name
Titania	Greek – giant
Toni	Short/pet form of Antonia. The spelling distinguishes it from the boy's name Tony
Tonia	Alternative spelling of Tanya
Tonya	Alternative spelling of Tanya
Topaz	Latin – gemstone
Topaza	Variant of Topaz
Tora	Old Norse – thunder
Tori	Japanese – bird
Toyah	Anglo-Saxon – whimsical, sporty
Tracey	Alternative spelling of Tracy
Tracy	Variant of Teresa (*Tracey, Trasey*)
Trasey	Alternative spelling of Tracy
Trilby	Italian – one who sings musical trills
Trina	Short/pet form of Catriona and Katrina; now an independent name
Trinette	Diminutive of Trina, meaning 'little maid'
Trista	Latin – sorrowful
Trixie	Derived from Beatrice/Beatrix

Trudi	Alternative spelling of Trudy
Trudie	Alternative spelling of Trudy
Trudy	Short/pet form of Ermintrude and Gertrude, now also an independent name (*Trudi, Trudie*)
Trula	Variant of Truly
Truly	True
Tryphena	Latin – dainty
Tuesday	Tuesday, the day of the week that honours the Teutonic god of war
Tulla	Gaelic – little hill
Twila	Alternative spelling of Twyla
Twyla	Anglo-Saxon – thread (*Twila*)
Tyanne	From Tyrus + Anne
Tyra	Old Norse – god of battle

TYRA

ULRIKA

VANESSA

VALENCIA

UV

Ula	Celtic – jewel of the sea *(Ulla)*
Ulla	Alternative spelling of Ula. Also Aborigine – a well
Ulrica	Old German – noble ruler *(Ulrika)*
Ulrika	Alternative spelling of Ulrica
Ultima	Latin – aloof
Una	Anglicized form of the ancient Gaelic name Oonagh
Undine	Latin – water sprite, of the waves *(Ondine)*
Unity	An abstract 'virtue' name brought into use by the Puritans during the 17th century. Derived from the Latin *unus* ('one')
Urania	Greek – heavenly, muse of astronomy
Uria	Hebrew – light of the lord
Ursa	Variant of Ursula
Ursala	Alternative spelling of Ursula
Ursel	Variant of Ursula
Ursella	Alternative spelling of Ursula
Ursie	Variant of Ursula
Ursula	Latin – female bear *(Ursala, Ursella)*
Usha	Sanskrit – the dawn
Vala	Anglo-Saxon – chosen
Valarie	Alternative spelling of Valerie
Valda	Old Norse – spirited warrior, power. Short/pet form: Val
Valencia	Variant of Valentina; a place name
Valentina	Feminine form of the boy's name Valentine, meaning 'strong', 'valorous'. Short/pet form: Val
Valeria	Originally the feminine form of a famous Roman family name, probably meaning 'to be strong/in good health'
Valerie	French form of Valeria. Short/pet form: Val *(Valarie, Valery, Vallerie)*
Valery	Alternative spelling of Valerie
Vallerie	Alternative spelling of Valerie
Valtina	Variant of Valentina
Vanda	Slavonic – wanderer
Vanessa	Greek – butterfly. Short/pet forms: Ness, Nessa, Nessie, Vanna, Vanni
Vannora	Alternative spelling of Vanora
Vanora	Scottish – white wave *(Vannora)*
Vanya	Russian – gracious gift of God
Vashti	Persian – beautiful
Velda	Alternative spelling of Felda
Velma	Derived from Wilhemina
Venetia	Latin – woman of Venice *(Venitia)*
Venitia	Alternative spelling of Venetia
Venus	Goddess of love and beauty in Roman mythology

VERITY VIVIANNE

VIOLETTA

Vera	Latin – truth, faith	**Vida**	Hebrew – life, or possibly
Verbena	Latin – species of plant		derived from Davida
Verena	Old German – defender	**Vidonia**	Latin – vine branch
Verita	Variant of Verity	**Vilma**	Derived from Wilhemina
Verity	Latin – truth. One of the many	**Vincentia**	Feminine form of Vincent
	'virtue' names given to girls by	**Viola**	Older Latin variant of Violet
	the 17th-century Puritans	**Violante**	Variant of Violet
Verna	Variant of Verona. This is also	**Violet**	Latin – species of flower. One of the
	the feminine form of the boy's		oldest of the flower names, Violet
	name Vernon, which means		symbolizes modesty. Also a colour
	'alder tree'		name. Short/pet form: Vi *(Violette)*
Verona	Variant of Veronica, and an Italian	**Violetta**	Variant of Violet
	place name	**Violette**	Alternative spelling of Violet
Veronica	Latin – true image. It was the	**Virginia**	Latin – maid, virgin. Short/pet
	name given to the woman who		forms: Ginnie, Ginny, Jinny
	wiped the face of Jesus with a cloth,	**Virida**	Latin – green
	which retained the image of his	**Viridienne**	French form of Virida
	face. Also a species of plant.	**Vita**	Latin – life, lively
	Short/pet forms: Ron, Ronna,	**Vivian**	Alternative spelling of Vivien
	Ronnie, Ronny	**Viviana**	Variant of Vivien
Véronique	French form of Veronica	**Vivianne**	Variant of Vivien
Vesta	Goddess of the hearth in Roman	**Vivien**	Feminine form of the boy's
	mythology, equivalent to the		name Vivian, meaning 'alive',
	Greek goddess Hestia		'lively'. Short/pet forms: Viv,
Victoria	Latin – victorious, conqueror.		Vivi, Vivia *(Vivian, Vyvyan)*
	Short/pet forms: Tor, Torie,	**Vivienne**	Variant of Vivien
	Vicki, Vickie, Vicky, Vikki	**Vivietta**	Variant of Vivien
Victorie	Variant of Victoria	**Vondra**	Slavonic – love of a woman
Victorine	Variant of Victoria	**Vyvyan**	*See* Vivien

WINONA

WENDELIN

WINIFRED

W

Wallice	Alternative spelling of Wallis
Wallis	Feminine form of the boy's name Wallace, meaning 'a foreigner' *(Wallice)*
Wambui	Kikuyu – singer
Wanda	Old German – kindred, stock
Warrah	Aborigine – honeysuckle
Wenda	Variant of Wendy
Wendelin	Anglo-Saxon – wanderer
Wendi	Alternative spelling of Wendy
Wendie	Alternative spelling of Wendy
Wendy	Possibly of Old German origins, the name was probably first used in 1904 by playwright JM Barrie for the heroine of *Peter Pan*. Possibly a short/pet form of Gwendolen *(Wendi, Wendie)*
Whitney	Anglo-Saxon – white island
Wilda	Anglo-Saxon – wild one
Wilhelmina	Feminine form of the boy's name Wilhelm, the German version of William. 'Wil' + 'helm' = will + helmet/protection, ie means 'determined protector'. Short/pet forms: Elma, Mina, Minnie, Willa

Williamina	Variant of Wilhelmina
Willow	Species of tree
Wilma	Derived from Wilhelmina *(Wylma)*
Wilona	Anglo-Saxon – desired
Winda	Swahili – hunt
Winema	Native American – female chief
Winifred	Anglicized form of the Welsh name Gwenfrewi, meaning 'blessed reconciliation'. Short/pet forms: Freda, Freddy, Win, Winnie
Winola	Old German – gracious friend
Winona	Native American – first-born daughter. Also US place name *(Wynona)*
Winter	Name of a season
Wylma	Alternative spelling of Wilma
Wyn	Alternative spelling of Wynn
Wynn	Welsh – fair, light complexion *(Wyn, Wynne)*
Wynne	Alternative spelling of Wynn
Wynona	Alternative spelling of Winona
Wyomia	Native American – expansive plain

XANTHE

YONAH

XY

Yonina	Hebrew – dove
Younice	Alternative spelling of Eunice
Yvette	French feminine form of the boy's name Yves, meaning 'archer', 'yew tree'
Yvonne	Another French feminine form of the boy's name, Yves, meaning 'archer', 'yew tree'

Xandy	Derived from Alexandra
Xanthe	Greek – golden yellow, making this a suitable name for a fair-haired child
Xena	Alternative spelling of Xenia
Xenia	Greek – guest, hospitality. Zenia/Zena are alternative spellings, which indicate the pronunciation (Xena)
Xylia	Greek – wood dweller
Xylona	Greek – from the forest
Yakini	Swahili – truth
Yamuna	Hindi – a sacred river
Yasmin	Alternative spelling of Yasmine
Yasmine	Arabic – jasmine flower (Yasmin)
Yekaterina	Russian form of Katherine
Yelena	Russian form of Helen
Yepa	Native American – winter princess
Yoko	Japanese – positive female child
Yolanda	Alternative spelling of Yolande
Yolande	A medieval French name, from the Greek Iole meaning 'violet flower' (Yolanda)
Yonah	Feminine form of the boy's name Jonah, meaning 'dove'

YOLANDA

ZAHARA

ZOHREH

Z

Zabrina	Alternative spelling of Sabrina
Zahara	Swahili – flower
Zaira	Variant of Zara and Sarah
Zakiya	Swahili – intelligent
Zandra	Alternative spelling of Sandra
Zara	Variant of Sarah. Also Arabic – splendour of the east, brightness
Zarah	Hebrew – coming of dawn
Zaza	Arabic – flowery
Zelda	Derived from Griselda/Grizelda
Zelia	Greek – ardent, zeal
Zellie	French form of Zelia
Zena	*See* Xenia
Zenia	*See* Xenia
Zerlinda	Hebrew – beautiful dawn

Zeta	Alternative spelling of Zita
Zeva	Greek – sword
Zevida	Hebrew – gift
Zia	Arabic – light
Zigana	Hungarian – gypsy girl
Zilla	Alternative spelling of Zillah
Zillah	Hebrew – shadow (*Zilla*)
Zina	Greek – from Zeus
Zinia	Alternative spelling of Zinnia
Zinnia	Latin – species of flower (*Zinia*)
Zita	Derived from Rosita (*Zeta*)
Zizi	Hungarian – dedicated to God
Zoë	Alternative spelling of Zoe
Zoe	Greek – life. It was equated with Eve as the 'mother of life' (*Zoë, Zoey, Zoie, Zowey*)
Zoey	Alternative spelling of Zoe
Zohar	Hebrew – light, brilliance
Zohreh	Persian – happy
Zoie	Alternative spelling of Zoe
Zola	Italian – ball of earth
Zona	Latin – a girth
Zora	Greek – dawn
Zorah	Variant of Zarah
Zoreen	Variant of Sarah
Zowey	Alternative spelling of Zoe
Zsa zsa	Hungarian form of Susan
Zuza	Slavonic form of Susan
Zuzanny	Variant of Susan